Property Rights in a Social and Ecological Context
Case Studies and Design Applications

Edited by
Susan Hanna
and
Mohan Munasinghe

Beijer International Institute of Ecological Economics
and
The World Bank

ISBN 0-8213-3416-6

CONTENTS

FOREWORD

Institutions are the rules of the game in a society or, more formally, are the humanly devised constraints that shape human interaction. In consequence they structure incentives in human exchange, whether political, social, or economic. Institutional change shapes the way societies evolve through time and hence is the key to understanding historical change.

Douglas North, Nobel Prize Laureate 1993
in *Institutions, Institutional Change and Economic Performance*
Cambridge University Press, 1990

When analyzing environmental problems, economists have traditionally searched for ways of extending the rules of social cost–benefit analysis so as to include the environmental side effects associated with investment projects. This they have done by estimating the "economic" value of side effects. Such side effects are often called "externalities" in the economics literature. Economists have also studied the efficacy of various policy instruments—such as the taxation of resource use or the use of tradeable permits for environmental pollution—for directing economic activity in decentralized economic environments. Recently economists have inquired into the environmental side effects of macroeconomic policies.[1] However, a more fundamental question, concerning the nature of the institutions of society that shape the use of environmental resources, has only recently begun to be studied.

One such program of research, conducted at the Beijer International Institute of Ecological Economics, on the ecology and economics of biodiversity loss, explored the notion that a significant cause of much biodiversity loss lies in inadequate institutions, in particular, ill-defined property rights.[2] It was a natural next step for the Institute to launch a more general program of research on property rights and environmental resources. Towards this end, the Institute was fortunate to receive generous economic support from the MacArthur Foundation in Chicago. Subsequently, this support was augmented by the World Bank's Vice Presidency on Environmentally Sustainable Development. This enabled the two institutions to work together in what we believe to be a vital area of concern. We are particularly grateful to Professor Susan Hanna of Oregon State University (also Director of the Property Rights Programme at the Beijer Institute), and to Dr. Mohan Munasinghe of the Environment Department of the World Bank (also Fellow of the Beijer Institute) for the able manner in which they have developed the joint program of activities and produced these two volumes.

Much remains to be done on the design of institutions that would improve upon the current patterns of use of environmental resources. For example, we need to better understand the relationship between various property rights regimes and the speed and direction of technological change because the use of environmental resources is greatly shaped by the technologies in operation. Future programs, both at the Beijer Institute and the World Bank, will hopefully address these issues.

---

1. See M. Munasinghe and W. Cruz, *Economywide Policies and the Environment* (Washington, D.C.: World Bank, 1994).

2. For an overview of this research program, see the special issue of *Ambio* 1993, and E. Barbier, J. Burgess, and C. Folke, *Paradise Lost* (London: Earthscan, 1994).

The subject of property rights covers a wide field, as reflected in these volumes. The relevance of property rights for any study of environmental problems should be self-evident. Nevertheless, the bulk of the efforts that have been made to date for improving the state of the environment in developing countries has been devoted to a support of appropriate investment projects. It is time to place more emphasis on aid that is directed at improving the institutional framework within which resources are used. Indeed, institutional reforms that are aimed at a better management and use of environmental resources should now complement those reforms that are usually called structural adjustment programs. These two volumes should be read with this background in mind.

Ismail Serageldin   Partha Dasgupta   Karl-Göran Mäler
Vice President   Chairman of the Board   Director
Environmentally Sustainable   Beijer International Institute   Beijer International Institute
   Development   of Ecological Economics   of Ecological Economics
The World Bank   Stockholm   Stockholm
Washington, D.C.

Janis B. Alcorn has been involved in environmental research and international development for the past twenty-five years, with emphasis on Asia and the Americas. She is Director of the Asia and Pacific program of the Biodiversity Support Program at World Wildlife Fund–US. Her publications include over fifty articles on biodiversity conservation, tropical forest management, tenure, and economic botany; and four books, including *Huastec Mayan Ethnobotany* and *Ethnobotany: Community, Culture and Biodiversity* (forthcoming).

Fikret Berkes is Professor and Director of the Natural Resources Institute, University of Manitoba. His research interests include common property resources, applied ecology, and ecological economics. He has been fascinated for a long time with the interface between natural systems and social systems, and reports in this volume on a research project that spans over twenty years in the James Bay area of Canada.

Manuel Bonifaz completed his Master of Environmental Management degree in 1993 in the Resource Economics and Policy Program of the School of the Environment, Duke University. His research and professional experience emphasizes environmental and resource economics and policy, and he is currently employed in this field in Quito, Ecuador.

Runar Brännlund is Associate Professor at the Department of Economics, University of Umeå, Sweden. His research interests are concentrated in the fields of environmental economics, applied production theory, and industrial organization.

Lloyd M. Dickie is Scientist Emeritus at the Bedford Institute of Oceanography in Nova Scotia. He was formerly Director of the Marine Ecology Laboratory at the Bedford Institute of Oceanography, Chairman of the Department of Oceanography at Dalhousie University, and Director of the Institute of Environmental Studies at Dalhousie University. For many years he worked with the Fisheries Research Board of Canada.

Madhav Gadgil is Professor of Ecology at the Indian Institute of Science in Bangalore and is involved in both field research and mathematical modeling in the areas of population biology, conservation biology, and human ecology. He has served as a member of the Science Advisory Council to the Prime Minister of India, and works actively with the voluntary sector in nature conservation and ecodevelopment efforts.

Ing-Marie Gren is Associate Professor of Economics at the Stockholm School of Economics and is also on the staff of the Beijer International Institute of Ecological Economics, the Royal Swedish Academy of Sciences. Her research has emphasized cost-effective achievement of environmental targets, choice of policy instruments and their enforcement, and valuation of complex ecosystems. She is currently conducting interdisciplinary research relating to water pollution.

Monica Hammer has a Ph.D. in natural resources management and is Researcher at the Department of Systems Ecology, Stockholm University, Stockholm, Sweden. Her research interests concern the interface between ecology and economics, with special reference to Baltic Sea fisheries, ecosystem resilience, biodiversity, and property rights issues.

Susan Hanna is Associate Professor of Marine Economics in the Department of Agricultural and Resource Economics at Oregon State University, and Director of the research program, Property Rights and the Performance of Natural Resource Systems, at the Beijer International Institute of Ecological Economics, the Royal Swedish Academy of Sciences. Her research areas are fishery economics, natural resource management, economics of common property resources, and the economic history of marine resource use.

Narpat S. Jodha is with the Social Policy and Resettlement Division of the Environment Department at the World Bank in Washington, D.C. His professional interests include agriculture and natural resource management in fragile areas. Formerly he has worked in the International Crop Research Institute for Semi-Arid Tropics (ICRISAT), the International Institute for Tropical Agriculture (IITA), and the International Center for Integrated Mountain Development (ICIMOD).

Mohan Munasinghe is Chief, Environmental Economics Division, the World Bank, and Fellow of the Beijer International Institute of Ecological Economics, the Royal Swedish Academy of Sciences. He is also Distinguished Visiting Professor of Environmental Management, University of Colombo, Sri Lanka. During 1982–1986, he served as Senior Advisor to the President of Sri Lanka. He has authored or edited more than fifty books and several hundred technical papers on environmental economics, energy, water resources, and informatics.

Gísli Pálsson is Professor of Anthropology at the University of Iceland. His writings include *Coastal Economies, Cultural Accounts: Human Ecology and Icelandic Discourse* (1991), *The Textual Life of Savants: Ethnography, Iceland, and the Linguistic Turn* (1995), and a number of articles published in anthropological journals. His major fields of research interest include ecological anthropology, fishing economies, cognition, and language. He is currently doing research on practical skills and quota management in Icelandic fishing.

Peter J. Parks is Assistant Professor of Environmental and Resource Economics in the Department of Agricultural Economics and Marketing at Rutgers University. His research examines local, regional, national, and global environmental consequences of land use, with a particular interest in the design policies and property rights systems that sustain environmental quality and resource productivity by influencing land use.

Samuel G. Pooley has been Industry Economist with the National Marine Fisheries Service's Honolulu Laboratory since 1981. He is responsible for their Fishery Management and Performance Investigation which monitors U.S. domestic fishing in the area around Hawaii. Most of his research has involved cost–earnings analysis of commercial fishing fleets and seafood market analysis with an orientation toward fishery management applications.

Ajay S. Pradhan is a Ph.D. student in the Environmental Science Program, School of Public and Environmental Affairs, Indiana University. His research concentrates on terrestrial ecological systems and human dimensions of environmental change. He was formerly a Fulbright Scholar at the School of the Environment, Duke University, before which he was with IUCN—the World Conservation Union's National Conservation Strategy Implementation Program in Nepal.

P. R. Seshagiri Rao is a practicing farmer, as well as a researcher in the area of human ecology and conservation biology. He is currently working on a doctoral dissertation on cooperation and conflict in the human use of natural resources at the Indian Institute of Science, Bangalore.

Kenneth Ruddle is Professor at the School of Policy Studies, Kwansei Gakuin University, Japan. His main research interest is coastal marine fisheries management in the Asia–Pacific Region, and particularly the modern role of traditional resources management and its supporting "local" knowledge base. He has also studied integrated systems of agriculture–aquaculture in China, Southeast Asia, and Africa, and is interested in tropical resources policy and management.

Tom Tietenberg is Mitchell Family Professor of Economics at Colby College in Waterville, Maine. He is the author or editor of seven books, including *Environmental and Natural Resource Economics*, and nearly fifty articles and essays on environmental and natural resource economics. Formerly President of the U.S. Association of Environmental and Natural Resource Economists, he has served as a consultant on environmental policy to international, national, and state governments.

Victor M. Toledo is a researcher at the Centro de Ecología at the Universidad Nacional Autónoma de México. He has carried out research on the ecological and economic relationships between Latin American peasant communities and their natural environment for over twenty years, and has published over 100 articles and numerous books on biogeography, tropical ecology, deforestation, and ethnoecology. He was recently awarded a Guggenheim Fellowship and is the founding editor of the journal *Etnoecológica.*

Ralph E. Townsend is Professor of Economics at the University of Maine. His research has focused on economic evaluation of alternative fisheries management institutions. Much of his current research is directed at the exploration of new approaches to economic management of fisheries, including ideas such as corporate management, transferable dynamic stock rights, bankable ITQs, and fractional licenses.

James A. Wilson is Professor of Resource Economics at the University of Maine. He has worked in the area of fisheries regulations and markets for about twenty-five years. His research has been directed principally at regulatory implications of complexity and unpredictability in both the ecosystems and human systems associated with fisheries.

Tomasz Żylicz is Professor of Economics at Warsaw University, and Advisor to the Minister of the Environment. Since 1974 he has taught at Warsaw University, where—from 1989 onward—he has been involved in an extensive curriculum reform. He was formerly Director of the Economics Department at the Ministry of the Environment, where, among other things, he was responsible for the design of several major policy reforms.

Introduction

1

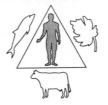

An Introduction to Property Rights in a Social and Ecological Context

Susan Hanna and Mohan Munasinghe

THIS BOOK AND ITS COMPANION VOLUME, *Property Rights and the Environment: Social and Ecological Issues,* concern the institutional dimensions of environmental sustainability. Humans interact with their environment through systems of property rights that are embedded in social, political, cultural, and economic context. The outcome of that interaction affects both the quantity and quality of environmental resources. It is becoming increasingly clear that although national and international economic policies have often ignored the environment, economic development ultimately depends on institutions that can protect and maintain the environment's carrying capacity and resilience (Arrow and others 1995). The knowledge of how property rights regimes, as particularly important types of institutions, function in relation to humans and their use of the environment is critical to the design and implementation of effective environmental protection.

The papers collected in these books are products of a research program of the Beijer International Institute of Ecological Economics, the Royal Swedish Academy of Sciences, Stockholm, Sweden. The research program "Property Rights and the Performance of Natural Resource Systems" began in 1993 with support from the World Environment and Resources Program of the John D. and Catherine T. MacArthur Foundation and the Environment Department of the World Bank. The program's goal is to further the scientific understanding of ways humans relate to their natural environments through the mechanism of property rights regimes. A major objective of the program is to bring together social scientists and natural scientists to address research questions in their full social and ecological dimensions.

More than fifty international scholars have participated in interdisciplinary research projects. These projects address questions of the design of governance systems for sustainability; the relationships among equity, stewardship, and environmental resilience; the use of traditional knowledge in resource management; the mechanisms that link humans to their environments; and the role played by poverty and population. The chapters in the companion volume, *Property Rights and the Environment, Social and Ecological Issues*, review the theoretical and conceptual background of these five general issues of property rights and the environment. The present volume contains a number of case studies that address questions of design application in the same five areas.

Sustainability, Sustainable Development, and Property Rights

Property rights regimes consist of *property rights*, bundles of entitlements defining rights and duties in the use of natural resources, and *property rules*, the rules under which those rights and duties are exercised (Bromley 1991). Property rights regimes matter to the use of environmental resources, a fact that has long been well established, if not well practiced. In 1911 Jens Warming wrote of the dangers of fisheries overexploitation without ownership, an argument enhanced by Scott Gordon in 1954 (Warming 1911; Gordon 1954). Garrett Hardin's

1968 article, "The Tragedy of the Commons," focused widespread attention on the problem of environmental degradation in the absence of rules governing use (Hardin 1968). For a number of years the general interpretation of Hardin's argument was that collectively owned property was the culprit and that private property was necessary to sustain environmental resources. However, a rapidly expanding body of scientific evidence indicates that sustaining environmental resources is not dependent on a particular structure of property regime, but rather on a well-specified property rights regime and a congruency of that regime with its ecological and social context.

Sustainability is a difficult concept because it has a wide range of meanings based on different disciplines and world views. What is being sustained, how it is to be sustained, and over how long a period of time are all open to interpretation. Regardless of the specific meaning used, it is clear that, to some extent, sustainability is a human construct. Humans use their environment for a range of objectives, including subsistence, commodity production, aesthetic pleasure, and indirect ecosystem services. These objectives have their basis in the desire to sustain human life, enhance standards of living, maintain culture, and protect environmental quality for generations to follow. The different objectives for the use of environmental resources lead to different expectations as to what is to be sustained, and who is to have claims on environmental services.

It is becoming increasingly clear that the question of sustainability is a complicated one whose answer involves more than the generic application of a property rights regime. Property rights regimes, to be effective in modulating the interaction between humans and their environment, must reflect both general principles and specific social and ecological contexts. General principles are the structural and functional attributes of property rights regimes which transcend a particular context. General principles are the necessary conditions of effective property rights regimes because a property rights regime cannot succeed over the long run without them. They include the congruence of ecosystem and governance boundaries; the specification and representation of interests; the matching of governance structure to ecosystem characteristics; the containment of transaction costs; and the establishment of monitoring, enforcement, and adaptation processes at the appropriate scale (Eggertsson 1990; Ostrom 1990; Bromley 1991; Hanna 1992).

General principles are necessary, but not sufficient in themselves for effective property rights regimes. In addition to the general principles, specific attributes of social and ecological context must be represented. Social contexts contain all the dimensions of the human relationship to environmental resources, including social arrangements, cultural practices, economic uses, and political constraints. Ecological contexts contain the structure of ecosystems in which humans live and work, as well as the particular functional properties of those ecosystems. The particular details of the social and ecological context are what give a human–environmental interaction its variety in detail. The match between a property rights regime and the contextual characteristics of the affected humans and ecosystems will determine success or failure in terms of sustainability.

The scientific (biogeophysical) concepts and measures of sustainability have been explored in a recent volume that made a number of recommendations and set out several areas for further study (Munasinghe and Shearer 1995). Meanwhile, those concerned with poverty and development are exploring how to implement some of these approaches to sustainability. The now well-known definition of sustainable development, succinctly paraphrased from the Bruntland Commission report as "meeting the needs of the present generation without jeopardizing the ability of future generations to meet their needs," must be elaborated further, for practical application (World Commission on Environment and Development 1987). The current concept of sustainable development encompasses three key elements—the economic, social, and environmental (Munasinghe 1993).

The *economic* approach to sustainability is based on the Hicks–Lindahl concept of the maximum flow of income that can be generated while at least maintaining the stock of assets (or capital) which yield these benefits. The *social* concept of sustainability is people-oriented, and seeks to maintain the integrity of social and cultural systems, including the reduction of destructive conflicts (Munasinghe and McNeely

1994). Equity is an important aspect of this approach. The *environmental* view of sustainable development focuses on the stability of biological and physical systems. The emphasis is on preserving the resilience and dynamic ability of such systems to adapt to change, rather than conservation of some "ideal" static state. Natural resource degradation, pollution, and loss of biodiversity reduce system resilience. Reconciling these various concepts and implementing them as a means to achieve sustainable development is a formidable task, since all three elements of sustainable development must be given balanced consideration.

The correct economic valuation of environmental and sociocultural assets, and their internalization in the price system is one means of ensuring that market forces lead to more sustainable resource use. The more equitable distribution of resources and assets is a step toward poverty reduction and social sustainability, as is greater participation and empowerment of disadvantaged groups. Clearly, property rights regimes that specify access to the natural resource base and rights of use have a crucial role to play in this context (Dasgupta 1993).

The body of research addressing questions of property rights and environmental resource use is growing, but there remain areas characterized by large gaps in knowledge. Five of these areas form the focus of the Beijer Institute's Property Rights Research Program and are represented by the sections of these books. These areas are the design of governance systems, the development of stewardship and equity in environmental management and its contribution to environmental resilience, the management role of traditional ecological knowledge, the mechanisms by which humans are linked to their environmental resource base, and the relationship between poverty, population, and environmental degradation.

The Volume on *Property Rights and the Environment: Social and Ecological Issues*

In the overview chapter of this book, **Hanna, Folke, and Mäler** summarize the findings on property rights and environmental resources—focusing on why property rights matter, the general problems they address, their structural forms, design principles, mechanisms by which they create linkages between human and ecological systems, and mechanisms by which they coordinate uses at different scales. They argue that policies addressing environmental problems must focus on general principles of property rights regimes and on the context in which such regimes are placed.

Governance

Questions of governance over environmental resources have to do with the ability to predict and oversee both human behavior and ecosystem behavior. Success in prediction and oversight depends on a number of variables. The complexity of the human systems and ecosystems affects the ability to extract consistent objectives, design meaningful control systems, and monitor response. The scale of the ecosystem in comparison with scales of social organization or legal jurisdiction determines the extent of the match between the human and environmental systems. The clarity of lines of authority over environmental decisions and the degree to which authority is coordinated or fragmented is critical to relating actions to outcomes. Finally, the ways in which governance is coordinated between authorities at different levels determine consistency across scales. **Ostrom** addresses both complexity and scale. Since many biological processes occur at small and medium, as well as large scales, governance arrangements that can cope with this level of complexity also need to be organized at multiple scales and linked effectively together. The importance of nested institutional arrangements is emphasized, with quasi-autonomous units operating at very small, up through very large, scales.

Two further chapters address the question of the distribution of authority. **Townsend and Pooley** present the concept of distributed governance—how rights and responsibilities are distributed among the central government, industry, and local communities—analyzing competing models of cooperative management, comanagement, and rights-based management in the context of fisheries. They pay attention to both internal and external governance issues. **Hanna**'s chapter focuses on the effect of distributed authority on governance efficiency and in particular on the role played by user participa-

tion in lowering management costs. The contribution of user participation to governance efficiency is analyzed in terms of the structure and function of user participation and its effect on management costs.

Kaitala and Munro's chapter addresses the question of governance coordination over multiple jurisdictions, as exemplified by transboundary fishery resources categorized as highly migratory fish stocks and straddling fish stocks. The high seas portion of the stocks are exploited both by coastal states and distant water fishing nations. The problem of managing such resources (characterized by ill-defined property rights over the high seas portion of the resources) is now seen as severe, and has become the focus of a major United Nations intergovernmental conference.

Equity, Stewardship, and Environmental Resilience

It is a general finding of the property rights literature that the degree of equity represented by a property rights regime helps create the incentive structure which either promotes or inhibits stewardship of environmental resources. The degree of stewardship practiced, in turn, affects the level of ecosystem resilience, or the ability of an ecosystem to absorb external shocks. Exactly how equity affects stewardship, and how specific stewardship practices affect resilience is still a matter of research. It is becoming clear that definitions of equity, stewardship practices, and environmental resilience reflect a combination of local context, appropriate incentive structures, and adaptation to environmental change.

The goals of equity and stewardship are commonly considered to be inconsistent with efficiency in environmental management. In a departure from the usual approach, **Young and McCay** look at efficiency-driven, market-based property rights systems and evaluate them for their ability to accommodate equity, stewardship, and resilience, offering suggestions about ways these criteria can be built into the design of adaptive and flexible management regimes. They consider a number of different types of property rights systems for a variety of resources.

Traditional Knowledge

Long-standing systems of environmental resource management and their use of traditional ecological knowledge are yielding insights into some current resource management problems. The documentation and use of traditional ecological knowledge is now a part of international environmental policy. **Cicin-Sain and Knecht** review and assess major developments at the international level that have recently emphasized the importance of reconciling systems of traditional knowledge with modern approaches to the management of natural resources. They look at the varying conceptions of the role of traditional knowledge and indigenous peoples in these international agreements, and analyze implementation challenges that both regional and national-level entities will face as they endeavor to enhance the role of indigenous knowledge and participation.

Linking Mechanisms

Linkages between humans and environmental systems operate in different ways according to their structure, the systems they link, and the process by which the linkage is made. Some linkages are constructed by the informal observation of environmental characteristics on the part of users, and the gradual evolution of behavioral response. Others are established as more rapid responses to change. In cases of environmental overuse, linking mechanisms are often weak or absent, cutting off the interaction between environmental condition and human response. The particular structure of a linking mechanism reflects the economic, social, and ecological context in which it is established. The structure determines what information will be monitored, how it will be monitored, and what will be done with the information once acquired. The key question is whether the governance system promotes or even allows behavioral adaptation to environmental change. Linkages affect both ecosystem and human system adaptation and evolution through the type of feedbacks allowed.

Folke and Berkes look at the structure and processes by which ecological systems and human systems are connected. They extract from the common property literature lessons about the interface between ecological and social systems.

A systems view of social and ecological interactions is presented, which stresses the need for active social adaptations to environmental feedbacks and the use of traditional ecological knowledge. Particular attention is paid to the lessons that can be learned to assist in the design of more sustainable resource management systems—improving their adaptiveness and resilience.

Poverty and Population

Population is importantly linked to poverty and the erosion of the environmental resource base. The population policy literature reflects the current conclusion that previous successes in population policy directed at family planning, the supply side of population growth, cannot be sustained without serious attention to the need to reduce both the demand for births and the momentum of population growth (Bongaarts 1994). Proposed policy foci include the education of women to enhance economic standing, incentives to postpone childbearing to later years, and establishment of formalized systems of property rights to resources (Bongaarts 1994; de Soto 1993).

Dasgupta applies economic analysis to rural households in poor countries to examine the forces underlying population growth—finding that it is in varying degrees linked to poverty, to gender inequalities in the exercise of power, to communal sharing of child-rearing, and to an erosion of the local environmental–resource base. These linkages suggest that population policy should contain not only such measures as family planning programs, improved female education, and employment opportunities, but also those measures that are directed at the alleviation of poverty—such as improved credit, insurance, and savings opportunities—and improved availability of basic household needs—such as potable water and fuel.

The Volume on *Property Rights in a Social and Ecological Context: Case Studies and Design Applications*

Governance

The first three illustrative case studies in this book apply various principles of governance to the environmental challenges of air pollution, fishery management, and pesticide use. **Tietenberg** examines the question of governance design and scale through an analysis of the use of market-based mechanisms in his chapter on the transferable permits approach to pollution control problems in the United States. From the various examples described, he extracts lessons for both the implementation process and program design.

Townsend and Pooley consider the question of appropriate levels of authority—through a potential application of the distributed governance concept to the lobster fishery of the Northwestern Hawaiian Islands. In their chapter, they pay particular attention to how rights and responsibilities would be distributed among central government, industry, and local communities.

Gren and Brännlund approach the issue of coordination by examining enforcement of regionally adjusted environmental regulations. Although geographic differences in environmental impacts may call for region-specific environmental regulations, regional differences in enforcement costs will lead to different levels of cost-effective regulation.

Equity, Stewardship, and Environmental Resilience

The next three chapters demonstrate the difficulties of crafting equitable schemes that promote better stewardship and resilience for the conservation of natural resources. **Gadgil and Rao** examine the incentives for managing biodiversity contained in India's folk traditions of nature conservation, in conjunction with a vigorous state-sponsored program of protected areas. They focus on the efficiency and equity gains possible through reestablishing conservation approaches based on positive incentives to local communities. This attractive option is contrasted with current unsuccessful regulatory methods that are too centralized, sectoral, and bureaucratic.

Żylicz looks at the difficulties posed by abrupt changes in property rights regimes for perceptions of equity, incentives for stewardship, and the maintenance of conservation goals. Analyzing an example of the conflict between conservationists and a municipality in Northeastern Poland, he illustrates how changing property

right regimes have influenced the social context of the protection of nature. Parts of national parks are being claimed by previous landowners who feel they were not reimbursed fairly, there are private or communal enclaves left within park boundaries, and neighboring landowners protest against development constraints implied by the park's existence. The fate of the protection of nature crucially depends on the ability of conservationists to demonstrate economic benefits from investing in natural capital, rather than letting it be degraded.

Parks and Bonifaz examine the incompatibility of incentives in the joint use of environmental resources by looking at the inconsistencies of short-term commodity production with long-term environmental sustainability in open-access Ecuadorian mangrove–shrimp systems. They identify incentives to maximize short-term profits through shrimp mariculture, which have led to destruction of larval-shrimp habitats as mangrove ecosystems were converted to shrimp ponds.

Traditional Knowledge

Three further case studies examine the use of traditional and nontechnical knowledge by itself, in combination with modern scientific knowledge, and in the restoration of previously established property rights. **Pálsson** considers the use of practical knowledge obtained by Icelandic fishing skippers in the course of their work, exploring how fishermen's knowledge differs from that of fishery scientists, and to what extent the former could be brought more systematically into the process of resource management for the purpose of ensuring resilience and sustainability. He outlines many of the benefits of engaging fishermen and using their practical knowledge of fishing for the purpose of sustainable resource use and responsible management.

Berkes presents a case study of Cree Indians from the Canadian subarctic, analyzing the evidence regarding the distinctions of the local indigenous knowledge from Euro-Canadian, science-based wildlife and fishery management knowledge. He notes that resource development policies have rarely taken into account local systems of knowledge and resource use. Along with increasing attention to the social impacts of development, there is more interest in traditional indigenous knowledge. Yet, concepts of traditional knowledge and resource management systems have remained elusive, not only for development policymakers, but also for scholars engaged in such research.

Ruddle focuses on the use of traditional knowledge to reestablish claims to former rights. For the New Zealand Maori, traditional property rights have been recognized by customary law. Bodies of local knowledge have been accepted as legal evidence in the process of restoring usurped rights. The codification of existing rights and customary laws within a system of statutory law in various cultural settings is a contemporary process in many nations in the Pacific Basin, which might provide useful precedents for application worldwide.

Linking Mechanisms

The question of linkages is addressed in four chapters that examine their function in nested forest tenure systems, fisheries, and joint farming–forestry systems. **Alcorn and Toledo** examine Mexican resource tenure systems, which function as "shells" that provide the superstructure within which activities are developed and operate. Such shells are linked in very specific ways to the larger "operating system" in which the shell is embedded. The evidence from Mexico suggests that the best course of action for promoting ecologically sustainable resource management is to support existing structures that have served this function earlier.

Hammer focuses on the links between ecological and social systems in Swedish fisheries, especially in the Baltic Sea. An important aspect of fisheries management is the degree to which property rights systems can be developed that reflect the ecological and socioeconomic context, and that sustain or improve the resilience of the life-supporting ecosystem. Hammer compares traditional small-scale and current large-scale management systems, in terms of how they promote linkages between social and ecological systems, and finds that large-scale systems are more vulnerable because of their failure to process ecosystem feedbacks.

Wilson and Dickie also look at fisheries. They present a view of social and ecological linkages that is based on the broader parametric effects of fishing on the whole biotic and environmental system. Fishing activity leads to a degradation of the biotic or physical environment of desirable species, upsetting their feeding patterns and disrupting normal life cycles. However, the fundamental cause of overfishing lies in the social institutions that either cannot grasp the complexities of biological interactions, or have insufficient means to control the inputs. This institutional difficulty, combined with the uncertainty characterizing marine systems, suggest the appropriateness of a multilevel governance system that captures the social–ecological linkages on different scales.

Pradham and Parks look at Nepal, where deforestation and forest land use change have both socioeconomic and environmental linkages. The interactions between forests and subsistence agricultural systems in Nepal's villages are influenced by the activities of rural farming communities that depend on the forest for various subsistence products. It is because of this reliance on forest resources that such communities often have been blamed for the country's deforestation problem and its associated environmental consequences. Recent government efforts to protect forest resources by excluding local communities have resulted in the opposite effect. Destruction of the social–ecological linkages at the local level has resulted in a new perception by village residents of forests as open-access resources, which has led to further environmental degradation.

Poverty and Population

The links among poverty, population, and the environment are explored in a case study that examines how poverty affects resource use behavior based on desperation. **Jodha** examines the current unsustainable pattern of resource use in the Himalayas—finding the root cause in the replacement of traditional conservation-oriented resource management systems with more extractive systems. He examines the driving forces that induced or forced the communities to treat natural resources differently under the traditional and current contexts, and discusses ways to restore some of the beneficial properties of the traditional systems.

Lessons Learned and Conclusion

These two volumes provide powerful evidence of the importance of both general principles and specific social and ecological context to the design, implementation, and maintenance of property rights regimes for environmental resources.

Governance: General principles of governance are discussed in relation to the need to match the scale and complexity of ecological systems with their property rights regimes, to ensure that the sets of rules are consistent across different levels of authority, to design a distribution of authority that achieves representation and contains transactions costs, and to coordinate between jurisdictions. Specific properties of governance are presented in the contexts of controlling air pollution, managing a fishery, and enforcing regional environmental regulations.

Equity, Stewardship, and Environmental Resilience: General principles are discussed in terms of the relationship between equity, stewardship, environmental resilience, and efficiency in property rights regimes designed for a range of environmental resources. Specific properties of equity, stewardship, and environmental resilience are presented in the contexts of traditional systems for maintaining biodiversity in India, changing property rights to national parks in Poland, and mangrove–shrimp production systems in coastal Ecuador.

Traditional Knowledge: General principles of traditional knowledge are discussed in terms of the interaction between international environmental policy on the use of traditional knowledge and the implementation of local-level resource management systems that use traditional knowledge. Specific properties of traditional knowledge are presented in the contexts of practical knowledge acquired by fishing skippers in Iceland, fishery and wildlife management in the Canadian subarctic, and the restoration of Maori property rights in New Zealand.

Linking Mechanisms: General principles of mechanisms that link humans to their environment are discussed in terms of their structures and the processes by which they allow humans to observe environmental change, adapt their behavior to reflect environmental change, and create knowledge in the process. Specific properties of linking mechanisms are presented in the contexts of forest tenure systems in Mexico, fisheries management in Sweden and elsewhere, and the interaction between agriculture and forestry in Nepal.

Population and Poverty: General principles of the connection between population and poverty are discussed in terms of the intermediate linkages of gender equality, child-rearing practices, women's education, and general employment opportunities. Specific properties of the population–poverty connection are presented in the context of the relationship of population growth to poverty and unsustainable forest practices in Nepal.

The chapters cover a wide range of general principles and specific contexts. Despite their diversity, the chapters are woven together by a common thread—the interaction of social and ecological systems through property rights to produce environmental outcomes. Each chapter demonstrates in its own way the importance of the social and ecological context. The ecological context shapes human organization and behavior, and the human context in turn shapes ecological organization and response. The structure of governance, values of equity and stewardship, traditional knowledge, linking mechanisms, and conditions of poverty and population all form a part of that context. It is, most important, the interaction of social and ecological contexts that determine the co-evolutionary path that humans and their environment follow. The more we understand about the mechanisms of their interactions and the role of property rights regimes in shaping that interaction, the better able we will be to structure that path.

The editors gratefully acknowledge the invaluable contributions of the chapter authors. Thanks are also due to Adelaida Schwab and Stephanie Gerard, as well as to Rebecca Kary and Jay Dougherty of Alpha-Omega Services, Inc., for assistance in the editing and production stage. Judith Smith of Soleil Associates designed the elegant cover.

Bibliography

Arrow, K., B. Bolin, R. Costanza, P. Dasgupta, C. Folke, C. Holling, B.-O. Jansson, S. Levin, K.-G. Mäler, C. Perrings, and D. Pimentel.

1995. "Economic Growth, Carrying Capacity, and the Environment." *Science* 268:520–21.

Bongaarts, J. 1994. "Population Policy Options in the Developing World." *Science* 263:771–76.

Bromley, D. W. 1989. *Economic Interests and Institutions: The Conceptual Foundations of Public Policy.* Oxford, U.K.: Basil Blackwell.

Bromley, D. W. 1991. *Environment and Economy: Property Rights and Public Policy.* Oxford, U.K.: Basil Blackwell.

Dasgupta, Partha. 1993. *An Enquiry into Well-Being and Destitution.* Oxford, U.K.: Oxford University Press.

de Soto, H. 1993. "The Missing Ingredient." *The Economist* 328(7828):8–12.

Eggertsson, T. 1990. *Economic Behavior and Institutions.* Cambridge, U.K.: Cambridge University Press.

Gordon, Scott. 1954. "The Economic Theory of a Common Property Resource: The Fishery." *Journal of Political Economy* 62(2):122–42.

Hanna, Susan. 1992. "Lessons for Ocean Governance from History, Ecology, and Economics." In B. Cicin-Sain, ed., *Ocean Governance: A New Vision.* Center for the Study of Marine Policy, Graduate College of Marine Studies, University of Delaware, Newark, pp. 23–25.

Hardin, Garrett. 1968. "The Tragedy of the Commons." *Science* 162:1243–48.

Munasinghe, Mohan. 1993. *Environmental Economics and Sustainable Development.* Washington, D.C.: World Bank.

Munasinghe, Mohan, and J. McNeely, eds. 1994. *Protected Area Economics and Policy.* Geneva and Washington, D.C.: World Conservation Union (IUCN) and World Bank.

Munasinghe, Mohan, and W. Shearer, eds. 1995. *Defining and Measuring Biogeophysical Sustainability.* Tokyo and Washington, D.C.: United Nations University and World Bank.

Ostrom, L. 1990. *Governing the Commons.* Cambridge, U.K.: Cambridge University Press.

World Commission on Environment and Development (WCED). 1987. *Our Common Future.* Oxford, U.K.: Oxford University Press.

Warming, Jens. 1911. "Om grundrente af fiskegrunde." *Nationalokonomisk Tidsskrift:* 495–506. Translated in P. Andersen, 1983, "On Rent of Fishing Grounds: A Translation of Jens Warming's 1911 Article, with an Introduction." *History of Political Economy* 15(3):391–96.

Governance

2

Design Lessons from Existing
Air Pollution Control Systems: The United States

Tom Tietenberg

Abstract

IN 1975 A VERY LIMITED transferable permits approach to air pollution control was implemented in the United States. From rather humble beginnings this approach has been expanded dramatically, encompassing not only a much wider set of pollutants, but also some rather different design characteristics. In this chapter, I describe the various applications of this approach to pollution control problems in the United States and extract the lessons for both the implementation process and program design that can be drawn from these applications.

Background

Beginning in 1975, burgeoning costs associated with the rigidities inherent in its traditional predominantly legal approach to controlling air pollution, led the U.S. Environmental Protection Agency (EPA) to start experimenting with an economic incentive approach now known as the **Emissions Trading Program**, a limited version of a system of transferable emissions permits. Since that time, the transferable emissions permit concept has been applied to several new areas of environmental policy and is currently being proposed for several more.

Support for the use of this market approach to environmental control has clearly grown in the United States, as reflected by the increasing number of applications by the federal government and by state governments. This political shift toward transferable permits has both benefited from and contributed to an increasingly favorable treatment in the popular business and environmental press. Some public interest environmental organizations have even adopted economic incentive approaches as a core part of their strategy for protecting the environment.

Overview

The intellectual foundation for this policy is provided by the economic concept known as the transferable permit. Knowledge about this particular form of control has grown rapidly in the two decades in which it has been implemented.

In this chapter, I will briefly describe the major programs that have made use of this concept to control air pollution and will provide a brief overview of some of the major lessons that have been learned about this approach.[1]

---

1. In the limited space permitted by this chapter, only a few highlights can be illustrated. All of the details of the proofs and the empirical work can be found in the bibliography at the end of the chapter. For a comprehensive summary of this work, see Dudek and Palmisano 1988; Hahn 1989; Hahn and Hester 1989a; Hahn and Hester 1989b; Tietenberg 1985; and Tietenberg 1990.

Applications of the Concept

The Traditional Approach

Stripped to its bare essentials, the U.S. prereform approach to pollution control relied upon a command-and-control approach to controlling pollution. Ambient standards, which establish the highest allowable concentration of the pollutant in the ambient air or water for each conventional pollutant, represent the targets of this approach.

To reach these targets, emissions or effluent standards (legal discharge ceilings) are imposed on a large number of specific discharge points, such as stacks, vents, outfalls, or storage tanks. Following a survey of the technological options of control, the control authority selects a favored control technology and calculates the amount of discharge reduction achievable by that technology as the basis for setting the emissions or effluent standard. Technologies yielding larger amounts of control and, hence, supporting more stringent standards are selected both for emitters in areas where is it very difficult to meet the ambient standard and for new emitters. The responsibility for defining and enforcing these standards is shared in legislatively specified ways between the national government and the various state governments.

Conventional Air Pollutants

In an attempt to inject more flexibility into the manner in which the objectives of the Clean Air Act were met during the last half of the 1970s, the EPA created what has become known as the emissions trading program. It attempts to facilitate compliance by allowing sources a much wider range of choice in how they satisfy their legal pollution control responsibilities than is possible in the command-and-control approach. Any source that chooses to reduce emissions at any discharge point more than is required by its emissions standard can apply to the control authority for certification of the excess control as an emissions reduction credit (ERC).

Defined in terms of a specific amount of a particular pollutant, the certified emissions reduction credit can be used to satisfy emissions standards at other, presumably more expensive to control, discharge points controlled by the creating source, or it can be sold to other sources. By making these credits transferable, the EPA allowed sources to find the cheapest means of satisfying their requirements, even if the cheapest means were under the control of another firm. The ERC is the currency used in emissions trading, and the offset, bubble, emissions banking, and netting policies govern how this currency can be stored and spent.[2]

The offset policy requires major new or expanding sources in nonattainment areas, those with air quality worse than the ambient standards, to secure sufficient offsetting emissions reductions, through the acquisition of ERCs, from existing firms so that the air is cleaner after their entry or expansion than before. This is accomplished by requiring new sources to more than offset any pollution they will add to the area. These sources must acquire ERCs for 120 percent of the amount they will emit. The extra 20 percent is gained as better air quality. Prior to this policy, no new firms were allowed to enter nonattainment areas on the grounds that they would interfere with attaining the ambient standards. By introducing the offset policy, EPA allowed economic growth to continue while insuring progress toward attainment.

The bubble policy receives its unusual name from the fact that it treats multiple emissions points, those that are controlled by existing emitters as opposed to those expanding or entering an area for the first time, as if they if they were enclosed in a bubble. Under this policy, only the total emissions of each pollutant leaving the bubble are regulated. Although the total leaving the bubble must be 20 percent less than the total permitted by adding up all the corresponding emissions standards within the bubble, emitters are free to control some discharge points fewer than dictated by the corresponding emissions standard, providing that sufficient compensating ERCs are obtained from other discharge points within the bubble. In essence, sources are free to choose the mix of control among the discharge points as long as the overall emissions reduction requirements are satisfied. Multi-plant bubbles are allowed, opening the possibility for trading ERCs among very different kinds of emitters.

Netting allows modifying or expanding sources, but not new sources, to escape from the need to meet the requirements of the stringent new source review process (including the need to acquire offsets) providing that any net increase in emissions, counting any ERCs earned elsewhere in the plant, is below an established threshold. Insofar as it allows firms to escape particular regulatory requirements by using ERCs to remain under the threshold that triggers applicability, netting is more properly considered regulatory relief than regulatory reform.

Emissions banking allows firms to store certified ERCs for subsequent use in the offset, bubble, or netting programs or for sale to others.

Lead in Gasoline

Following the path established by the Emissions Trading Program, the government began applying the transferable permit approach more widely. In the mid-1980s, prior to the issuance of new, more stringent regulations on lead in gasoline, EPA announced the results of a cost-benefit analysis of their expected impact. The analysis concluded that the proposed .01 grams per leaded gallon (gplg) standard would result in $36 billion (1983 U.S. dollars) in benefits, from reduced adverse health effects, at an estimated cost to the refining industry of $2.6 billion.

Although the regulation was unquestionably justified on efficiency grounds, EPA wanted to allow flexibility in how the deadlines were met without increasing the amount of lead used. Some refiners could meet early deadlines with ease, but others could do so only with a significant increase in cost. Recognizing that meeting the goal did not require every refiner to meet every deadline, EPA initiated the lead banking program to provide additional flexibility in meeting the regulations.

Under this program, a fixed amount of lead rights, which authorized the use of a fixed amount of lead over the transition period, were allocated to the various refiners. Refiners who did not need their full share of authorized rights, owing to earlier or larger reductions, could sell their rights to other refiners.

Refiners had an incentive to eliminate the lead quickly because early reductions freed up rights for sale. Their acquisition of credits made it

---

2. The details of this policy can be found in "Emissions Trading Policy Statement." (Dec. 4, 1986) *Federal Register, 51,* 43829.

possible for other refiners to comply with the deadlines, even in the face of equipment failures or acts of God. Fighting the deadlines in court, the traditional response, was unnecessary. Designed purely as a means of facilitating the transition to the new regime, the lead banking program ended as scheduled December 31, 1987 (Nussbaum 1992).

Ozone-Depleting Chemicals

Responding to the threat to the ozone shield, twenty four nations signed the Montreal Protocol in September 1988. According to this agreement, signatory nations have to restrict their production and consumption of the chief responsible gases to 50 percent of 1986 levels by June 30, 1998. Soon after the protocol was signed, new evidence suggested that it had not gone far enough; the damage apparently was increasing more rapidly than previously was thought. In response, fifty nine nations signed a new ozone agreement at a London conference in July 1990. This agreement called for the complete phaseout of halons and chlorofluorocarbons (CFCs) by the end of this century. Moreover, two other destructive chemicals, carbon tetrachloride and methyl chloroform, were added to the protocol and are scheduled to be eliminated by 2000 and 2005, respectively.

The United States has chosen to use a transferable permit system to implement its responsibilities under the protocols. On August 12, 1988, the Environmental Protection Agency issued regulations implementing a tradable permit system to achieve the targeted reductions (*Federal Register, 53,* 30598). According to these regulations, all major U.S. producers and consumers of the controlled substances were allocated baseline production or consumption allowances, using 1986 levels as the basis for the proration. Each producer and consumer is allowed 100 percent of the baseline allowance initially, with smaller allowances being granted after predefined deadlines. These allowances are transferable within producer and consumer categories, and production allowances can be transferred across international borders to producers in other signatory nations if the transaction is approved by EPA and results in the appropriate adjustments in the buyer or seller production allowances in their respective countries. Production allowances can be augmented by

demonstrating the safe destruction of an equivalent amount of controlled substances by approved means, but thus far no means have been approved.

Although transfers of the production allowances are allowed, even across international borders, they are severely constrained. The regulations allow any producer to increase its production allowance by any means, including transfer of a portion of another producer's allowance, by a maximum of 10 percent of its apportionment before 1998 and 15 percent of its apportionment after that date.

Because the demand for these allowances is inelastic, supply restrictions increase revenue. By allocating allowances to the seven major domestic producers of CFCs and halons, EPA was concerned that its regulation would result in sizable windfall profits, estimated to be billions of dollars, for those producers. EPA handled this problem by imposing a tax on the rents created by the regulation-induced scarcity. The Revenue Reconciliation Act of 1989 includes an excise tax imposed on all ozone-depleting chemicals sold or used by manufacturers, producers, or importers of these chemicals. The tax is imposed at the time the importer sells or uses the affected chemicals and is computed by multiplying the chemical's weight by the base tax rate and the chemical's ozone depletion factor. In addition to soaking up some of the regulation-induced scarcity rent, this tax provides incentives to switch to less harmful and, therefore, untaxed substances.

The application is unique in two senses. It not only allows international trading of allowances, but it also involves the simultaneous application of permit and tax systems.

Acid Rain

A version of the emissions-trading concept also has been incorporated into the U.S. approach for achieving further reductions in those electric utility emissions contributing to acid rain. Under this innovative approach, allowances to emit sulfur oxides have been allocated to older plants; the number of allowances will be restricted to ensure a reduction of 10 million tons in emissions from 1980 levels by the year 2010. The allowances, which provide a limited authorization to emit 1 ton of sulfur, are defined for a specific calendar year, but unused allowances can be carried forward into the next year, and they are transferable among the affected sources. Any plants reducing emissions more than required by the allowances could transfer the unused allowances to other plants. Emissions may not legally exceed the levels permitted by the allowances allocated plus acquired. An annual year-end audit balances the emissions with allowances. Utilities that emit more than authorized by their holdings of allowances must pay a $2,000-a-ton penalty and are required to forfeit an equivalent number of tons in the following year (Kete 1992; Kete 1994).

An important innovation in this program was the assurance of the availability of allowances through the institution of an auction market. Each year, EPA withholds 2.24 percent of the allocated allowances for the auction. These withheld permits are allocated to the highest bidders, with successful buyers paying their bid price. The proceeds are refunded to the utilities from whom the allowances were withheld, on a proportional basis.

Private allowance holders also may offer allowances for sale at these auctions. Potential sellers specify minimum acceptable prices. Once the withheld allowances have been disbursed, EPA matches the highest remaining bids with the lowest minimum acceptable prices on the private offerings and matches buyers and sellers until all remaining bids are less than the remaining minimum acceptable prices. This auction design, unfortunately, is not particularly efficient because it provides incentives for inefficient strategic behavior (Cason 1993; Hausker 1992).

Smog Trading

All of the above programs were initiated and promoted by the federal government. The newest programs, however, have arisen from state initiatives. Faced with the need to reduce ozone concentrations considerably in order to comply with the ozone ambient standard, states have chosen to use trading programs as a means of facilitating drastic reductions in precursor pollutants.

One of the most ambitious of these programs is California's Regional Clean Air Incentives Market (RECLAIM) established by the South Coast Air Quality Management District, the district responsible for the greater Los Angeles

area (Robinson 1993). Under RECLAIM, each of the almost 400 participating industrial polluters are allocated an annual pollution limit for nitrogen oxides and sulfur, which will decrease by 5 percent to 8 percent each year for the next decade. Polluters are allowed great flexibility in meeting these limits, including purchasing credits from other firms that have controlled more than their legal requirements.

The RECLAIM program shares with the sulfur allowance program the characteristic that it sets a cap on total emissions from the controlled group rather than on emissions from each source. This cap ensures that expansion must be accommodated within the cap, by cutting back a compensating amount somewhere else, rather than by allowing emissions to increase.

In an importance sense, the RECLAIM program changes the nature of the regulatory process: the burden of identifying the appropriate control strategies has been shifted from the control authority to the polluter. In part, the shift was a necessity because traditional processes were incapable of identifying enough appropriate technologies to produce sufficiently stringent reductions. In another part, it was motivated by a desire to make the process as flexible as possible.

As a result of the flexibility that became possible from the shift in the burden of choosing appropriate responses, many new control strategies are emerging. Instead of the traditional focus on end-of-pipe control technologies, pollution prevention has been given an economic underpinning by the program. All possible pollution reduction strategies, for the first time, can compete on a level playing field.

Mobile Sources

As a result of emissions reductions achieved from stationary sources, mobile sources in many regions of the United States now account for a high percentage of the remaining pollution. Although individual new vehicles also have been controlled for many years, an increase in both the number of vehicles and the amount of mileage the average vehicle is driven has offset to a large degree the gains achieved from the production of cleaner vehicles.

The desire to reduce mobile source pollution, beyond what can be achieved with traditional emissions standards, has motivated recent attempts to include them in emissions-trading programs designed to reduce ozone (Boyd 1993; Kling 1994). Because remote sampling of in-use vehicles has confirmed that in many cases a substantial proportion of the mobile source pollution is coming from a relatively small number of vehicles, one approach specifically targets those vehicles for early retirement.[3]

Under this approach, credits can be created by any source that acquires and retires high-emissions vehicles. The number of credits is determined by estimating the emissions avoided by vehicle retirement, which involves combining actual emissions tests on the retired vehicle with estimates of the number of miles the vehicle could have been driven over its remaining useful life and subtracting the emissions expected to be added by a replacement vehicle to produce the expected net emissions reduction per vehicle. After aggregating the results over the fleet of retired vehicles and discounting the aggregated estimated reduction to account for uncertainties in the estimation process, credits are issued for the adjusted aggregate net emissions reduction.

In California, for example, the UNOCAL Corporation, in cooperation with the California Air Resources Board, initiated a vehicle scrappage program. Offering $700 for pre-1971 vehicles, the program ultimately was responsible for retiring some 8,000 vehicles (Dudek and other 1992).

Vehicle retirement strategies are not the only way to include mobile sources within an emissions-trading program. A credit system can be used to provide manufacturers an incentive to produce cleaner cars than required by law (Rubin and Kling 1993) or to reward fleet operators for driving cleaner cars than required by law.

A Proposed Application: Global Warming

The proposed application of the emissions-trading concept to global warming could have large international consequences, particularly for developing countries. The possibility of using emissions trading in controlling greenhouse

gases was established by the Climate Change Convention, which went into force March 21, 1994. Reducing carbon dioxide emissions to 1990 levels by the end of the decade was specified as a voluntary target within the convention. Limiting carbon emissions to specific levels now appears to be an internationally-recognized objective.

The convention identified nations (listed in Annex I of the convention proceedings) that were committed to achieving a stabilization of carbon dioxide emissions by 2000. As Annex I nations seek to reduce emissions sufficiently to meet the target, they have two choices: they can either find reductions within their own borders, or they can seek them in other nations. An official process, known as joint implementation, has been established to explore and develop a set of procedures for transborder transfers of reduction offsets. Pilot projects, funded by the Global Environment Facility (GEF), have been initiated in China, Jamaica, Mexico, and the Philippines (Bertram 1992; OECD 1992; Rose and Tietenberg 1993; United Nations Conference on Trade and Development 1992). Although any initial trading is likely to take place among the industrialized nations, in the future, trades that include developing countries are a distinct possibility (Tietenberg 1994).

Design Elements of the Transferable Permit System

Two distinct forms of trading currently are in use, but the general evolution has been from credit trading to allowance trading. Although they are similar in many ways, the differences are subtle and significant. The variations in design that have been implemented in the United States provide a menu of possibilities as well as opportunities for assessing the consequences of various choices.

Credit Denomination

In the original emissions trading program, the credits were typically denominated in terms of a pollutant flow, such as tons per year. The newer programs are based on allowances defined in discrete terms—for example, tons rather than tons per year. Whereas the former confers a continuing entitlement to a flow, the latter is a

---

3. Interim EPA guidance for mobile source crediting can be found in the *Federal Register*, 58, 11134 (Feb. 23, 1993).

one-time entitlement to emit 1 ton. Once the authorized ton has been emitted, the allowance is surrendered. Authorizing additional emissions requires the issuance of new allowances. In general, this is done well in advance according to specific schedules so that emitters have reasonable security for pollution control investment planning. Allocating allowances in advance has also facilitated the development of futures markets.

One of the big differences between the two types of credits involves the capacity of the new definition to accommodate the creation and transfer of discrete emissions reductions. One of the original criteria used by EPA for approving credits was that the emissions reductions supporting them must be permanent. Many useful strategies to reduce emissions, such as meeting a deadline early, produce temporary, rather than permanent, reductions. As noted above, the ability to set an earlier deadline in the lead phaseout program was made possible by the flexibility inherent in an allowance program. With an allowance program, the tons saved by early compliance can free up a discrete number of allowances.

Baseline

Credit trading, the approach taken in the bubble and offset policies, allows emissions reductions, above and beyond legal requirements, to be certified as tradeable credits. The baseline for credits is provided by traditional technology-based standards. Credit trading presumes the preexistence of these standards, and it provides a more flexible means of achieving the aggregate goals that the source-based standards were designed to achieve.

Allowance trading, used in the acid rain–lead phaseout program and RECLAIM in California, assigns a prespecified number of allowances to polluters. Typically, the number declines over time, and the initial allocations are not necessarily based on traditional technology-based standards; in most cases, the aggregate reductions implied by the allowance allocations exceed those achievable with technology-based standards.

Despite their apparent similarity, the difference between these two types of trading systems should not be missed. Credit trading depends upon the existence of a previously determined

set of regulatory standards. Allowance trading does not. Once the aggregate number of allowances is defined, they can, in principle, be allocated among sources in an infinite number of ways. The practical implication is that allowances can be used even in circumstances where a technology-based baseline either has not been, or cannot be, established.

Caps

Allowances and credits differ in another significant way. Allowances systems set a cap on aggregate emissions that cannot be eroded by economic growth. This characteristic is not shared either by traditional technology-based, source-specific emissions standards or, in the absence of other constraints, by an emissions credit system that is linked to technology-based standards. Because emissions standards are source-specific, they exert no control over the aggregate amount of emissions from all sources. As the number of sources increases, the aggregate level of emissions increases. Similarly, credit trading that is based on these standards will allow aggregate emissions increases unless some additional constraint is built into the system.

In the United States, the additional constraint was that all new or expanding sources in nonattainment areas were required to offset all emissions increases by acquiring sufficient credits from existing emitters so that air quality would improve as a result of their entering the area or expanding their operations. No such constraint was mandatory in attainment areas so that credit trading could lead to emissions increases in those areas as the number of sources increased.

Allocation Method

In principle, entitlements could either be auctioned off, with the sources purchasing them from their respective governments at the market-clearing price (Lyon 1989; Lyon 1990), or distributed to each source on the basis of some allocation rule, which typically, but not inevitably, is based on historical use. Only a transferable permit system that allocates permits free of charge to sources on the basis of their historic emissions rate would guarantee that existing sources would be no worse off than they would under a command-and-control system imposing the same degree of control. The financial outlays associated with acquiring allowances or credits in a traditional auction market, or a comparable emissions charge, would be sufficiently large that sources typically would have lower financial burdens with the traditional command-and-control approach than with these particular economic incentive approaches (Atkinson and Tietenberg 1982; Atkinson and Tietenberg 1984; Hahn 1984; Harrison 1983; Krupnick 1986; Lyon 1982; Palmer et al. 1980; Seskin, Anderson, and Reid 1983; Shapiro and Warhit 1983).

From the point of view of the source that is required to control its emissions, two components of financial burden are significant: controlling costs and controlling expenditures on permits. Although only the first represents real resource costs to society as a whole—the latter merely represents transfers from one group in society to another—both represent a financial burden to the source. The empirical evidence suggests that when a traditional auction market is used to distribute permits or, equivalently, when all uncontrolled emissions are subject to an emissions tax, the permit expenditures (tax revenue) frequently would be larger in magnitude than the control costs. The sources would spend more on permits, or pay more in taxes, than they would on the control equipment. This characteristic has inhibited the adoption of these approaches within the United States.

Under the traditional command-and-control system, firms make no financial outlays to the government. Although control costs are necessarily higher with the command-and-control system than with a marketable permit system, they are not so high as to outweigh the additional financial outlays required in an auction market permit system or an emissions tax system. For this reason, existing sources understandably oppose distributing permits by a traditional auction market despite its social appeal, unless the revenue derived is used in a manner that is approved by the sources, and the sources with which it competes are required to absorb similar expenses.

Both free distribution and the auction market have significant disadvantages. A main disadvantage of the free distribution approach is that it does not generate any revenue for the government. A main disadvantage of the auction approach is that it raises the financial burden of the polluting firms, a significant deterrent in an increasingly competitive global market (Tietenberg 1990).

In the absence of either a politically popular way to use the revenue or assurances that competitors will face similar financial burdens, the political opposition could be reduced substantially by distributing the permits free to existing sources on the basis of a grandfather rule. Under grandfathering, sources only have to purchase additional permits they may need over and above the initial allocation, as opposed to purchasing all permits in an auction market. Grandfathering is *de facto* the approach taken in all of the programs.

Grandfathering, however, has disadvantages. Although reserving some permits for new firms is possible, this option is rarely exercised in practice. As a result, under the free distribution scheme, new firms typically have to purchase all permits, whereas existing firms get an initial allocation free. Thus, this free distribution system imposes a bias against new sources in the sense that their financial burden is greater than that of an otherwise identical existing source, even if the two sources install exactly the same emissions control devices. The evidence suggests that this new source bias has retarded the introduction of new facilities and new technologies (Maloney and Brady 1988; Nelson, Tietenberg, and Donihue 1993).

As the auctions in the sulfur allowance program have made clear, it is possible to combine these approaches in a useful way. Although that program bases the allowance distribution in part on historical emissions, it also requires some of those allowances to be put up for sale each year. Because the proceeds from the auction are returned to the original holders of the auctioned allowances, the financial burden associated with this auction is no greater than that associated with a pure grandfathered system.

Coping with Spatial Issues

Transferable permits seem to have worked particularly well for trades involving uniformly mixed pollutants—those for which only the level of emissions matters—and for trades of nonuniformly mixed pollutants—those for which emissions location also matters—involving contiguous discharge points.

The plurality of consummated trades in the emissions-trading program have involved uniformly mixed pollutants. Because dispersion modeling is not required for uniformly mixed pollutants, even when the trading sources are somewhat distant from one another, trades involving these pollutants are cheaper to consummate. Additionally, trades involving uniformly mixed pollutants do not raise concerns about local air quality deterioration because the location of the emissions is not a matter of policy consequence.

But when emissions location does matter, the dominance of economic instruments over traditional command-and-control strategies is less clear cut in practice than it might appear from theory. Although the fully cost-effective system is relatively easy to define in this circumstance (Montgomery 1972), implementing such a system imposes a large administrative burden. Because the economic and environmental benefits from allowing trading both in the short run and the long run, particularly their ability to stimulate technological progress and pollution prevention, are so large, attempts to implement second-best designs are justified. All second-best designs involve an element of compromise with the cost-effectiveness goal, but they still can represent an improvement, sometimes a substantial improvement, over more traditional approaches.

The menu of promising second-best strategies is growing (Atkinson 1994; Tietenberg, forthcoming). Although the most commonly discussed second-best strategies all have problems, slight modifications of those approaches, as embodied in the new generation of approaches, do appear to offer the prospect for significant reductions in compliance costs, while assuring environmental improvement.

Space does not permit an elaboration of all the possibilities here, but one approach can be illustrated. The starting point for this approach is the assumption that it is better to implement a basic system built around standard emissions permits, dealing individually with those trades that would result in hot spots or excess pollution at the most severely affected receptors, rather than to establish wholesale restrictions on trades.

One illustration of how this type of constrained trading could be implemented has surfaced in the United States in the trading rules developed by a new entity for controlling tropospheric ozone, the Ozone Transport Commission (OTC). Attempting to implement a truly regional strategy that deals realistically with the spatial elements of the problem, the commission, which has jurisdiction over the northeastern United States from Washington, D.C., to Maine, has allowed regional trading of NOx offsets, subject to some specific trading constraints.

Because the ozone plume typically moves in a particular direction, and not all emissions in a region affect nonattainment status equally, without any constraints it would be possible for offset trades to actually worsen the degree of nonattainment. To allow interstate trading while ensuring environmental improvement in the most severely affected areas, the OTC plan imposes two restrictions on trading: offsets must come from an area with equal or more severe nonattainment,[4] and offsetting reductions must have contributed to violations of the ambient standard in the area of the new emissions. The first restriction offers protection against trades which worsen pollution in the most severely affected areas, while the second, in effect, creates trading zones that conform to wind flow patterns.

Compared to an unrestricted trading area, these rules have the effect of reducing the size of trading areas and, hence, the number of possible trades. However, they do allow trades across large distances and offer better environmental protection than an unrestricted system.

Dealing with Market Power

One of the fears that is expressed in almost any new discussion of transferable permits involves the degree to which this approach may either facilitate market power or be rendered ineffective by the existence of market power. In general, these fears have not been substantiated by experience.

The first type of market power involves the ability of participants to manipulate prices strategically in the permit market, either as a

---

4. Nonattainment areas are further classified into five categories, depending on current ozone concentration levels: marginal, moderate, serious, severe, and extreme. These designations affect both the deadlines for achieving the ambient ozone standards and the rules affecting offset trading.

monopolistic seller or a monopsonistic buyer. Although only a few studies of the empirical impact of market power on emissions trading have been accomplished, their results are consistent with a finding that market power does not seem to have a large effect on regional control costs in most realistic situations (Hahn 1984).

Within the class of grandfathered distribution rules, some rules create a larger potential for strategic price behavior than others. In general, the larger the divergence between the number of permits received by the price-searching source and the cost-effective number of permits, the larger the potential for market power. When allocated an excess of permits by the control authority, price-searching firms can exercise power on the selling side of the market, and when allocated too few permits, they can exercise power on the buying side of the market.

According to the existing studies, it takes a rather considerable divergence from the cost-effective allocation of permits to produce much difference in regional control costs. Because most realistic rules used to distribute permits are estimated to affect control costs to only a small degree, the deviations from the least-cost allocation caused by market power pale in comparison to the much larger potential cost reductions achievable by implementing a marketable emissions permit system.

Strategic price behavior is not the only potential source of market power problems. Firms could conceivably use also permit markets as a vehicle for driving competitors out of business. (Misiolek and Elder 1989). This problem is relatively rare (Tietenberg 1985).

Even when the possibility of market power exists, the consequences frequently can be limited by proper program design. For example, the sulfur allowance program has two design components that would diminish the ability of any participant to exercise market power of either form. First, the auction market provides a continuous alternative source of permits. Second, the program contains a set-aside of allowable permits that the government can sell at $1,500 a ton, should the need arise.

Shut-Down Credits

From an economic point of view, how the credits are created or allowances freed up for sale does not really matter. Experience has shown, however, that from a political point of view it does. And, among the various ways of creating credits, shut-downs seem to have generated the most dissatisfaction.

When a source shuts down its operations, its emissions will drop to zero. Normally, the allowable emissions granted to that plant would become available for transfer. Some states, however, have shown a reluctance to allow the unrestricted sale of allowances from a shut-down. The reluctance is based not only on the desire to avoid any appearance that policy may be implicitly subsidizing shut-downs, but also on the belief that the economic incentive should be targeted at positive actions to reduce pollution, such as investing in new control equipment or changing the production process to reduce emissions, not to reduce shut-downs. Shut-downs are considered an artifact of other economic decisions, rather than a positive action to reduce pollutants.

A variety of methods have been developed to deal with these concerns while attempting to maintain the integrity of the system. In the two limiting cases, all shut-down credits could either revert to the control authority, or they could be authorized for unrestricted sale. In practice, most areas make finer distinctions. For example, firms which are selling their shut-down facilities to another firm commencing operations at the same site may be allowed to include the allowance entitlements in the sale. Or, if the firm that is shutting down its operations wants to commence operations elsewhere in the state, it may be allowed to carry its allowances from the shut-down with it.

Other allowances may revert to the state, either to be retired, thereby producing better air quality, or sold, thereby facilitating economic development. If they are retired, then the supply of allowances is reduced. In areas with very stringent controls, shut-down credits may be a major source of available allowances, and their retirement could have a significant effect on the number available for trading.

Opt-in Provisions

Each program applies to an eligible population. For example, the sulfur allowance system applies to the slightly more than 800 electric utilities in the United States, and the RECLAIM program applies to approximately 400 industrial polluters. Usually, the eligible population is not the sole source of the pollutants being controlled, but for monitoring or other reasons, the remaining sources are not included. Leaving them out, unfortunately, reduces the set of control opportunities and, therefore, increases the resulting cost.

This problem is reduced by creating a process by which polluters that are not part of the eligible population can voluntarily opt-in, or join, the process. Usually, in opt-in procedures, applicants face the burden of proving that they can satisfy the basic conditions of participation. Individual emitters who fulfill the conditions may join. The sulfur allowance program, for example, has opt-in provisions for industrial boilers.

Why would any initially ineligible individual source want to join? In many cases, individual emitters are capable of reducing emissions well below their allowable levels. As long as they are not in the program, surplus reductions are not rewarded. Once in the program, however, surplus reductions become transferable and can either be sold or used by the plant owners in other locations.

Conclusions and Policy Implications

Substituting for vs. Complementing Traditional Regulation

Whereas the early programs complemented traditional regulation by making it more flexible, later programs represent a more radical departure from traditional regulation. They are beginning to substitute for traditional regulation.

The earliest use of this concept, the emissions-trading program, overlaid credit trading on an existing regulatory regime and was designed to facilitate implementation of that program. Trading baselines were determined on the basis of already determined, technology-based standards, and created credits could not be used to satisfy a number of these standards. The requisite technology had to be installed.

More recent programs, such as the sulfur allowance and RECLAIM programs, replace, rather than complement, traditional regulation. Allowance allocations for these programs were not based on preexisting technology-based standards. In the case of RECLAIM, the control

authority, the South Coast Air Quality Management District, could not have based allowances on predetermined standards even if they had been inclined to do so. Defining a complete set of technologies that offered the necessary environmental improvement and yet were feasible in both an economic and engineering sense proved impossible. Traditional regulation was incapable of providing the degree of reduction required by the Clean Air Act.

The solution was to define a set of allowances that would meet the environmental objectives, leaving the choice of methods for living within the constraints imposed by those allowances up to the sources covered by the regulations. This approach fundamentally changes the nature of the control process. The historical approach involved making the control authority responsible, not only for defining the environmental objectives and performing the monitoring and enforcement activities necessary to assure compliance with those objectives, but also for defining the best means for reaching those objectives. The allowance program transfers the last of these responsibilities to the private sector and retains for the public sector both the responsibility for defining the environmental target and performing the monitoring and enforcement function.

Pursuing Cost-Effectiveness

A vast majority, though not all, of the relevant empirical studies in the United States have found control costs to be substantially higher with the regulatory command-and-control system than the least-cost means of allocating the control responsibility (Tietenberg 1985). This is an important finding because it provides the motivation for introducing a reform program; the potential social gains, in terms of reduced control cost, from breaking away from the status quo are sufficient to justify the trouble. Although the estimates of the excess costs attributable to a command-and-control system, presented in the numerous studies, overstate the cost savings that would be achieved by even a completely unrestricted permit market (a point discussed in more detail below), the general conclusion that the potential cost savings are large from adopting economic incentive approaches seems accurate, even after correcting for overstatement.

The emissions-trading program is the basis for most existing empirical work because of its longevity. When judged from the perspective of whether the emissions-trading program improved the system that preceded it, the answer is certainly yes! Judged by whether it has achieved full cost-effectiveness, the answer is no!

The program has unquestionably and substantially reduced the costs of complying with the requirements of the Clean Air Act. Most estimates place the accumulated capital savings for all components of the program at over $10 billion. This does not include the recurring savings in operating costs.

On the other hand, the emissions-trading program did not produce the magnitude of cost savings that was anticipated by most proponents at its inception. Part of this failure to fulfill expectations can be explained as the result of unrealistically inflated expectations. More restrictive regulatory decisions than expected and higher than expected transaction costs also bear some responsibility.

The models used to calculate the potential cost savings were not, and are not, completely adequate guides to reality. The cost functions in these models are invariably *ex ante* long-run cost functions. They implicitly assume that the modeled plant can be built from scratch and can incorporate the best technology. In practice, of course, many existing sources cannot retrofit these technologies, and, therefore, their *ex post* control options are much more limited than implied by the models.

The models also assume all trades are multilateral and are simultaneously consummated, whereas actual trades are usually bilateral and sequential. The distinction is important for nonuniformly mixed pollutants because bilateral trades frequently are constrained by concerns about decreasing air quality at the site of the acquiring source. With multilateral trades, the concerns would frequently be allayed by compensating reductions coming from other near-by sources. In essence, the models implicitly assume an idealized market process, which is only remotely approximated by actual transactions. The amount of potential cost savings that is sacrificed in bilateral, sequential trading of nonuniformly mixed pollutants is apparently large (Atkinson and Tietenberg 1991).

In addition, some non-negligible proportion of the expected cost savings recorded by the models is attributable to the substantially larger amounts of emissions allowed by the modeled permit equilibrium (Atkinson and Tietenberg 1987). For nonuniformly mixed pollutants, for example, the cost estimates imply that the control authority is allowed to arrange the control responsibility in any fashion that satisfies the ambient air quality standards. In essence, the models allocate more uncontrolled emissions to sources with tall stacks because those emissions can be exported. Exported emissions avoid control costs without affecting the readings at the local monitors. The portion of the cost savings estimated by the models that is due to allowing increased emissions is not acceptable to regulators. Some recent work has suggested that the benefits received from the additional emissions control required by the command-and-control approach may be justified by the net benefits received (Oates, Portney, and McGartland 1989). The regulatory refusal to allow emissions increases may not have been such a bad idea.[5]

Certain types of trades that were assumed to be permissible under the models were prohibited in the emissions-trading program. New sources, for example, were not allowed to satisfy the New Source Performance Standards, which imply a particular control technology, by choosing some less-stringent control option and making up the difference with acquired emissions reduction credits; they must install the degree of technological control necessary to meet the standard. Typically, this is the same technology used by EPA to define the standard in the first place.

In the emissions-trading program, much uncertainty was associated with emissions reduction credit transactions because they depend so heavily on administrative action. All trades required approval by the control authorities. When the authorities were not cooperative, or at least consistent, the value of the created emissions reduction credits was diminished or even destroyed.

---

5. Not all of the cost savings, of course, results from the capability to increase emissions. The remaining portion of the savings, which results from taking advantage of opportunities to control a given level of emissions at a lower cost, is still substantial and can be captured by a well-designed permit system that does not allow emissions to increase beyond the command-and-control benchmark. See the calculations in Atkinson and Tietenberg (1987).

Reducing Transactions Costs with Program Design

The emissions-trading program resulted in fewer trading opportunities than had been anticipated, as noted above. Therefore, although the program did produce considerable savings, it fell far short of achieving full cost-effectiveness.

One of the lessons derived from the evolution of these programs is that some of the high transactions costs experienced by the emissions-trading program can be decreased with proper program design. Providing better information to participants is the key.

Price Revelation

One of the specific problems with the early system was that prices were determined in private during bilateral negotiations. Because the results of those negotiations typically were not revealed publicly, the prices associated with ERCs were not known generally.

Inadequate knowledge about prices not only makes negotiations more complicated than necessary for the parties involved, but it makes pollution control investment planning more difficult for all sources. Because equilibrium prices should reflect marginal control costs, knowing these prices and how they are changing over time provides a great deal of information on the desirability of future control investments. Prices in the $5,000-a-ton range suggest a very different set of control options than prices in the $250-a-ton range.

The sulfur allowance program rectifies this deficiency by initiating both spot and future auctions for sulfur allowances. One of the side benefits of this auction is that it reveals both current and future prices to everyone, thereby improving information considerably.

Even in cases where auctions may not be practical, it is possible to get better price information. For example, whenever sources that have acquired credits seek to use them to fulfill regulatory requirements, they could be required to provide price information that would be shared in annual reports to the public.

Clearinghouse

Another strategy for lowering transactions costs is to provide a clearinghouse for all buyers and sellers to learn about trading possibilities.

One-stop shopping for allowances represents a considerable improvement over the previous practice of hiring brokers to ferret out possible sources. Although brokers were a market response to high transactions costs, providing a clearinghouse makes it easier, quicker, and cheaper for all parties.

Shifting the Payoff

The demonstration that the traditional regulatory policy was not cost-effective had two mirror-image implications. It either implied that the same air quality goals could be achieved at lower cost, or that better air quality could be achieved at the same cost. The earlier programs were designed to exploit the first implication; the later programs attempted to produce better air quality and lower cost.

Trading programs were used to produce better air quality in many ways. The lower costs offered by trading were used in initial negotiations to secure somewhat more stringent pollution control targets, as in the acid rain and RECLAIM programs, or earlier deadlines, as in the lead phaseout program. Offset ratios for trades in nonattainment areas were set at a ratio greater than 1.0, implying that a portion of each acquisition would go for better air quality. Environmental groups are allowed to purchase and retire sulfur allowances at the auction.

This shift toward sharing the benefits has had two consequences. Cost savings are lower than they would have been without benefits sharing, but the public support, and particularly the support from environmental organizations, has been increased greatly. Politically, this means that it is now easier to implement trading programs because the potential common ground has been expanded.

Encouraging Technological Progress

Transferable permits encourage more technological progress in pollution control than the command-and-control system (Milliman and Prince 1989). The anecdotal evidence seems to suggest that it not only bolsters the rate of change in pollution control, but it influences the direction and structure of control approaches. Traditional command-and-control policies usually base standards on technologies known to the regulators. Meeting those standards can be accomplished simply by adopting the identified technology. Adopters have little incentive to search for superior technologies.

With transferable permits, adopters not only have an incentive to search for new technologies that reduce the cost of compliance of meeting the mandated standard, they also have an incentive to search for technologies that can reduce emissions more than is required by the standard. Selling the emissions reduction credits, or unused allowances, produces revenue that can be used to finance the new technologies.

Allowances have facilitated the transition to new areas of pollution control. most notably in the area of pollution prevention. Whereas, under traditional regulation, firms saw their role as merely adopting the end-of-pipe technology suggested by the federal or state control authority, now they have begun to scrutinize their entire production process. Strategies that prevent pollution, such as process changes, free up valuable allowances and, hence, become more attractive to the adopting source.

Combining Policy Instruments

If raising revenue became an important component in the coalition-building strategy followed by negotiators, the revenue could be raised by levying a low annual fee on each entitlement, even while using a grandfathered entitlement system. The revenue could be used to finance the monitoring and enforcement system, be retained by the community, or be dedicated to other worthy purposes without jeopardizing the cost-effectiveness of the system.

Although an annual fee is not a necessary component of a transferable entitlement system, it can be added if so desired. This combined system would leave the control of emissions to the quantity-based entitlements, and would use the fee to raise revenue.

Coupling a low annual fee with a free distribution of permits provides an attractive alternative to both auctioned entitlements and an emissions charge. Because of political reluctance to establish rates as high as would be required to achieve conventional emissions reduction targets, emissions charges have traditionally not been effective in producing the desired level of emissions reduction. They have, however, been effective in raising revenue for environmental purposes, particularly in Europe (OECD 1989).

Conversely, although grandfathered entitlements have been effective in producing the desired level of control, they produce no revenue. The combined system provides more assurance of sufficient emissions reduction and of raising revenue.

Because per unit annual fees applied to the emissions authorized by the allowances do not affect the cost-effectiveness of the system, the fee can be as low or as high as necessary to achieve the desired revenue result. Although the fees do lower the entitlement price, they do not affect the incentive to trade. The incentive is preserved by the fact that a seller not only receives the price for the entitlement, but is able to avoid paying the annual fee any longer on the transferred entitlements.

Merging Equity with Cost-Effectiveness

Because transferable entitlement systems allow the issue of who will pay for control to be separated from who will undertake control, they allow distributional and cost-effectiveness goals to be pursued simultaneously. They also facilitate technology transfer by providing a means for cost-sharing and risk-sharing.

Regardless of the initial allocation of permits, the trading that would subsequently take place would provide the means for control of greenhouse gases to be accomplished cost-effectively. This is a particularly important feature when concerns about fairness and affordability preclude simple solutions, such as equal proportional reductions. Even very complex allocations of the control responsibilities, which are sensitive to a host of individual fairness concerns, can be fully compatible with achieving the desired emissions target at the lowest possible cost.

Sharing the Risk

Risk-sharing can be achieved even for very limited versions of transferable entitlement systems. In the United States, for example, some sulfur oxide control equipment manufacturers have indicated a willingness to install the pollution control equipment free of charge, taking only the sulfur oxide allowances in return.[6] In this way, the recipient utility incurs neither a

---

6.   I am indebted to Dan Dudek of the Environmental Defense Fund for pointing this out.

financial burden nor a financial risk; the equipment supplier is willing to accept both by accepting the allowances as payment.

Can This System Be Used in Developing Countries?

Although no definitive answer can be given to this question because developing country implementation experience is lacking, some grounds for optimism exist. To start with, it certainly appears that attempts to use this type of system in a developing country context are merited. In developing countries, where the opportunity cost of capital is high, it makes especially good sense to assure that investments, including pollution control investments, are made wisely. The cost-effectiveness properties of tradable permits, therefore, make them especially attractive. Furthermore, the powerful incentive effects provided by transferable permits could stimulate much more rapid development and implementation of new, innovative control technologies and strategies, such as pollution prevention. By stimulating technological progress, a transferable permits approach can contribute to the lowering of long-run as well as short-run costs. These potential cost savings should provide considerable motivation to adapt the strategy for use in developing countries.

Transferable permits also offer the possibility for raising revenue for environmental protection in countries were government revenue is a serious constraint. Combining fees with transferable permits allows an additional source of funding. In the United States at the moment, much of the financial responsibility for funding the monitoring and enforcement system has been transferred from the taxpayers to the pollution sources by means of fees on permits.

The most serious concerns about the transferability of this approach to developing countries have to do with whether developing countries have sufficient organizational resources to manage this approach (Lyon 1989). When this question is raised, the questioner usually is making the implicit assumption that the organizational resources in developing countries are homogeneous and insufficient. They are not homogeneous, of course. Some countries have sufficient resources now, and others could use a program such as this to begin the process of

accumulating sufficient resources over time, little by little.

My experience in the United States leads me to believe that the infrastructure that would be necessary to run a transferable permit program is not, over the long run, greater than those necessary to run an equally effective traditional regulation system, but the nature of that infrastructure may differ.

One misleading myth about conventional regulation holds that mere verification that the correct control equipment has been acquired by the source and that it has been installed correctly is a sufficient enforcement strategy. Although it is possible to set up a regulatory system where enforcement takes this form, those systems are rarely effective (Russell, Harrington, and Vaughan 1986). Initial compliance does not ensure continuing compliance. Installing the right equipment certainly does not guarantee that it is operated and maintained correctly; effective enforcement requires continuous monitoring of some form. In this respect, transferable permits and traditional regulation share the same requirements.

As a practical matter, however, reasonable monitoring systems are not very burdensome for a control authority. Most emissions monitoring is based upon a system of self-reporting (Russell, Harrington, and Vaughan 1986). Although self-reporting systems immediately raise concerns about possible abuse, in practice they work remarkably well, particularly when complemented by an effective system of criminal penalties for falsification.

Furthermore, it is possible to design limited resource enforcement systems that can be effective (Harrington, 1988; Russell, Harrington, and Vaughan 1986). The secret to this design is to target more resources on repeat offenders. Among other characteristics, this approach discourages sources from becoming repeat offenders so they can avoid the hassle of intense scrutiny.

The skills involved in running these two types of programs are rather different. Under traditional regulation, the responsibility for defining appropriate control technologies falls on the regulatory authority. With transferable permits, it falls on the private sources. Therefore, with transferable permits, the control authorities need fewer staff trained in environmental engineering.

The remainder could be dedicated to the monitoring and enforcement functions.

Finally, the public monitoring and enforcement infrastructure can be bolstered by allowing some degree of private enforcement (Naysnerski and Tietenberg 1992). Allowing private enforcement to complement public enforcement increases the amount of resources dedicated to monitoring and enforcement and allows public resources to be used more effectively. An effective self-reporting system, as described above, makes this private enforcement possible.

It probably will not be long before we have implementation experience from developing countries. Chile recently passed an Environmental Framework Law that requires the use of transferable permits. In its effort to implement this law, Santiago is likely to become the world leader in crafting versions of this approach that are appropriate in a developing country context. At that point, we thankfully will be able to replace speculation with experience.

Concluding Comment

The transferable permit programs in the United States have improved upon the command-and-control program that preceded them. The documented cost savings are large and the flexibility provided has been important. To be sure, the program is far from perfect, but the flaws should be kept in perspective. Although the emissions-trading program loses its utopian luster upon closer inspection, it has nonetheless made a lasting contribution to environmental policy.

Bibliography

Atkinson, Scott E. 1983. "Marketable Pollution Permits and Acid Rain Externalities." *Canadian Journal of Economics* 16(4):704–22.

———. 1994. "Tradable Discharge Permits: Restrictions on Least Cost Solutions." In G. Klaassen and Finn Førsund, *Economic Instrument for Air Pollution Control*. Boston: Kluwer Academic Pubishers, pp. 3–21.

Atkinson, Scott E., and Tom H. Tietenberg. 1982. "The Empirical Properties of Two Classes of Designs for Transferable Discharge Permit Markets." *Journal of Environmental Economics and Management* 9(2):101–21.

———. 1984. "Approaches for Reaching Ambient Standards in Non-Attainment Areas: Financial Burden and Efficiency Considerations." *Land Economics* 60(2):148–59.

———. 1987. "Economic Implications of Emission Trading Rules for Local and Regional Pollutants." *Canadian Journal of Economics* 20(2): 370–86.

———. 1991. "Market Failure in Incentive-Based Regulation: The Case of Emissions Trading." *Journal of Environmental Economics and Management* 21(1):17–31.

Bertram, G. 1992. "Tradeable Emission Permits and the Control of Greenhouse Gases." *Journal of Development Studies* 28(3):423–46.

Boyd, James D. 1993. "Mobile Source Emissions Reduction Credits as a Cost-Effective Measure for Controlling Urban Air Pollution." In Richard F. Kosobud, William A. Testa, and Donald A. Hanson, eds., *Cost-Effective Control of Urban Smog*. Chicago: Federal Reserve Bank of Chicago.

Cason, T. N. 1993. "Seller Incentive Properties of EPA's Emission Trading Auction." *Journal of Environmental Economics and Management* 25(2):177–95.

Dudek, Daniel J., Joseph Goffman, Dean Drake, and Tom Walton. 1992. *Mobile Emissions Reduction Crediting*. New York: Environmental Defense Fund and General Motors.

Dudek, Daniel J., and John Palmisano. 1988. "Emissions Trading: Why is this Thoroughbred Hobbled?" *Columbia Journal of Environmental Law* 13(2):217–56.

Feldman, Stephen L., and Robert K. Raufer. 1987. *Emissions Trading and Acid Rain: Implementing a Market Approach to Pollution Control*. Totowa, NJ: Rowman & Littlefield.

Hahn, Robert W. 1984. "Market Power and Transferable Property Rights." *Quarterly Journal of Economics* 99(4):753–65.

———. 1989. "Economic Prescriptions for Environmental Problems: How the Patient Followed the Doctor's Orders." *The Journal of Economic Perspectives* 3(2):95–114.

Hahn, Robert W., and Gordon L. Hester. 1989a. "Marketable Permits: Lessons from Theory and Practice." *Ecology Law Quarterly* 16:361–406.

———. 1989b. "Where Did All the Markets Go? An Analysis of EPA's Emission Trading

Program." *Yale Journal of Regulation* 6(1):109–53.

Harrison, D., Jr. 1983. "Case Study 1: The Regulation of Aircraft Noise." (p. 41–143) In Thomas C. Schelling, ed., *Incentives for Environmental Protection*. Cambridge, Mass: MIT Press.

Hausker, K. 1992. "The Politics and Economics of Auction Design in the Market for Sulfur Dioxide Pollution." *Journal of Policy Analysis and Management* 11(4):553–72.

Harrington, W. 1988. "Enforcement Leverage When Penalties Are Restricted." *Journal of Public Economics* 37:29–53.

Kete, Nancy. 1992. "The U.S. Acid Rain Control Allowance Trading System." (p. 69–93) In Tom Jones and Jan Corfee-Morlot, eds., *Climate Change: Designing a Tradeable Permit System*. Paris: Organization for Economic Co-operation and Development.

———. 1994. "Air Pollution Control in the United States: A Mixed Portfolio Approach." (p. 122–44) In Ger Klaassen and Finn R. Førsund, eds., *Economic Instruments for Air Pollution Control*. Boston: Kluwer Academic Publishers.

Kling, C. L. 1994. "Emission Trading vs. Rigid Regulations in the Control of Vehicle Emissions." *Land Economics* 70(2):174–88.

Krupnick, Alan J. 1986. "Costs of Alternative Policies for the Control of NO2 in the Baltimore Region." *Journal of Environmental Economics and Management* 13(2):189–97.

Lyon, R. M. 1982. "Auctions and Alternative Procedures for Allocating Pollution Rights." *Land Economics* 58(1):16–32.

———. 1989. "Transferable Discharge Permit Systems and Environmental Management in Developing Countries." *World Development* 17(8): 1299–1312.

———. 1990. "Regulating Bureaucratic Polluters." *Public Finance Quarterly* 2:198–220.

Maloney, Michael and Gordon L. Brady. 1988. "Capital Turnover and Marketable Property Rights." *The Journal of Law and Economics* 31(1):203–26.

Milliman, Scott R., and Raymond Prince. 1989. "Firm Incentives to Promote Technological Change in Pollution Control." *Journal of Environmental Economics and Management* 17(3):247–65.

Misiolek, W. S., and H. W. Elder. 1989. "Exclusionary Manipulation of Markets for Pollution Rights." *Journal of Environmental Economics and Management* 16(2):156–66.

Montgomery, W. D. 1972. "Markets in Licenses and Efficient Pollution Control Programs." *Journal of Economic Theory* 5(3):395–418.

Naysnerski, W., and T. Tietenberg. 1992. "Private Enforcement of Environmental Law." *Land Economics* 68(1):28–48.

Nelson, Randy, Tom Tietenberg, and Michael R. Donihue. 1993."Differential Environmental Regulation: Effects On Electric Utility Capital Turnover and Emissions." *Review of Economics and Statistics* 75(2):368–73.

Nussbaum, Barry D. 1992. "Phasing Down Lead in Gasoline in the U.S.: Mandates, Incentives, Trading and Banking." (p. 21–34) In Tom Jones and Jan Corfee-Morlot, eds., *Climate Change: Designing a Tradeable Permit System*.Paris: Organization for Economic Co-operation and Development.

Oates, W. E., and A. M. McGartland. 1985. "Marketable Pollution Permits and Acid Rain Externalities: A Comment and Some Further Evidence." *Canadian Journal of Economics* 18(3):668–75.

Oates, W. E., P. R. Portney, and A. M. McGartland. 1989. "The Net Benefits of Incentive-Based Regulation: The Case of Environmental Standard Setting." *American Economic Review* 79(5):1233–42.

OECD. 1989. *Economic Instruments for Environmental Protection*. Paris: Organization for Economic Cooperation and Development.

———. 1992. *Climate Change: Designing a Tradeable Permit System*. Paris: Organization for Economic Cooperation and Development.

Palmer, Adele R., William E. Mooz, Timothy H. Quinn, and Kathleen A. Wolf. 1980. *Economic Implications of Regulating Chlorofluorocarbon Emissions from Nonaerosol Applications*. Washington, D.C.: U.S. Environmental Protection Agency.

Robinson, Kelly. 1993. "The Regional Economic Impacts of Marketable Permit Programs: The Case of Los Angeles." In Richard F. Kosobud, William A. Testa, and Donald A Hanson, eds., *Cost-Effective Control of Urban Smog*. Chicago: Federal Reserve Bank of Chicago.

Rose, Adam and Tom Tietenberg. 1993. "An International System of Tradeable CO2 Entitlements: Implications for Economic Development." *Journal of Environment and Development* 2(1):1–36.

Rubin, Jonathan and Catherine Kling. 1993. "An Emission Saved Is an Emission Earned: An Empirical Study of Emission Banking for Light-Duty Vehicle Manufacturers." *Journal of Environmental Economics and Management* 25(3):257–74.

Russell, Clifford S., Winston Harrington, and William J. Vaughan. 1986. *Enforcing Pollution Control Laws.* Washington, D.C.: Resources for the Future, Inc.

Seskin, Eugene P., Robert J. Anderson, Jr., and Robert O. Reid. 1983. "An Empirical Analysis of Economic Strategies for Controlling Air Pollution." *Journal of Environmental Economics and Management* 10 (2):112–24.

Shapiro, M., and E. Warhit. 1983. "Marketable Permits: The Case of Chlorofluorocarbons." *Natural Resource Journal* 23(5):577–91.

Tietenberg, Tom H. 1985. *Emissions Trading: An Exercise in Reforming Pollution Policy.* Washington, D.C.: Resources for the Future.

———. 1989. "Acid Rain Reduction Credits." *Challenge* 32(2):25–29.

———. 1990. "Economic Instruments for Environmental Regulation." *Oxford Review of Economic Policy* 6(1):17–33.

———. 1994. "Implementation Issues for Global Tradeable Permits." (p. 119–49) In Ekko C. Van Ierland, ed., *International Environmental Economics: Theories, Models, and Applications to Climate Change, International Trade and Acidification.* New York: Elsevier.

———. 1995. "Economic Instruments for Pollution Control When Emission Location Matters: What Have We Learned?" *Environmental and Resource Economics* 5(2):95–113.

United Nations Conference on Trade and Development. 1992. *Combating Global Warming: Study on a Global System of Tradeable Carbon Emission Entitlements.* New York: United Nations.

3

Distributed Governance in the Northwestern Hawaiian Islands Lobster Fishery

Ralph E. Townsend and Samuel G. Pooley

Abstract

ALTERNATIVE MANAGEMENT APPROACHES for the governance of the lobster fishery of the Northwestern Hawaiian Islands (NWHI) are considered. These alternatives are analyzed within the framework of distributed governance: how rights and responsibilities are distributed among the central government, the industry, and local communities.

The analysis presented herein does not represent the official position of the National Marine Fisheries Service.

This research was supported in part by the National Oceanographic and Atmospheric Administration (NOAA), the National Sea Grant Program, Department of Commerce, under Grant NA36RG0110-01 through the Maine/New Hampshire Sea Grant Program, Project R/FMD-237, and in part by the research program in Property Rights and the Performance of Natural Resource Systems of the Beijer International Institute of Ecological Economics, the Royal Swedish Academy of Sciences, Stockholm, Sweden, with support from the World Environment and Resources Program of the John D. and Catherine T. MacArthur Foundation and the World Bank. Ralph Townsend was supported by two National Marine Fisheries Service summer fellowships while part of this work was completed.

Townsend and Pooley (1995) suggested the idea of distributed governance as a criteria by which to analyze governance of fisheries. Distributed governance examines how rights and responsibilities are distributed among and within the government, the fishing industry, and fishing communities. This analysis of governance of fisheries must ultimately be applied within the specific circumstances of individual fisheries. The present analysis applies the concept to the lobster fishery of the NWHI.

The NWHI Lobster Fishery and Its Management

The NWHI lobster fishery harvests two species of lobsters, spiny lobsters (*Panulirus marginatus*) and slipper lobsters (*Scyllarides squamosus*).[1] The fleet operates in an archipelago of small islands and atolls that stretches north and west of the main Hawaiian Islands for over 1,000 miles to Kure and Midway Islands. A small fleet of fifteen boats makes trips of four to ten weeks to harvest these lobsters. Total landings are small in comparison to many other fisheries, varying from a high of 2.3 million pounds in 1985 to no catch in 1993 because of a closure. However, the catch is quite valuable, with average prices of $5.81 per pound (round weight) for spiny lobsters and $3.65 per pound for slipper lobsters in 1994. Most of the catch has been sold as a frozen product on the U.S. mainland.

Management of this fishery under the U.S. Magnuson Fishery Conservation and Management Act began in 1983. Regulation initially was confined to reporting catch and effort data and to biological measures, such as minimum size limits and protection of egg-bearing females. Trap design also was regulated, in part to reduce any potential for incidental mortality of monk seals, an endangered species.

In 1991, the management structure changed dramatically, when the industry proposed a limited entry plan. In large part, the industry wanted to prevent mining of the resource by vessels from other fisheries and especially by potential entrants from the longline fishery for large pelagics, which was facing its own moratorium on entry and restrictions on fishing areas. Fishery biologists recommended an annual quota in the lobster fishery and a limited fishing season in response to what was believed to be an unusual decline in the lobster biomass.[2] The limited entry and quota regulations were adopted by the Western Pacific Regional Fishery Management Council (the council) in 1991 and were implemented by the National Marine Fisheries Service (NMFS) for the 1992 fishing season. Fifteen boats qualified for permits under these regulations.

The quota for the NWHI lobster fishery is set in a two-step procedure. A preliminary or forecast quota is announced in the spring, prior to the opening of the fishery on July 1. The final quota is set by August 15 and is based in part upon catch-per-trap-haul from the first month of the season.

The fishery opened under quota regulation in July 1992, with a preliminary quota of 750,000 lobsters. The final quota was revised downward to 438,000 lobsters. The fishing season was not closed prematurely, because the quota was not reached. Final landings for 1992 were 424,000 lobsters. In 1993, due to poor stock conditions, the fishery was closed to fishing. The closure in 1993 was a particular burden for some small vessels that had few short-term options.

The preliminary quota for 1994 was set at 200,000 lobsters, and five vessels chose to participate in the fishery. However, the final quota was revised downward to 20,900 lobsters, and the fishery was closed in August 1994 by emergency rule. Because the vessels had operated for six weeks before the closure was announced, the total catch was actually 130,000 lobsters. Separate concerns by the industry about the large in-season quota reduction and by NMFS about exceeding the final quota led to a review of the quota setting process.

The limited-entry plan originally contained a requirement that a permit be used at least once

---

1. Descriptive information and data on this fishery are primarily from the annual reports on the fishery, the most recent of which is Dollar (1993). The regulatory structure is described in the Crustacean Fisheries Management Plan (Western Pacific Regional Fishery Management Council, 1994).

2. Polovina and Mitchum (1992) and Polovina and others (1994) subsequently attributed this decline to a deterioration of the carrying capacity of the environment, which was caused by changes in nutrient levels associated with atmospheric and oceanographic cycles.

every two years. Each vessel was required to land a minimum of four lobsters per registered trap—approximately 4,000 lobsters for most boats—every other year to meet this requirement. This use-it-or-lose-it provision had unintended consequences because some permit holders, who otherwise would have been voluntarily idle, were forced to fish. (The use-it-or-lose-it provision was rescinded by the council following the 1994 fishing season.)

The immediate prospects for the NWHI lobster fishery seem to be poor. The combination of uncertainty created by changing biological conditions and administrative inflexibility are creating economic hardships. A cost and earnings study by Clarke and Pooley (1988) indicates that the average vessel would break even at catch rates and prices that prevailed in the 1980s. The catch rates were 1.27 lobsters per trap haul for 1985–89, and they fell to 0.63 lobsters per trap haul for 1990–94. Real prices have fluctuated in a narrow band over the past ten years, so price levels have not offset the decline in catch-per-unit-effort. The use-it-or-lose-it provision added to the economic hardship by increasing costs and catch competition. With fewer vessels, lower total costs, and higher catch rates, the fishery certainly would generate significant rents under favorable stock conditions. It also probably would support a small, marginally profitable fleet under poorer stock conditions.

The history of management of the NWHI lobster fishery supports three conclusions. First, the general structure of the current management system for this fishery, which includes limited entry and quotas, ought to be a solid foundation for management. But, secondly, ancillary rules and administrative complexity, including the use-it-or-lose-it requirement and the within-season quota adjustments, have combined to create unnecessary uncertainty and hardship in the fishery.

Third, the fishery is both small and, from a management point of view, relatively noncomplex. Only two species are harvested, and there are almost no interactions with other fisheries. All lobsters are landed in Honolulu, so the cost of monitoring quotas is relatively low. As a trap fishery, a relatively good index of fishing effort is available in traps, and enforcement of trap limits is simplified by the distant water nature of the fishery. The hard question of who gets rights under any new management approach has largely been answered in the existing limited-entry program. These factors create a favorable environment for many alternative approaches to management.

Governance Alternatives in the NWHI Lobster Fishery

The balance of this chapter examines how alternative approaches to distributed governance might be applied to this fishery. We will examine external governance arrangements and internal governance arrangements.

External Governance Alternatives

Rights-based management

The NWHI lobster fishery is subject to limited entry, so a form of rights-based management is already in place. The question is whether a more elaborate rights-based regime should be considered for the fishery. Either an individual transferable quota (ITQ) or an individual transferable input (ITI) approach would be a logical, evolutionary path in the management of the NWHI lobster fishery. The main limitation to this evolutionary approach is apparent in the current system: it is very difficult for the government to determine which regulations will accomplish biological objectives without imposing unnecessary costs and inconvenience on the industry. As long as fishery management is basically an adversarial relationship between government and the industry, the confrontational game is likely to produce unnecessarily high transactions costs.

For a number of reasons, ITQ management is an attractive option in the NWHI lobster fishery. The often-difficult ITQ allocation problem is simplified because a well-defined pool of recipients already exists: the fifteen limited-entry permit holders. However, allocating the quota among the fifteen permit holders may be contentious. Usually, quota allocations are based on the historical record of landings. The difficult question is which part of history. In the NWHI lobster fishery, how to treat the fishing years of 1992 and 1994, which were subject to quota regulation and to use-it-or-lose-it permit requirements and which also had poor stock conditions, may be difficult. Using the years prior to 1991 would generally favor the larger, non-Honolulu boats.

Including the 1992 and 1994 years would generally favor the smaller, Honolulu boats that had lower fixed costs and could survive on lower catches. The decision is ultimately a political one. An equal division among all fifteen boats might be a viable alternative.

An overall quota is required to determine annual quota allocations from ITQ shares. The quota-setting history in the fishery has been controversial, particularly in light of the quota revisions in 1994. Although the quota-setting problem is not unique to ITQs (it would also arise under the continuation of the current overall quota), quota setting under ITQ management is likely to be more sensitive because fishers feel a direct effect between the total quota and their allocations. Moreover, the current within-season adjustment process would be difficult, and probably impossible, to implement under ITQs. If fishers expect that the quota will be revised downward during the season, every boat will rush to exhaust the initial ITQ before it is revoked. Although the current quota-setting process may be very annoying even under the current regulations, it would be untenable under ITQs. Hence, some revision to the process would be necessary.

Enforcement of ITQs is always a critical issue. They are very valuable, with annual lease values often running to 50 percent of landed value. The net (not gross) return to unreported landings is as much as 50 percent of market value of the fish. Moreover, income tax obligations are reduced by not reporting landings. The incentive to cheat is great. Even if as little as 5 percent or 10 percent of total landings were diverted to an unreported channel, the corrosive effect on other participants' willingness to cooperate with enforcement would be severe. Because all NWHI lobsters are landed in Honolulu and within a relatively short season, dockside monitoring of landings is relatively easy. Because this is a small, distant water fleet, unscheduled port calls—landing without reporting—could probably be monitored by electronic "black boxes." Whether a black box could detect off-loading to other vessels may be less clear.

Individual transferable input programs are probably also feasible in the NWHI lobster fishery. If the experience in other lobster fisheries around the world is an indication, the number of traps in the NWHI lobster fishery may be a relatively good input index (Bell 1972; Morgan 1980). An individual transferable trap (ITT) program may provide an adequate index of fishing effort. A somewhat better index of effort might be trapdays or trapmonths, the number of traps fished times the number of days or months of fishing. Because all traps are returned each trip, monitoring trap numbers is somewhat simpler in this fishery than in coastal trap fisheries.

Because the enforcement problems of ITQs seem generally manageable, there are no significant advantages of an ITT program. Because an ITT will create some incentives for boats to increase non-trap inputs, it will create some distortions. Although it is fully feasible and has some advantages over the current system, the ITT approach will probably yield less economic benefit than the ITQ approach.

Comanagement

The NWHI lobster fishery already involves a degree of comanagement. Authority is legally shared between the Western Pacific Regional Fisheries Management Council and the National Marine Fisheries Service. The council has twelve members, apportioned among Hawaii, American Samoa, the Northern Marianas, Guam, and federal agencies. In recent years, two of the four public Hawaii members of the council have been lobster permit holders. Given the deference that non-Hawaii members of the council usually accord Hawaii's representatives on the management of Hawaii's fisheries, these two members have significant influence in the lobster management policy process.[3] That influence is reflected in the implementation of the limited-entry plan for NWHI lobsters. However, the fact that NMFS was able to insist upon a quota-setting regime that has been troublesome for the industry indicates the extent of NMFS influence.

An obvious step would be to create a formal organization that represents all fifteen permit holders in negotiations with government agen-

3. It should be noted that some proposed amendments to the Magnuson Fishery Conservation and Management Act would restrict the ability of fishing industry members to serve as public members or to vote on issues that directly affect the individual council member. Passage of such amendments would reduce the degree of comanagement created by the act.

cies. Such an organization perhaps could be advisory to the current council process. How to move beyond a merely advisory role into a position of coauthority is more difficult to identify, whether under the council process or not. Perhaps the most obvious U.S. model might be agricultural marketing orders, which permit groups of farmers to petition the government for creation of what are essentially marketing monopolies. But even agricultural marketing orders lack the kind of flexibility that would be necessary to respond to the dynamic changes in fisheries in general and in the NWHI lobster fishery in particular.

As Townsend and Pooley (1995) suggested, it is very difficult to frame institutions of comanagement that create equality for the central government and the industry in the governance process. There are no special circumstances in this fishery that avoid this fundamental difficulty. The strength of the contractual management approach, to which we now turn, is that it delineates distinct functions for the central government and for the industry, rather than trying to create some kind of dynamic equality of the two organizations over a wide range of decisions.

Contractual management

Two factors make the NWHI lobster fishery well-suited to contractual management. First, the fishery is relatively self-contained with little direct interaction with other fisheries. It has an extremely limited impact on the local economy and a similarly small social impact. Second, the industry is both small and relatively undifferentiated. There are common interests across all fishers, so joint decisionmaking will not be difficult. As discussed below, these common interests, under either corporate or cooperative governance, are likely to produce a clear mandate for efficient management.

The permanent right that would be bestowed under contractual management would be the right of ownership or membership in a fisheries management corporation or cooperative. To protect minorities, the corporation or cooperative would be required to bestow fishing privileges only in proportion to ownership or membership rights.

The government would negotiate and administer an operating contract with the corporation or cooperative that regulated interactions of the fishing fleet with the environment of the NWHI. The contract would specify, for example, the current gear design restrictions that limit interactions with monk seals and the current area closures around coral reefs. The contract would also identify information, both biological and economic, that must be provided by the industry organization to the government.

For the NWHI lobster fishery, a contract of twelve years would seem appropriate. That contract length should provide the industry organization with a period sufficiently long that decisions about investments in both physical capital and in resource status can yield adequate returns. This period covers between one and three recruitment cycles for the lobster fishery. Under the staggered renewal process proposed by Townsend and Pooley (1995), contract renegotiation would occur at year six.

Internal Governance Alternatives

The real choice in internal governance for the NWHI lobster fishing industry is between cooperative and corporate governance. Because the local community has very little stake in the fishery, communal governance is not really an important alternative. Inasmuch as the existing limited entry program has already defined the participants, there is no new self-organizing group waiting to form. The government might well leave some of the details of the internal organization to the industry, but the government will also shape that institution by how it defines rights and responsibilities.

In this fishery, there is likely to be relatively little difference in the short run between cooperative and corporate management. Fifteen voting members of a cooperative or fifteen equal shareholders in a corporation are certain to reach very similar conclusions. The real differences between cooperative and corporate management are likely to arise over a longer term, as changes in ownership and membership occur.

Transfers, effort reduction, and divisions of interests are all easier under corporate governance than under cooperative governance. Effort reduction is an issue in this fishery, even in the short run. If members can freely transfer and divide shares, the consolidation of fishing effort will be easiest. Given the need to deal with effort reduction, transfers, and divisions of interests, a cooperatively organized industry is likely over time to accede to economic pressures and to move closer to the corporate model. Although corporate governance from the time of initiation may be preferable, even an initial choice of cooperative governance may ultimately mean something very close to corporate governance.

Townsend and Pooley (Manuscript) have proposed a detailed model of corporate governance for the NWHI lobster fishery, which could be modified slightly to accommodate cooperative governance. Each of the current fifteen limited-entry license holders would receive an equal number of shares. Because the shares would be distributed to the current limited-entry permit holders, who have an existing usufruct interest, the government would probably not receive compensation. The owners probably should be expected to pay for any administrative, research, and enforcement services that would continue to be provided by the government. All shares would be freely transferable, subject only to restrictions embodied in securities law. The management corporation would be able to elect a representative board of directors. To protect minorities, the bylaws of the management corporation would contain two constraints. First, any fishing benefits bestowed by the management corporation must be in proportion to share ownership. Second, fees imposed to finance the management corporation must be either in proportion to ownership shares or in proportion to landings.

The management corporation or cooperative for the NWHI lobster fishery would be responsible for making all resource management decisions, subject to the operating contract. The management corporation would determine the level of fishing activity. Within this structure, the management corporation would have an internal economic interest in efficient management of the lobster resource. For example, the cost of enforcing the regulations, which would be borne by the management corporation or cooperative, would be one economic consideration. The management corporation or cooperative could evaluate alternatives, such as overall quotas, closed seasons, minimum sizes, ITQs, and trap limitations. For exactly the same reasons that ITQs and ITTs seem feasible under rights-based management, they may also minimize the corporation's or cooperative's costs of supervising the fishing activities of individual boats.

Conclusions and Policy Implications

This analysis has obvious policy implications for the governance of the lobster fishery of the NWHI. But the analysis also suggests a general approach for policy analysis in fisheries.

Because of the relatively simple nature of the NWHI lobster fishery, a wide array of governance structures could be applied to this fishery. If management options are limited to the traditional rights-based approaches, either ITQ management or transferable trap regulation could be expected to increase the economic rents that the industry would earn. The administration of either type of rights-based management would be relatively straightforward in this fishery. On the other hand, this fishery presents a unique opportunity to move beyond government-centered, rights-based management to a contractual model of management between the government and a local cooperative or corporation.

The current literature on governance of common pool resources suggests a fundamental dissatisfaction with the governance dynamics that are inherent in command-and-control regulation. But to move away from command-and-control regulation, new governance structures must be proposed and tested. There will be no theoretical proof of the efficacy of alternative models of distributed governance that will dissuade governments from continuing with government-centered solutions. Rather, alternative models, such as contractual external governance and corporate internal governance, must be tested and demonstrated in the real world. The application of these concepts to small resource management problems, such as management of the NWHI lobster fishery, are crucial demonstration projects in the evolution of these new ideas.

Bibliography

Bell, F. W. 1972. "Technological Externalities and Common Property Resources: An Empirical Study of the U.S. Northern Lobster Fishery." *Journal of Political Economy* 80:148–58.

Clarke, R. P., and S. G. Pooley. 1988. *An Economic Analysis of NWHI Lobster Fishing Vessel Performance.* Honolulu, Hawaii: U.S. Department of Commerce, NOAA–TM–NMFS–SWFC–106.

Dollar, R. A. 1993. *Annual Report of the 1992 Western Pacific Lobster Fishery.* Honolulu, Hawaii: Southwest Fisheries Science Center Administrative Report H–93–09.

Morgan, G. R. 1980. "Increases in Fishing Effort in a Limited Entry Fishery—The Western Rock Lobster Fishery 1963–1976." *Journal du Conseil International pour l'Exploration de la Mer* 39:82–87.

Polovina, J. J., and G. T. Mitchum. 1992. "Variability in Spiny Lobster *Panulirus Marginatus* Recruitment and Sea Level in the Northwestern Hawaiian Islands." *Fishery Bulletin* 90:483–93.

Polovina, J. J., G. T. Mitchum, N. E. Graham, M. P. Craig, E. E. Martini, and E. N. Flint. 1994. "Physical and Biological Consequences of a Climate Event in the Central North Pacific." *Fisheries Oceanography* 3(1):15–21.

Townsend, R. E., and S. G. Pooley. 1995. "Distributed Governance in Fisheries." In S. Hanna and M. Munasinghe, *Property Rights and the Environment: Social and Ecological Issues.* Washington, D.C.: World Bank.

———. Manuscript. "A Proposal for Corporate Management of the Northwestern Hawaiian Islands Lobster Fishery."

Western Pacific Regional Fishery Management Council. 1994. "Amendment 8: Fishery Management Plan for the Crustacean Fisheries of the Western Pacific Region." Honolulu.

4

Enforcement of Regional Environmental Regulations: Nitrogen Fertilizer in Sweden

Ing-Marie Gren and Runar Brännlund

Abstract

ONE DIFFICULTY WITH INTRODUCING regional adjusted environmental regulations within a nation is the enforcement of compliance. An appropriate design of regulations among regions then calls for the introduction of enforcement costs into the decision problem. The analytical results in this study indicate that the introduction of enforcement cost changes the cost-effective allocation of abatement between regions when the marginal environmental impacts and the marginal enforcement costs are not perfectly correlated. The simple analysis is applied to regional regulation of nitrogen fertilizers in Sweden. According to the results, the impact on total costs of including enforcement costs in the decision problem is relatively small for the entire country. On the other hand, for some of the regions, total costs may change by about 50 percent when enforcement costs are included in the decision problem.

Like many other pollutants, the environmental damages of nitrogen fertilizers depend on the location of the pollution source. As one of several causes of eutrophicated coastal waters, nitrogen fertilizer stimulates the production of algae, which in turn causes oxygen deficits at sea bottoms and hence reductions in the stock of certain species of fish, such as cod.

According to a ministerial declaration in 1989, the Nordic countries agreed to reduce the load of nitrogen in all coastal waters by 50 percent. However, the impact on the coast of particular deposits of nitrogen within a drainage basin on coastal waters depends on such factors as soil quality and hydrology, which differ in various basins. Thus, an efficient regulation of nitrogen requires adjustments to the leaching conditions of each drainage basin.

The design of policy instruments to take into account regional environmental differences has been recognized in several studies (see, for example, Tietenberg 1979; Siebert 1992). A common result is that the policy instrument should be designed in order to account for these regional differences. The losses, as compared with cost-effective allocation of abatement between regions, might otherwise be high. One important argument against differentiated policy schemes is that they usually require more monitoring and supervision and, hence, the enforcement costs can be relatively high. The enforcement costs associated with a differentiated regulation scheme may then outweigh the gains from lower abatement costs.

The purpose of this study is to analyze under what conditions enforcement costs are important for a cost-effective allocation of abatement measures when the spatial allocation of abatement measures matters for the environmental impact. The analysis is applied to the regulation of nitrogen fertilizers in Sweden. The chapter is organized as follows. First, a simple model is presented, which is used for identifying under what conditions the introduction of enforcement costs is likely to have relatively large impacts on the regional allocation of abatement measures. Next, an application is made to the Swedish farmers' use of nitrogen fertilizers. The chapter ends with a summary.

The Model

A simple model for cost minimization is used to identify various conditions for relatively large impacts of the introduction of enforcement costs. It is then assumed that the environmental target at the recipient in question is a function of the loads of pollutants from all regions q^j, where $j=1,...,k$ regions. The load of pollutants to the ecosystem from a certain region is, in turn, determined by total emissions of firms within the region, E^{ij} where $i=1,..,n$ firms, minus abatement, Y^{ij}. The environmental quality of the ecosystem can then be written as

$$Q=q(\Sigma_j q^j(\Sigma_{ij}(E^{ij}-Y^{ij}))) \tag{1}$$

The abatement cost of a firm is described by $C^i(Y^i)$ where $\dot{Y}$ is the level of abatement and $i=1,...,n$ are the firms. It is further assumed that $C_y>0$ and $C_{yy} \geq 0$. For each region there exists a cost function for enforcement, $C^j(R^j)$ where R^j is the level of enforcement, which is assumed to be increasing in Y. The level of enforcement needed to achieve full compliance depends on several factors, such as choice of policy instrument, the enforcement weapons available to the regional agency, and the number of firms being regulated and their associated costs of compliance (see, for example, Andréasson-Gren 1992. Here it is simply assumed that the level of enforcement can be written as a function of the total abatement within the region.

$$R^j=r^j(\Sigma_i Y^{ij}) \tag{2}$$

The decision problem of the national environmental agency is then formulated as a choice of the allocation of Y^{ij}, which minimizes total costs subject to Equation (1) where total costs are written as

$$\underset{Y^{ij}}{Min} \quad \Sigma_j C^j(r^j(\Sigma_i Y^{ij}))+\Sigma_i C^i(N^i) \tag{3}$$

The first-order conditions are written as

$$\frac{(\partial C^j/\partial r^j)(\partial r^j/\partial Y^{ij})+\partial C^i/\partial Y^{ij}}{(\partial Q/\partial q^j)(\partial q^j/\partial Y^{ij})} = \lambda \qquad (4)$$

where λ is the Lagrange multiplier for the restriction in emissions Equation (1). A cost-effective allocation of regional abatement occurs where the marginal cost of abatement is equal to λ for all regions and firms. The numerator consists of two parts: the enforcement cost of a marginal abatement and the firm's marginal cost for abatement at the emission source. The marginal enforcement cost is, in turn, determined by two factors: the marginal increase in enforcement and the associated marginal enforcement cost. The former is determined, as mentioned above, by the regulated firm's violation behavior. The denominator measures the marginal impact on the environmental quality of a certain ecosystem. The whole expression thus measures the cost for a unit improvement of the environmental quality, that is, λ. The condition for cost-effectiveness is that these marginal costs shall be equal.

Let us for a moment ignore the enforcement cost. The abatement level of each emission source is then determined by the relation between marginal cost at the source and impact on the environment. The higher the impact on the environment of a the abatement of a specific emission source, ceteris paribus, the higher is the level of abatement, and vice versa.

When introducing the enforcement cost, the associated impact on the allocation of abatement measures of enforcement depends on the relation between the marginal enforcement costs and the marginal environmental impacts. For two different regions, l and m, this can be written as

$$\frac{(\partial C^l/\partial r^l)(\partial r^l/\partial Y^{il})}{(\partial Q/\partial q^l)(\partial q^l/\partial Y^{il})} \underset{<}{>} \frac{(\partial C^m/\partial r^m)(\partial r^m/\partial Y^{im})}{(\partial Q/\partial q^m)(\partial q^m/\partial Y^{im})} \qquad (5)$$

When equality holds so that the marginal enforcement cost as related to the marginal environmental impact is the same in all regions, the allocation of measures remains unchanged. This occurs when the marginal enforcement costs and the marginal environmental impacts are perfectly correlated between regions. That is,

in regions with high marginal enforcement costs the marginal impacts of abatement measures are also high. When equality does not hold, the impact on the allocation of abatement measures is relatively small if the levels of the marginal enforcement costs in all regions are low as compared with the abatement costs. Thus, the introduction of enforcement costs is important for the regional allocation of abatement measures when they differ between regions and when the size of the enforcement cost is not negligible in at least one region.

Two cases are then identified; the correlation of marginal enforcement cost and marginal environmental impacts is positive or negative. The level of abatement is reduced in regions with relatively high marginal enforcement costs and vice versa. Note that the introduction of enforcement costs is an argument in favor of uniform policy instruments for all regions if the inequality holds and when the marginal abatement costs and marginal environmental impacts are negatively correlated. The efficiency losses of a uniform regulation scheme are reduced when the marginal enforcement costs are relatively high in regions with relatively low abatement costs and vice versa.

An Application to Nitrogen Fertilizers

Sweden is divided into seven main drainage basins: the Bothnian Bay, the Bothnian Sea, Mälar region, Baltic Proper South, the Sound, Kattegatt, and Skagerack. These drainage basins differ with respect to several factors, such as soil conditions, climate, and farm management practices. In general, the soil in the south of Sweden is more fertile. We would expect differences in farmers' costs of reducing the use of nitrogen fertilizers in various drainage basins. In this study, abatement costs are calculated as a reduction in producer surplus from decreases in the use of nitrogen fertilizers. Changes in producer surplus are calculated by means of input demand functions estimated by econometric methods. Input demand functions and associated costs functions for decreases in the use of nitrogen fertilizers are estimated for each drainage basin (see Appendix 4–A).

By enforcement cost we mean the regional authorities' costs of monitoring and supervising compliance, and the cost for prosecution and final conviction. The enforcement cost is determined by violation behavior by the farmers and the associated cost for perfect compliance. In order to estimate the cost function for enforcing reductions in the use of nitrogen fertilizers, we thus need to know farmers' compliance as a function of the enforcement level, and the regional agency's costs as a function of the enforcement level. Ideally, we would have sufficient data for the estimation of these functions from actual regulations on nitrogen fertilizers. Unfortunately, such data are not available. Instead, the estimation of cost is based on data available from investigation of enforcement of all current environmental regulations (Statistics Sweden 1993).

Traditionally, enforcement of regulations include decisions on penalties and the detection rate (see, for example, Becker 1968). In Sweden, however, the determination of penalties is regulated by the law, which implies that changes in the detection rate can be regarded as the only enforcement tool available to regional environmental agencies. The regional agencies supervise compliance by visits and inspections of some of the firms subjected to environmental regulations. Costs of enforcement are thus calculated by means of econometric estimates (see Appendix 4–A).

Unfortunately, the data do not allow us to estimate compliance as a function of the detection rate. Therefore, a linear relation is assumed between the detection rate and compliance rate. The detection rate is calculated as the amount of visits divided by the total amount of regulated firms, and the compliance rate is calculated as the amount of complying firms divided by the total amount of regulated firms.

Recall from the foregoing section that the condition for cost effectiveness is determined by three factors: the marginal environmental impact, the marginal enforcement cost, and the marginal abatement cost. Here, the marginal environmental impact is defined as the share of a certain nitrogen deposition within a drainage basin that reaches the coastal water. Note that it is then assumed that the impacts on the marine waters are independent on where along the coast the nitrogen is deposited. This is probably not true, but currently there are no measurements of the nitrogen retention capacities of different coastal waters. Therefore, we disregard this aspect. In Table 4–1, nitrogen fertilizer loads, the estimated marginal environmental impacts, marginal abatement costs, and marginal enforcement costs are presented for different drainage basins.

The use of nitrogen fertilizers in the Baltic Proper South catchment region accounts for about one-third of the total use. The next important region is Kattegatt where the use of nitrogen fertilizers corresponds to about one-fourth of the total use. Due to the relatively high rate of retention, 0.40, the role of the Baltic Proper region is reduced when comparing loadings to the coastal waters. However, the total use of nitrogen in these two regions and the associated load to coastal water account together for about 50 percent and 66 percent of total use and load, respectively. The total minimum costs for reduction in nitrogen use and load to coastal waters are thus to a large extent determined by the costs in the Baltic proper and the Kattegatt regions.

When comparing the marginal enforcement costs with the marginal environmental impact, we identify different patterns. The marginal enforcement cost is relatively high in regions such as the Bothnian Sea, Kattegat, and the Mälar region where the marginal environmental impacts are low. The reverse is true for the Sound region. We therefore expect that the introduction of an enforcement cost will have some impact on the cost-effective allocation of nitrogen reductions among the regions.

As mentioned earlier, the Nordic ministerial declaration indicated a 50 percent reduction of nitrogen loads to all coastal waters. Therefore, minimum costs for a 50 percent reduction in the use of nitrogen fertilizers are calculated for two scenarios: with and without the inclusion of the enforcement costs. We assume that the environmental agency's exclusion of enforcement costs in the decision problem does not imply that these costs do not exist. The associated enforcement costs are therefore calculated for this scenario. As mentioned above, we would expect that the introduction of enforcement costs into the decision problem would have an impact on the allocation of nitrogen between the regions, since there is a negative correlation between marginal environmental impacts and marginal enforcement costs for some of the regions. The results are presented in Table 4–2.

According to the results presented in Table 4–2, there is only a small increase in total costs under the two policy scenarios. Total annual costs amount to 536.2 million SEK when enforcement costs are included in the decision problem, and to 557.1 million SEK when they are not. The increase corresponds to about 4 percent. One important reason for the relatively small difference in costs is that the abatement cost dominates under both scenarios. The abatement costs account for about 85 percent of total costs when enforcement costs are included and for 80 percent when they are not included.

We can also see from Table 4–2 that the impact on five drainage basins is relatively small: Bothnian Bay, Bothnian Sea, Baltic Proper, Mälar region, and Skagerack. The main changes occur for the Kattegat and the Sound regions. The enforcement costs are relatively low in the Sound region, which implies that the nitrogen reduction and associated costs are higher under the policy, with explicit inclusion of the enforcement costs. The total cost for this region increases by about 50 percent when enforcement costs are included in the decision problem. The reverse is true for the Kattegat region where the enforcement costs are relatively high. An introduction of the enforcement costs reduces the total costs by about 45 percent for this region.

Summary

The purpose of this chapter has been to analyze the impact on total costs of the explicit inclusion of enforcement costs in the decision problem. The decision problem was formulated as minimizing total costs for obtaining certain environmental improvements in different regions. The analysis was applied to the regulation of nitrogen fertilizers in Sweden. According to the analytical results, the introduction of enforcement costs is likely to change the allocation of abatements between regions when there is a negative correlation between the marginal enforcement costs and marginal environmental impacts. The impact on total costs is also determined by this factor and on the size of the enforcement costs as compared with the abatement costs.

The application on the regulation of nitrogen fertilizers in Sweden indicated a negative corre-lation between the marginal enforcement costs and the marginal environmental impacts for only some of the regions. Because of this result, the cost-effective allocation of nitrogen abatement among five of the seven drainage basins remained, in principle, unchanged when enforcement costs were introduced. However, the impacts of nitrogen reduction and associated costs were considerable for the two remaining regions. For one region, the Sound, with relatively low marginal enforcement costs and high marginal environmental impact, the introduction of enforcement costs into the decision problem increased total costs by about 50 percent. The marginal enforcement costs were relatively high and the marginal environmental impact low in the other region, Kattegat, where instead total costs were reduced by 45 percent when enforcement costs were introduced into the decision problem. It should be noted, however, that the differences in total costs, abatement, and enforcement costs were small between the two policy scenarios, decreasing by about 3 percent when enforcement costs were included into the decision problem. One important reason is that the shares of enforcement costs are low in both scenarios.

Bibliography

Andréasson-Gren, I-M. 1992. "Profits from Violating Controls on a Polluting Input." *Environmental and Resource Economics*.

Becker, G. 1968. "Crime and Punishment: An Economic Approach." *Journal of Political Economy* 76:169–80.

Braden, J. B., R. S. Larson, and E. E. Herricks. 1991. "Impact Target versus Discharge Standards in Agricultural Pollution Management." *American Journal of Agricultural Economics* (73)2:388–97.

Brännlund, R., I-M. Gren, and K. Elofsson. 1994. "Uniform versus Differentiated Charges. An Application to a Nitrogen Fertilizer Charge in Sweden." Presented at the European Association of Environmental and Resource Economics (EAERE) Fifth Annual Conference, Dublin, June 22–24, 1994.

Elofsson, K., and I-M. Gren. 1994. "Cost Effective Reductions in the Agricultural Load of Nitrogen to the Baltic Sea." Beijer International Institute of Ecological Economics,

Royal Swedish Academy of Sciences. Unpublished.

Kneese, A. V. 1964. The Economics of Regional Water Quality Management. Baltimore, Md: Johns Hopkins University Press.

Lau, L. J. 1978. "Applications of Profit Functions. In M. Fuss and D. McFadden (eds.), *Production Economics: A Dual Approach to Theory and Applications*, Volume 1. Amsterdam: North-Holland.

Miltz, D., J. B. Braden, and G. V. Johnson. 1987. "Standards versus Prices Revisited: The Case of Agricultural Non-Point Source Pollution." *Journal of Agricultural Economics*:360–368.

Siebert, H. 1992. *Economics of the Environment—Theory and Policy.* Berlin and Heidelberg: Springer Verlag.

Statistics Sweden and Swedish Environmental Protection Agency. 1990 and 1993. "Application of the Swedish Environment Protection Act 1989 and 1990." Report Na 34, SM 9301, Stockholm, Sweden. In Swedish.

Tietenberg, T. H. 1979. "On the Efficient Spatial Allocation of Air Pollution Control Responsibility." In H. Siebert, I. Walker, and K. Zimmerman (eds.), *Regional Environmental Policy: The Economic Issues*. New York: Pergamon Press, pp. 79–93.

Table 4–1: Nitrogen Fertilizer Use, Marginal Coastal Impact, Marginal Abatement, and Enforcement Costs for Different Swedish Drainage Basins

Region	Use tons of N	Marginal coastal[a] impact	Marginal[b] abatement SEK/ton	Marginal[b] enforcement SEK/ton
Bothnian Bay	2,607	0.03	7,568	1,669
Bothnian Sea	13,129	0.05	5,632	6,092
Mälar Region	31,448	0.02	6,600	10,491
Baltic Proper	68,648	0.07	7,000	7,294
The Sound	23,172	0.21	15,972	1,913
Kattegatt	51,171	0.10	7,722	12,445
Skagerrack	3,708	0.17	4,246	7,194
Total	193,833			

a. Share of the use of nitrogen that reaches the coast (Elofsson and Gren (1994)).
b. Evaluated at a 50 percent reduction in the respective basin's current use.

Table 4–2: Regional Costs, Millions of Swedish Crowns (SEK), Regional Nitrogen Reductions in Percent under Two Policies Reducing the Nitrogen Load to the Coastal Water by 50 Percent

Region	Including enforcement costs			Excluding enforcement costs		
	Abatement cost	Enforcement cost	N reduction %	Abatement cost	Enforcement cost	N reduction %
Bothnian Bay	1.0	0.2		10	0	0
Bothnian Sea	7.9	1.4	17	11	2.7	23
Mälar Region	0	0	0	0	0	0
Baltic Proper	145.0	12.8	44	123.2	10.1	38
The Sound	193.0	12.7	56	132.9	3.7	43
Kattegatt	110.0	25.4	34	179.8	66.9	58
Skagerack	15.8	11.0	100	15.8	11	100
Total	472.7	63.5	50	462.7	94.4	50

Appendix 4–A: Calculation of Abatement and Enforcement Costs

The costs for reducing the use of fertilizers are calculated as the associated decreases in profits from yield. The production of yield is a function of the vectors of variable and fixed inputs, X, and F, respectively, which is written as

$$Q = f(X, F) \qquad (A1)$$

In addition to nitrogen, the variable production factor included here is labor. The fixed production functions are land and supply of manure. Assuming given prices of outputs and inputs and that farmers maximize profits, the nitrogen demand, N, can be specified as a function of the prices of variable inputs nitrogen and labor, P^N and P^L, respectively, the output price, P^Q, and the supply of manure and arable land, M and HA (see, for example, Lau 1988). The regression equation is then written as

$$N = h(P^N, P^L, P^Q, M, HA, \epsilon) \qquad (A2)$$

where ϵ is the error term. When estimating the regional demand functions, the SURE-estimator (for "seemingly unrelated regression equations") is used in order to account for simultaneous error between the equations. In Table 4–A1, the results from estimation of the linear equations are presented.

Most of the estimated nitrogen price coefficients are significant on a 5 percent level. For three region, however, the results are rather poor. In spite of the poor estimates, all the estimated price coefficients are used for calculating cost functions. The quadratic cost functions are calculated by solving for P^N in all regression equations and integrating over N.

The Swedish Statistics and the Environmental Protection Agency have in a joint project investigated the level of compliance, enforcement options, and costs for twenty-four Swedish counties during the years 1989 and 1992. Thus there are forty-eight observations on costs and the number of visits. This is not sufficient to estimate enforcement cost functions for different drainage basins. A fixed effect model is therefore applied to account for different drainage basins where BS is Bothnian Sea, BP is Baltic Proper, MR is Mälar region, KAT is Kattegat, SKA is Skagerack, and SU is the Sound. In order to account for the different years of investigation, a dummy, DUM, is introduced for 1989. Since the regression model reveals heteroscedasticity, weighted least square is used where the amount of regulated firms constitute the weights. The estimated result is

$$E = 11261 + 0.0008*(V)^2 - 10028*DUM - 725.2*BP$$
$$\quad (5.46) \quad (4.80) \qquad (8.15) \qquad (0.29)$$

$$- 479.4*BS + 1958*MR - 323*KAT$$
$$\quad (0.91) \qquad (0.73) \qquad (0.14)$$

$$+ 5877*SKA + 11383*SU$$
$$\quad (2.61) \qquad (4.93) \qquad \text{Adj. } R^2 = 0.98$$

where E is enforcement cost and V visits for each county. Numbers in parentheses denote t-statistics. The regression performs well with a significant impact on costs of visits, and the adjusted R^2 is high.

When estimating cost functions for enforcing nitrogen reductions, two components are needed: the estimated cost function for changes in the detection rate and the impact on compliance of changes in the detection rate. A simple linear relation is assumed between compliance and the detection rate, which is obtained by dividing the compliance rate by the detection rate.

Cost functions for enforcing nitrogen fertilizer reductions are then obtained by first expressing the coefficient and the variable V^i in use of nitrogen per farm. It is further assumed that there is no fixed cost component in enforcing reductions of nitrogen. The compliance rate, detection rate, and nitrogen fertilizer use per farm are shown in Table 4–A2.

Table 4–A1: Results from Nitrogen Demand Regressions

Region	Constant	P^N	P^Q	P^L	M	HA	R^2
Bothnian Bay	1,266	-5.95	-89.5	.93	.47	.03	0.52
t-statistic	.73	-1.18	-3.11	1.92	1.19	1.82	
Bothnian Sea	13,942	-54.5	-233.9	5.27	.37	.06	0.69
t-statistic	1.91	-2.63	-1.94	2.47	.54	.84	
Mälar region	-1,612	-96.05	-708.9	7.57	-1.42	0.16	0.86
t-statistic	(-.12)	(-2.99)	(-3.90)	(2.43)	(-1.31)	(8.44)	
Baltic Proper South	91,786	-188.5	-1,092.2	2.76	0.18	0.034	0.81
t-statistic	3.73	-4.42	-6.14	0.77	1.01	1.22	
The Sound*	-24,807	-421.5		99.0	-3.89	.33	0.72
t-statistic	-1.54	-.69		2.67	-4.17	4.90	
Kattegatt	54,828	-119.3	-1174	3.69	-.01	.06	0.79
t-statistic	3.16	-2.64	-7.67	1.77	-.02	2.51	
Skagerack	5,921	-32.2	-117.2	.28	-.25	.11	0.82
t-statistic	3.59	-7.69	-5.20	0.70	-0.40	3.43	

* For the Sound Region, the general specification gives poor estimates. The input prices divided by the output price generates a better fit for the Sound.

Table 4–A2: Detection Rates, Compliance Rates, Enforcement Costs, and Number of Farms

Region	Detection rate	Compliance rate	Tons of N/farm
Bothnian Bay	0.39	0.62	0.62
Bothnian Sea	0.30	0.57	1.01
Mälar Region	0.40	0.47	2.01
Baltic Proper	0.28	0.47	3.96
The Sound	0.32	0.56	5.54
Kattegatt	0.31	0.40	2.57
Skagerack	0.53	0.48	4.62

Equity and Stewardship

5

Designing Incentives to Conserve India's Biodiversity

Madhav Gadgil and P. R. Seshagiri Rao

Abstract

INDIA HAS VIBRANT FOLK TRADITIONS of nature conservation, as well as a vigorous state-sponsored program of protected areas. However, there are signs that the current centralized, sectoral, bureaucratic regulatory approach to conservation is facing serious difficulties. We suggest that it would be far more efficient and equitable to replace it with an approach based on positive incentives to local communities. This would entail local communities being conferred (a) greater control over public lands and waters in appropriately defined territories, (b) enhanced capacities to add value to local biodiversity, and (c) specific financial rewards linked to conservation value of elements making up biological communities within their territories.

We are grateful to the Ministry of Environment and Forests, Government of India, for financial support.

Technical inputs from the national or global level would be needed to establish a system of assigning conservation value and of monitoring the levels of biodiversity throughout the countryside. Such a system based on redeployment of funds currently being spent on a bureaucratic, regulatory approach would create a very efficient market for conservation performance, as well channelize rewards for conservation action to relatively poorer communities living close to the land.

✧

Conserving India's biological diversity is a staggering challenge. For it must address itself to the task of protecting populations of organisms as diverse as soil amoebae and sea urchins, rock bees, and Gangetic dolphins. It must strive to maintain a whole spectrum of habitats from coral reefs and rain forests of Andaman to high altitude lakes and meadows of Kashmir. It must try to promote continued cultivation of thousands of land races of rice and husbanding of hundreds of different breeds of cattle. This it must accomplish in a variety of human settings: from the thinly populated Mizoram, with its largely autonomous communities of swidden agriculturists to the Rajasthan desert dominated by nomadic herders; from the thickly settled Gangetic plains with complex stratified societies of cultivators to the modern metropolises of Delhi and Bangalore.

Over millennia Indian society has evolved a variety of biodiversity-friendly practices. Thanks to these, myriads of banyan and peepal trees dot the Indian countryside, while thousands of troops of langurs and macaques roam freely in the towns and villages. The Indian lion survives in the Gir National Park, protected against heavy odds by the Nawab of Junagarh in what was once a princely hunting preserve. Today India has a well dispersed network of wildlife sanctuaries, national parks and biosphere reserves, covering over 4 percent of the land surface. This is indeed a most creditable performance in an old, densely settled country (Gadgil 1991).

But the current state-sponsored approach to biodiversity conservation is evidently under serious strain (Singh 1995). It has tended to focus on elimination of subsistence demands of local communities as a major conservation measure, a focus that has brought in its wake serious conflicts. It has attempted to divorce conservation from development, and is today facing the threat of opening large tracts of nature reserves to mining and other development (Nambiar 1993). It has paid little attention to the significant levels of biodiversity in areas outside nature reserves, whether it be in wetlands or on farm bunds. It has completely ignored issues such as *in situ* conservation of land races of husbanded plants and animals. And finally, it has treated with contempt folk practices like sacred groves, as well as extensive practical ecological knowledge of large numbers of Indians living close to the earth.

Indeed, it is time we begin to seek alternative paradigms to conserve the natural heritage of this diverse country. Such a new paradigm could attempt to involve as partners the masses of Indian people brought up in a biodiversity-friendly culture, to marry conservation with development, and to employ positive rewards in place of bureaucratic regulations as the main instrument of conservation (Gadgil and Rao 1994). It is our purpose here to outline such an alternative approach.

Current Approach

State Monopoly

Today, the formal responsibility for conserving India's biological diversity rests solely with the state apparatus. Indeed, since independence, India's state apparatus has tended to assume responsibility for a very wide range of activities: manufacturing steel and generating power, providing education and health care, broadcasting news, and protecting forest resources. While greatly broadening its range of functions, the state apparatus has continued many of its colonial traditions. In particular, these include maintenance of a distance from the people at large and a lack of transparency in function. It has therefore developed into a massive apparatus, with a monopoly over provision of many goods and services and extensive powers of regulation. Although democracy has struck roots in India, the functioning of the state has not been adequately opened to public scrutiny.

In this atmosphere of lack of public accountability, the state apparatus has tended to concentrate on growing in size and power. Its functioning has become highly compartmentalized, with little coordination among the many different ministries and departments. It has gone on accumulating excessive levels of regulatory powers. All of this has inevitably been at the cost of services it is expected to deliver (Gadgil and Guha, in press).

This way of functioning is reflected in the way the state apparatus has gone about the business of conserving the country's heritage of biological diversity. Given its interest in the accumulation of regulatory powers, and its narrow sectoral preoccupations, interests of conservation have been viewed as diametrically opposed to the basic subsistence demands of local people, as well as development aspirations of the larger society. Such an attitude implies that there are very large opportunity costs attached to any conservation effort. Consequently such efforts enjoy the support of a relatively narrow segment of the society, mostly among urban middle classes. In particular, there is little support to state-sponsored conservation efforts by the local people. Conservation is therefore forced to rely on guns and guards, making it a very expensive proposition. Furthermore, given its lack of accountability, the state apparatus in charge of conservation tends to squander much of the resources made available to it on salaries and perquisites, buildings, and vehicles. There is little doubt, then, that India, like many other countries, goes about the business of conservation in a highly wasteful and inefficient manner.

The Bharatpur Tragedy

On top of this, the business of conservation is often conducted in simply a wrong-headed fashion. For conservation involves management of complex, little understood natural ecosystems. The science of ecology has simply no broad generalizations that can be applied to make detailed management decisions at the field level (Ludwig, Hilborn, and Walters 1993). Rather, such management is best based on long-range, locality-specific observations of the behavior of particular ecosystems, adjusting human interventions in light of the observed effects. The state apparatus has little of such information available, and most conservation prescriptions therefore tend to be arbitrary, and often result in wholly undesired consequences.

The deficiencies of this approach are evident in what has happened at the Bharatpur Bird Sanctuary over the last twelve years. Bharatpur is a wetland of several hundred hectares created by damming a tributary of the river Yamuna some 150 years ago. The impounded waters have always been used for irrigation in the dry months of the summer, and the wetlands themselves have provided excellent grazing for cattle and especially water buffaloes. These wetlands have been attracting enormous numbers of aquatic birds, supporting a large heronary of residents breeding in the monsoon, and an even greater number of migrants in the winter. The locality served as a hunting preserve of the Maharaja of Bharatpur in the pre-independence days, supporting shoots of tens of thousands of ducks and teals in a single day. The significance of this wetland as a bird refuge has been increasing with time, with other wetlands in the region being brought under cultivation.

Following independence, Bharatpur wetlands came to constitute one of the first wildlife sanctuaries of the country. This, of course, led to the suspension of winter shoots. But the use of water for irrigation and grazing by livestock continued. In the 1960s, some scientific studies were initiated at Bharatpur, but these focused on ringing migrant birds to trace them to their summer breeding grounds in the north, and did not provide any information on the functioning of the wetland ecosystems. In particular, there was no scientific information pertaining to the impact of grazing on the ability of the locality to support breeding and wintering bird populations. It was nevertheless assumed by scientists as well as forest managers—Indian as well as from abroad—that elimination of grazing would be highly desirable. Bharatpur used to support Siberian cranes in the winter, and scientists of the U.S.-based Crane Foundation wrote to the Prime Minister, Mrs. Indira Gandhi, urging her to ban grazing in the sanctuary.

As a result of these demands, the government imposed a ban on grazing in November 1983. The local villagers, whose several hundred cattle and buffaloes grazed in the sanctuary, were never consulted; no provisions were made for alternative fodder supply for these animals. As a result, the villagers protested against the ban, and there was an altercation with the police in which several people were killed. The ban was upheld, but it turned out that the ban was counter-productive from the perspective of the birds, especially the wintering waterfowl. In the absence of grazing, a grass, *Paspalum*, grew unchecked, choking out the wetland. Other birds also suffered, for instance, some songbirds that nested in the hollows formed by buffalo hoof marks. Money must now be spent to engage bulldozers to remove the grass. But the bulldozers are nowhere as efficient as the buffaloes, and Bharatpur continues to deteriorate as a bird habitat (Vijayan 1987). The Siberian cranes, for instance, have now ceased to visit Bharatpur. While the precise reasons for this are not clear, they could be linked to the overall habitat change.

Bharatpur has several lessons. The assumption that all human use is detrimental to conservation was evidently invalid. The local villagers need not have been forced to pay the opportunity cost of desisting from grazing in the sanctuary. The additional expenses in protection and now use of bulldozers that this policy has entailed is a wasteful use of scarce resources that are deployed to support conservation. Finally, respected scientists and managers gave completely inappropriate advice on the basis of some general and, as it turns out, mistaken notions of incompatibility of human use and conservation objectives.

While conservationists have thus succeeded in lobbying for elimination of subsistence demands from protected areas, they have had less success in resisting the demands of the industrial sector. Consider, for example, the case of the Dandeli wildlife sanctuary, once the most extensive of India's protected areas, encompassing over 5,000 square kilometers of the hill tracts of Western Ghats in the Uttara Kannada district of Karnataka. In areas once within the sanctuary, exhaustive harvesting of bamboo was permitted to supply the West Coast Paper Mill, at rates, incidentally, of less than 0.1 percent of the market price. Also permitted were mining for manganese and construction of a series of reservoirs on the Kali river and its tributaries. The area of the sanctuary is now reduced to 800 square kilometers.

Sacred Groves and Safety Forests

The state machinery managing the forests and now entrusted with the task of conserving biodiversity has from the very beginning treated traditional folk practices of conservation with contempt. One such practice is that of setting aside parts of the landscape as sacred groves from which little or no harvests would be permitted. Notably enough, in 1801, Francis Buchanan (1870), a surgeon of the British East India Company asked to survey the newly conquered territory, wrote of a sacred grove as a "contrivance" by the local villagers to prevent the company from claiming its rightful property. It is no wonder, then, that in 1883 Dietrich Brandis (1897), the first Inspector General of Forests in India, remarked that the network of sacred groves that once covered much of the country was already in poor shape. Brandis was especially impressed by the excellent state of the sacred groves of Coorg, a hill tract at the junction of Karnataka, Kerala, and Tamilnadu. Following independence and the growing demands of the plywood industry, the forest department opened up the sacred groves of Coorg to commercial fellings in the 1970s. It turns out that the relatively few remaining sacred groves today harbor climax species that have largely disappeared elsewhere. Indeed, scientists from the Botanical Survey of India discovered a few years ago a new species of the first-ever record of a leguminous genus, *Kunstleria*, in a sacred grove in the thickly populated west coast plains of Kerala (Mohanan and Nair 1981). But these significant practices continue to be largely ignored by and receive scant support from the state machinery charged with conservation of biodiversity.

The traditional network of sacred groves remained relatively intact in may parts of northeastern India until independence. These remote hill areas continued up until that time to harbor largely autonomous tribal groups of shifting cultivators outside the fold of the mainstream society. Soon after independence, these people came into contact with the larger economy, and were simultaneously converted to Christianity. On conversion, they abandoned many traditions, including that of protection of sacred groves, and they liquidated many of them. Over the years, however, they noticed that this destruction of sacred groves, which earlier covered more than 10 percent of the land area, had many adverse consequences. In particular, in their absence, fire began to spread to the villages. Many groups in the states of Mizoram and Manipur have therefore revived protection to some forest patches, especially those surrounding the villages. In the new context, these protected areas are termed "safety" rather than "sacred" forests. However, the community-level mechanisms of ensuring the protection of these forests remain as before (Malhotra 1990). Notably enough, protection of these safety forests is often as stringent as prohibition of harvests—even of rattan, which has a ready market. It is notable that this revival of protection has been possible because land largely remains under community control in northeastern India.

Growing Problems

There are many signs that the current centralized, sectoral, economically wasteful, anti-development, anti-people, bureaucratic, regulatory approach to conservation is facing serious difficulties. On the one hand, it is beset with growing opposition from local communities, as manifest in tribals setting fire to large tracts of Kanha tiger reserve and Nagarhole National Park. On the other hand, it is losing out to pressures of commercial interests, with large tracts being opened up to development, as in the case of Narayansagar National Park. Evidently, the time has come to look for alternative paradigms (Singh 1995).

An Alternative

Efficiency and Equity

Any alternative approach must aim at greater efficiency by keeping the costs of conservation as low as possible. It should also serve the interests of equity by passing on the costs to those who would benefit from the conservation effort, and those who are wealthier and therefore in a better position to bear such costs to promote long-term, socially desirable objectives. The costs of conservation may be reduced in five ways: (a) by accepting that conservation may be combined with certain economic pursuits and then promoting those pursuits that are most compatible with the conservation objectives; (b) by assigning the role of custodians of biodiversity to those involved in some of the economic pursuits compatible with conservation, so that the custodians are willing to perform for

relatively modest levels of compensation; and (c) by assigning the role of custodians to those in intimate contact with the biological communities being managed, so that the custodians can perform their role more effectively; (d) by assigning the role of custodians to the economically underprivileged, so that the custodians are willing to perform for relatively modest levels of compensation; and (e) by establishing a firm link between conservation performance and the compensation paid to the custodians.

The interests of equity would be served in ways compatible with promoting efficiency by preferentially involving the economically weaker sections of the society in economic activities deemed compatible with maintenance of high levels of biodiversity and as custodians of biodiversity who may receive some compensation for their role.

Empowering Local Communities

We must then stand the current system of managing biodiversity on its head, and assign the role of custodians of biodiversity to local communities of people who live close to the earth: to the tribals, peasants, herders, fishers, and rural artisans. These are the people who depend for their day-to-day survival on the biological resources of their immediate surroundings. They have for centuries obtained livelihoods without destroying the natural diversity of their environment; its rapid erosion has largely followed large-scale commodification of nature in the last two centuries. Their traditions, such as sacred groves, have permitted survival of species such as *Kunstleria keralensis* in coastal plains of Kerala with human population densities exceeding 1,000 per square kilometer. They have an intimate knowledge of natural resources, albeit often in very limited localities. They are amongst the poorest of Indian people and would be willing to perform for relatively low levels of remuneration.

Experience of recent years has shown that communities of such people, the ecosystem people of Dasmann (1988), are often willing and even eager to take on the role of custodians of local natural resources when permitted to do so. The most notable instance of this is the experiment of joint forest management initiated some twenty years ago in the predominantly tribal

Midnapore district of West Bengal. The natural vegetation of this tract is dominated by sal (*Shorea robusta*), an excellent coppicer. Large tracts of sal forest of Midnapore had been reduced to poor scrub growth by the mid 1970s, although the tree root stock remained intact. Some imaginative forest officials therefore offered the local communities a share in the timber if they accepted the responsibility of protecting a forest patch and if they ensured good coppice growth. This approach was successful because the local tribal communities were relatively homogeneous, because the State Government of West Bengal had introduced a system of decentralized governance that helped local communities get organized to deal effectively with the bureaucracy, and because protection led to rapid tangible results in the form of coppice growth of sal (Deb and Malhotra 1993). The success of their West Bengal experience persuaded the State Government of West Bengal to formally recognize the role and rights of village-level forest committees. This in turn prompted the Government of India to issue in June 1990 an order urging other state governments to formulate rules encouraging the operation of village-level state forest departments in programs of joint forest management. The response to this initiative has been remarkable, and the last few years have witnessed the spontaneous formation of several thousand village forest committees spanning the length and breadth of the country (Poffenberger and McGean, in press).

Villagers participating in such joint management programs are motivated by their interest in more assured access to enhanced levels of plant biomass, for fulfilling their subsistence needs of food, fuel, fodder, drugs, leaf mulch, etc., as well as higher levels of income through marketing of nontimber forest produce such as sal leaf plates and eventually mature timber. They utilize a considerable variety of species for subsistence, as well as market a great diversity of nontimber forest produce. The village forest committees therefore do promote much higher levels of diversity than the state forest departments, which tend to focus on a few commercial species, such as teak or eucalyptus. The village forest committees have been working without any financial inputs on the part of the state, organizing themselves and managing the resource on a voluntary

basis. Empowering local communities to control and benefit from the local natural resource base is thus a powerful, highly efficient route to conservation of biological diversity.

Focusing on Biodiversity

There is, however, a distinct limitation to the range of diversity that the villagers would thus be motivated to protect on the grounds of utility. The larger interest in protection of the entire spectrum of biodiversity would obviously encompass many additional elements of no immediate utility to the local communities. Thus, dead trees left standing for years are an important habitat for a whole range of wood-eating insects, wood-rotting fungi, and hole-nesting birds that may play no role in village economy. Villagers would then be inclined to quickly harvest such dead trees and use them as timber or fuelwood. If we wish to motivate the villagers to conserve such habitats, we need to offer them additional incentives. Indeed, it is clear that if the rationale for conservation of biological diversity includes retaining options for future economic use, or ethical or aesthetic grounds, then simply assuring access to villagers for immediate use would lead to socially suboptimal levels of biodiversity conservation. The larger Indian (or global) society must then mobilize additional resources to raise the level of conservation efforts towards socially desirable levels. Today such additional resources are indeed being made available and used in a highly wasteful manner by the state bureaucracy. It is our contention that they should instead flow to local communities, which would use them in a far more effective fashion.

Building Institutions

We then visualize the additional resources mobilized by the state flowing to the local communities to encourage them to adopt resource use practices that would promote biodiversity. This proposal is clearly analogous to the subsidies farmers in some countries receive to adopt land use practices in the broader interests of soil conservation or payments made by the Nature Conservancy in the United States to landowners to adopt land use practices compatible with conservation of biodiversity. Our focus is on communities, rather than on private parties, for the proposal concerns public lands and waters. To operationalize such a proposal would require answers to a whole series of questions, such as:

- How are local communities to be bounded? How many households should they involve? How homogeneous must such communities be?

- How are parcels of land and water to be assigned to particular local communities to manage in the interests of biodiversity?

- How should the national or global society go about assigning conservation value to different elements of biodiversity? How should this information be shared with local communities?

- How can local communities be organized on different spatial scales to enable them to manage local natural resources effectively in the interests of biodiversity?

- How are the levels of financial or other incentives to be awarded to local communities to conserve biodiversity to be arrived at?

- How can the conservation performance of local communities be firmly linked to the level of rewards flowing to them?

- How can the funds used to promote biodiversity be generated?

Evidently we need to design and build a series of alternative institutions to manage the country's biodiversity, while dismantling part of the current wasteful, inequitable machinery. We suggest below a broad approach to such a task. It is important that care be taken to ensure sufficient flexibility to permit the emergence of institutions appropriate to the local conditions.

Linking Land and People

The basic unit of human society is a group of people in day-to-day, face-to-face contact, somewhere between 20 to 200 households living in a hamlet or a small village. Each unit would be relatively homogeneous, economically and culturally, and likely to act in a cohesive fashion. Such a group should constitute the basic element of a community-based resource management system. It should be authorized to manage all the public lands and waters within a defined territory, and to coordinate actions of private land owners within the bounds of such a territory. This management would of course operate within a broader, socially acceptable framework which may specify that no public lands or wetlands should be brought under cultivation, or that no trees belonging to the genus *Ficus* should be felled. The local communities should be organized into larger and larger groups within a nested hierarchy, with the larger groups serving to coordinate the activities of component neighboring groups and to resolve disputes. The larger resource management groups should form appropriate links with political institutions at corresponding levels: panchayat or village-cluster level corresponding to a population of around ten thousand, taluk or county level corresponding to a population of around a hundred thousand, and district level corresponding to a population of around a million.

A number of difficulties would of course arise pertaining to the complexities of social organization and to the overlap of areas of resource use by neighboring communities. Special cases of overlap would involve nomadic herder communities. It would be best to create institutions for finding locality-specific solutions to such difficulties. We have elsewhere provided much more detailed suggestions on such an institutional framework (Rao and Gadgil 1995).

Valuing Biodiversity

The local natural resource management groups would each have their own system of valuing biodiversity, based on utility, culture, and religion. The values may change with time, as when allopathic drugs supplement the use of herbal remedies. These local systems would be inadequate guides to organizing a national, or a global, effort at conservation of biodiversity. It is therefore necessary to set priorities at a larger level and to ensure that these provide the framework for the local conservation efforts. Such priorities may be set at many different scales: at the level of specific genes, of individuals of specific species, or of specific types of ecological habitats. In general, elements representing more isolated evolutionary lineages, such as those with restricted geographical ranges, under greater threats of extermination, or of greater economic utility, would tend to be valued more. Establishment of such priorities is a technical exercise and might have to be organized by a technical body such as the Subsidiary Body on Scientific, Technical, and Technological Advice to the Conference of Parties of the International Convention on Biological Diversity. It is, however, important that the relevant information from such an exercise of setting conservation priorities should ultimately reach local communities. Educational institutions at various levels, ranging from universities to village primary schools, could play a vital role in this process. Indeed, information on the conservation value of different species of living organisms or different types of habitats could constitute an important component of the environmental education curriculum at all levels.

Rewarding Conservation Efforts

Armed with information on the conservation values of different elements of local ecology, and with authority to manage public lands and waters in their immediate neighborhoods, local communities could design management strategies that would preserve and even enhance the total conservation value of biological communities within their territories. Indeed, we believe that local communities in continual touch with the local biological communities would be best equipped to do so. They could then continually adjust their resource use strategies in the interest of biodiversity, provided that they are adequately rewarded. The perception of local people as to the adequacy of such external rewards would to a great extent depend on their ability to directly benefit from biodiversity. An important component of rewards for conservation efforts could then be building the capacity of local communities to add value to local biodiversity. This may, for instance, involve preparing alcohol extracts of ingredients used in the pharmaceutical industry, or organizing ecotourism. Over and above that, the local communities may need to be compensated for foregoing some opportunities for economically more rewarding uses of land or water within their territory. Exactly what level of rewards the local communities receive and what level of conservation effort they put in would depend on the demand for conservation generated at the national or global level and on the supply of conservation effort offered at the local levels. However, we believe that such a system would deliver conservation effort in a far more cost effective fashion than the current system of investing in regulatory efforts by a bureaucracy which is not accountable for what it ultimately delivers.

Ensuring Accountability

Ensuring accountability in the proposed alternative system would depend on periodic monitoring with adequate independent checks of the biological communities within the territories of the various local communities. The system for organizing such monitoring would, of course, have to be designed at the national or global level, and then adapted to local conditions. Its implementation in the field would best involve local lower-level educational institutions guided by appropriate higher-level institutions. Indeed, such a program could form a valuable component of the teaching of ecology at all levels. It would, of course, be necessary to guard against local schools overestimating local levels of biodiversity in order to attract higher levels of rewards to their own territory. This could be ensured by organizing exchanges of students and teachers across districts or states to serve as independent auditors of the monitoring process. Such visits, too, would have considerable educational value.

Generating Finances

India as a nation state is already investing substantial amounts of state revenue in conservation efforts. Its population is further contributing by accepting costs of conservation, whether it be through foregoing some economically more attractive development options, or tolerating crop damage by elephants. What we propose is that these financial inputs be organized as a national biodiversity conservation fund, perhaps with contributions from international sources such as the Global Environment Facility. These funds could then be rationally allocated to the various local communities spread across the nation in relation to the levels of conservation value of biological communities in their respective territories. We have suggested elsewhere fuller details of how this system may be organized (Rao and Gadgil 1995).

Conclusions and Policy Implications

Biodiversity elements of value are by no means confined to extensive tracts of pristine ecosystems; they occur even in the midst of extensively humanized landscapes, as with wild relatives of paddy and climax rain forest species in sacred groves on the densely populated coastal plains of Kerala. Nor has conservation of biodiversity been the exclusive concern of a specialist bureaucracy, as is seen with the banyan and peepal trees belonging to the keystone resource genus *Ficus* dotting the entire countryside of India. In fact, the bureaucratic attempts at conservation of biodiversity have many glaring deficiencies and are extremely wasteful of resources. Conservation of biodiversity must therefore be made a people's movement, as forest protection has been made with the joint forest management program. Times are particularly opportune for such an initiative, since the 73rd amendment to the Indian constitution has set the stage for a decentralized system of governance, including management of natural resources, throughout the country.

The focus of biodiversity conservation efforts must therefore shift from a small number of protected areas, guarded with the force of arms by a state apparatus alienated from local people, to attempts to maintain substantial levels of biodiversity throughout the countryside by providing positive incentives to local communities.

Local communities should be conferred much greater control over public lands and waters in their own localities by extending systems such as joint forest management and farmers' guilds to manage irrigation waters.

Local communities should be encouraged to manage both public and private lands and waters in their own localities in a biodiversity-friendly fashion by enhancing their capacity to add value to biodiversity, be it through supplying processed material for pharmaceutical industry or through ecotourism.

Local communities should be further encouraged to maintain high levels of biodiversity through financial rewards, linking payments to conservation value of elements making up biological communities within their territories.

The efficacy of funds being deployed towards conservation efforts today in the form of salaries and perks of bureaucrats and technocrats, including their jeeps and guns and buildings to house them, should be critically assessed. It would undoubtedly be found to be exceedingly low. These funds should then be redeployed over a period of time to provide positive incentives to local communities to maintain biodiversity elements of high value to conservation.

Technical inputs from the national or global level would be required to decide on a common system of assigning conservation value to specific elements of biodiversity and to organize a reliable, transparent system of monitoring biodiversity levels within the territories assigned to various local communities. Educational institutions at all levels, from village primary schools to universities, could play an important role in this effort. Indeed, these exercises could become very valuable components of environmental education curricula.

In the long run, only a very lean bureaucratic apparatus should be retained to play a coordinating, facilitative role and to ensure that local communities can effectively enforce a desired system of protection and management of the natural resource base.

Such a system would create a very efficient market for conservation performance so that funds earmarked to promote biodiversity would flow to localities and local communities endowed with capabilities of conserving high levels of biodiversity.

This system would also channel rewards for conservation action to relatively poorer communities living close to the earth, thereby serving ends of social justice, and creating in the long range a situation more favorable to the maintenance of biodiversity on the earth.

Bibliography

Brandis, D. 1897. *Indian Forestry*. Woking: Oriental Institute.

Buchanan, F. D. 1870. *A Journey from Madras Through the Countries of Mysore, Canara and Malabar*. Vol. 2. Madras: Higginbothams.

Dasmann, R. F. 1988. "Towards a Biosphere Consciousness." In D. Worster, ed., *The Ends of the Earth*. Cambridge, United Kingdom: Cambridge University Press, pp. 277–288.

Deb, D. and K. C. Malhotra. 1993. "People's Participation: The Evolution of Joint Forest Management in Southwest Bengal." In S. B. Roy and A. K. Ghosh, eds., *People of India: Biocultural Dimensions*. New Delhi: Inter India Publications, pp. 329–42.

Gadgil, M. 1991. "Conserving India's Biodiversity: The Societal Context." *Evolutionary Trends in Plants* 5:3–8.

Gadgil, M. and R. Guha. In press. *Ecology and Equity: The Use and Abuse of Nature in Contemporary India*. London: Routledge.

Gadgil, M., and P. R. S. Rao. 1994. "A System of Positive Incentives to Conserve Biodiversity." *Economic and Political Weekly*. August 6:2103–2107.

Ludwig, D., R. Hilborn, and C. Walters. 1993. "Uncertainty, Resource Exploitation and Conservation: Lessons from History." *Science* 260:17–36.

Malhotra, K. C. 1990. "Village Supply and Safety Forest in Mizoram: A Traditional Practice of Protecting Ecosystem." in Abstracts of the Plenary, Symposium Papers and Posters Presented at the V International Congress of Ecology, Yokohama, Japan. 439.

Mohanan, C. N., and N. C. Nair. 1981. *Kunstleria Prain—A New Genus Record of India and a New Species in the Genus*. Proceedings of the Indian Academy of Science, B-90:207–10.

Nambiar, P. 1993. "A Change for the Worse." *Down to Earth*, November 15:45.

Poffenberger, M., and B. McGean. In press. *Village Voices—Forest Choices: Joint Forest Management in India*. New Delhi: Oxford University Press.

Rao, P. R. S., and M. Gadgil. 1995. "People's Nature, Health and Education Bill." *Hindu Survey of the Environment*, pp. 217–223.

Singh, T., ed. 1995. "Parks and People: A Symposium on Resource Use Around Our Protected Areas." *Seminar* 426:72. New Delhi.

Vijayan, V. S. 1987. *Keoldeo National Park*. Bombay: Bombay Natural History Society.

6

Will New Property Right Regimes
in Central and Eastern Europe
Serve the Purposes of Nature Conservation?

Tomasz Żylicz

Abstract

IN THIS CHAPTER, an example of the conflict between conservationists and a rural municipality in Northeastern Poland, is analyzed in order to illustrate how changing property right regimes after the collapse of communist rule in 1989 have influenced the social context of nature protection. The municipality resists establishing the Mazurian National Park, whose presence would imply certain economic restrictions. The pattern emerging from this case study is a complex one.

This research was sponsored by the Beijer Institute, The Royal Swedish Academy of Sciences, with support from the World Environment and Resources Program of the John D. and Catherine T. MacArthur Foundation and the World Bank. The research was conducted as part of the program Property Rights and the Performance of Natural Resource Systems. The case study in this chapter received funding from the Pew Scholar Program in Conservation and the Environment.

On the one hand, any development constraints are perceived as more severe now than before when there was little private entrepreneurship around. On the other hand, however, the enforceability of law—including environmental regulations—has improved as a result of increased transparency of public decisionmaking. Thus, the fate of nature protection crucially depends on the ability of conservationists to demonstrate economic benefits from investing in natural capital rather than letting it be degraded. A project is under way to identify local sustainable development options and to show that land use restrictions, when combined with a larger package of social and economic improvements, can turn out to be an asset rather than a liability. The project is used by conservationists to seek support of the local population for the national park idea.

◆

Nature Protection in Poland

When the communist political system in Europe collapsed in 1989, the gravity of the environmental destruction in this part of the world could finally be ascertained with some degree of scientific veracity. Most of the earlier assessments were largely inaccurate because of inadequate information supply resulting from the communist censorship or lack of reliable monitoring. One of the reasons for such policies of the old regimes was to portray their countries as environmental trouble-free. Ironically, this approach proved totally counterproductive and triggered even more curiosity from western journalists. It also stimulated a great deal of one-sided reporting and stigmatized the region with an image of the most devastated piece of land.

This overall image has determined thinking of the Polish natural environment both domestically and in the West. As a result, the Poles tend to view their environmental predicament in catastrophic terms, but they largely fail to have a comprehensive and consistent picture of what went wrong, which are the greatest risks, and how to redress the situation. At the same time, they overlook the fact that because the communist industrialization concentrated in areas of traditionally high intensity of production, vast regions remained largely underdeveloped. These regions and their almost intact natural capital represent an asset which is becoming increasingly scarce in Europe. However, because of the *cliché* of disruption, not only average citizens but also those environmentally concerned citizens are not fully aware of the value of their natural heritage (Żylicz 1994).

In Poland, experts estimate that about 8.5 percent of the area of the country remains relatively unscathed by development. Commercial forests and farms operating within sustainable and ecologically acceptable principles include about 19 percent of the Polish territory. Hence, over a fourth of Poland represents an asset that many areas of Europe no longer have. Poland's biological diversity is high, particularly with respect to forest and bog communities. According to a recent study (Andrzejewski and others 1992), in the last 400 years, the Polish vertebrate fauna has lost fifteen species (2.5 percent), including three mammals, eleven birds and one fish species. At the same time, the Polish flora has lost thirty-one species of vascular plants. Sad as they are, these figures turn out to be much less alarming than in other, more developed, European countries in the same biogeographical zone. For instance, a sister study for Germany found that—apparently due to the longer and more intensive industrialization period—the biodiversity loss has been much more acute. In the last 150 years, 28 species of vertebrates (6 percent) have become extinct, comprising 7 mammals (8 percent), 19 birds (8 percent), and 2 fishes, along with 58 vascular plant species.

The ecological value of Poland's natural capital has been internationally recognized. Most of its twenty national parks are on the IUCN list, as they meet all the criteria for this highest degree of protection. Three of them have been included by UNESCO in a network of biosphere reserves representing typical, well-preserved examples of the world's ecosystems. One of them—the Białowieża National Park (whose natural extension in Belarus has enjoyed the status of a national park, too)—has been declared an object of exceptional importance to the World Heritage, as the last remaining area of the characteristic Central European lowland primeval forest. Also, a number of smaller objects, "nature reserves," were found to be of international importance, some of them being protected under the Ramsar Convention on wetland ecosystems.

Table 6–1 presents the development of national parks in Poland in recent years. Between 1988 and 1993 their number grew from fourteen to nineteen. The total area almost doubled, which was achieved both by adding new parks and augmenting some of the old ones.

Apart from the network of national parks, covering the area of 244,000 hectares (0.8 percent of the country area), Poland has an even larger system of "landscape parks." In 1993 there were ninety-one such parks, comprising as much as 1,726,809 hectares (5.5 percent of the country area). The difference between a national and a landscape park is in the scope of protection as well as in the legal authority. While the former is established by a decree of the Council of Ministers (the central government), the latter is enacted by a decision of a regional administrator (there are forty-nine such administrative regions in Poland). The former is financed from the central budget directly. The financial status of the latter is more complex. Even though most subsidies that landscape parks receive originate from the central budget, regional administrators are supposed to contribute to their accounts too. However, the most crucial difference between the two types of parks is that only the national ones have the authority to issue regulations, within well-defined legal limits, which otherwise fall within the competence of regional administrators. In particular, directors of national parks have the right to license economic activities carried out within the park boundaries and to influence land-use patterns in their parks' buffer zones.

Most examples of the country's unique and unspoiled ecosystems have already been given the status of a national park (Nowicki 1993). There are only a few areas—usually protected as landscape parks—which are considered candidates for becoming national parks. The Mazurian Landscape Park is the site of a major conflict between conservationists, who urge turning it into a national park, and a part of the local population, who fear that the new status will make them worse off. The opposition comes from Piecki (pronounced *Pee-etzkee*), one of the three rural municipalities where the Mazurian Landscape Park is located. The conflict reveals in a transparent form what can be found in the existing national parks in a more or less latent

form, and its successful resolution can thus be instructive for other areas in Poland.

Quite paradoxically, the natural capital which survived several decades of communist mismanagement is now under the serious threat of a new sort of development. Even though the logic of market economies is likely to lead to a more efficient use of resources, at the same time, it exposes these resources to new pressures resulting from their opening up to large scale international tourism and international real estate markets. The ecologically valuable areas—especially those in Western and Northern Poland—are reportedly experiencing tourism pressure which increased rapidly after the collapse of the Berlin Wall.

Conservation and Property Right Issues

At first glance, nature conservation seems to have been easier under the central planning regime. Even though most of the land was always in private hands in Poland (unlike in other Central and Eastern European countries), the nondemocratic governments that ruled in 1945–1989 had little respect for owners' rights. Establishing a nature reserve or a national park was thus just an administrative decision. As a result, many patches of private property within national park boundaries were left. State policy towards buying these pieces of land was inconsistent, and quite often real estate owners could neither sell nor develop their lots. This contributed to tensions between park managers and the local populations.

Table 6–2 presents the ownership structure of the Polish national parks in 1992. As seen from the table, state property accounts for over 93 percent of the total area, mainly because of the high share of the forest land in the parks. Most of the nonstate enclaves are farms whose operators still hold ownership title to the land. The most typical conflicts include crop damages done by game animals, for which the parks serve as safe havens, constraints on the use of chemicals, and unclear prospects for the future. What could have been hushed up under the communist regime emerged as an open conflict after 1989. Thus national park directors started to face serious problems despite the fact that the agricultural land accounts for a minor fraction of the total area.

Another, perhaps an even more serious, conflict exists where the agricultural enclaves are left as a communal property. Here park directors are challenged not by individual farmers but rather by strong collectives with a long tradition and a sense of self-identity. This type of conflict has been best known from the Tatra Mountains National Park located on the border with Slovakia (where the other part of the range, also protected as a national park, is situated). The park was established in the first, most brutal, decade of communist rule in Poland. This fact has often been recalled in order to portray the conflict merely as the heritage of an insane political regime. The conflict, however, cannot simply be solved by compensating the original owners. The true struggle is not for a reimbursement for victims of unfair administrative decisions. What is at stake here is who will control the local assets which can generate decent revenues in the long run if well managed, and enormous yet unsustainable short-term profits.

The predicament resembles much of the tragedy of the commons. In fact, the community went through this in the nineteenth Century. One of the fertile valleys (Dolina Jaworzynki) was overgrazed. Once green slopes were turned into barren rock. The community does not want to acknowledge its contribution to the erosion process and insists on increasing the number of sheep allowed in the national park or "recommunalization" of some of the valleys. For the time being, the limit set at 1,000 sheep is seen by the park as ecologically safe and preserving the historical landscape. The culture of the region, which is one of the most popular in Poland, has been closely linked to pastoralism and to the gorgeous diversified landscape which depends on the land use. (Without sheep, all the foothills, now a major floristic attraction, would be covered by forest.)

The grazing conflict should not be overemphasized in the Poland of the 1990s any more. After all, agriculture provides an ever-decreasing share of the local incomes. Of great concern now is the ecological integrity of the Tatra range commons. The region is a top tourist attraction. The local population has been known for their entrepreneurial skills, and the supply of capital is not a constraint; almost every family has at least one member who earns income in the United States (mainly in the construction business), either temporarily or permanently. There is strong pressure to invest money in creating sport and tourist infrastructure modeled after the Alps ski resorts. What is overlooked in these plans is the scale of the Tatra mountains. The entire range (less than 30 kilometers long) could be contained in one of the many Alpian valleys, some of which were developed into large recreation factories and some of which were preserved. Building roads, luxury hotels, and a system of cable cars—as envisaged by local leaders—would give investors high short-term revenues but only at the cost of an irreversible degradation of the Tatra ecosystem. In the long run, such a scenario would seriously reduce the attractiveness of the region for visitors and thus undermine the local economy.

It is a pity that the conflict affects a region where both natural and cultural capital are so rich and outstanding. Besides, they seem to have successfully coevolved until the middle of the twentieth Century (with one exception of an overgrazing incident in the nineteenth Century). This coevolution and creative coexistence is considered to be a key element of a sound management of landscape and biodiversity resources (Berkes and Folke 1992, Nelson and Serafin 1992). It does not even help much that the present director of the Tatra National Park, who holds a Ph.D. in ecology, was born in one of the best-known and best respected shepherd families in the region. The director faces a real danger of physical attack on himself and his estate. Apparently, the stakes are so high that they will not let the parties calm down and cooperate.

The lesson learned from the Tatra National Park experience is fourfold. First, it proves that the establishment of some parks by the old political regime stigmatized them permanently with the image of an external intrusion which makes rational cooperation difficult. Second, no realistic compensation scheme for the previous owners of assets protected by a national park is likely to solve some of the conflicts. Third, encroaching on the park land gradually becomes of lesser importance (even though local poachers can be a serious problem in some places). The main conflict is over the pattern of development in the park neighborhood with or without taking advantage of the continued presence of its natural assets. Fourth, comanagement (McCay 1993)—understood as a regime entailing a mixture of local governance with an external authority based on mutual trust and recognition of each other's role in preserving resources—is the only viable form of control.

A practical lesson learned from this experience is that carrying out a successful conservation project calls for cooperation of conservationists and the local population from the outset. Otherwise, the project may be doomed to a lasting conflict, and its conservation objectives will be difficult to achieve.

McKean (1993) observes that "public ownership may be the most preferred form when a resource system is so threatened, so abused that (or so close to that point) that most uses and harvesting must be prohibited for the time being." Indeed, in Poland in some instances the predicament of the natural capital assets calls for public ownership. At the same time, however, the local pressure on the resource system calls for "the cooperation of local people so that they become coenforcers with the government, rather than perpetual encroachers" (McKean). Thus, comanagement emerges as a preferred form of control once again.

Nature protection under the old nondemocratic regime was easier only formally. Actually, the neglected property right issues were a source of tensions in the past, as they are now. The Tatra region conflict shows how bad things can become, even though in most cases they do not deteriorate. A more typical conflict entails a bit of poaching, illegal construction of small scale objects in the park's buffer zone, controversies about carrying out agricultural activities on private land in the park, and the general lack of interest in taking advantage of the protected natural capital in the neighborhood.

The respect for private and communal property rights reestablished under the post-1989 regime makes the position of national park authorities more difficult. From now on, they must prove the legality of all decisions taken. At the same time, however, they have an opportunity to become local community leaders by demonstrating development options linked to the preservation of natural capital. There was no demand earlier for such a role to be played by conservationists, since little entrepreneurship was allowed, economic decisionmaking was

heavily centralized, and development was seen as a matter of bringing industry into the region. Many ecologically valuable regions in Poland happen to be located in economically depressed areas without clear perspectives for attracting external investors. It is here where a skilled national park manager can win local support for conservation measures when they bring jobs, visitors, and capital.

The Case of Piecki

When the initiative of establishing the Mazurian National Park in lieu of the existing Mazurian Landscape Park was first officially discussed in 1993, it met with various reactions. Two out of three municipalities involved decided to support it. The representatives of the third one, Piecki, announced that they would not let their municipality be included in a national park. Several informal consultations were held, yet without any effect on the municipality's position. Facing such strong local opposition, the Ministry of Environment asked the Warsaw Ecological Economics Center for assistance in discussing with the local leaders the costs and benefits that would result from having the national park. The following summary is based on the assessment (Kaczanowski and others 1994) prepared in response to that request.

The assessment starts with general characteristics of Piecki and with the municipality's list of development constraints and other adverse effects expected from the national park's presence.

General Characteristics

The municipality of Piecki is located in the northeastern part of the country, referred to as "The Green Lungs of Poland" because of the abundance of forests and diversified, near-pristine ecosystems. It belongs to the Great Mazurian Lakes district, and it is adjacent to Śniardwy, Poland's largest lake. The area of Piecki is 31,500 hectares, and its population (as of the end of 1993) is 7,766, which gives average density of twenty-five persons per square kilometer, that is, one fifth of the country average and one half of the density recorded in the district. The sparse population and the lack of large enterprises are reflected in the breakdown of the municipal budget (Table 6–3).

In 1993, the municipal budget revenues in Piecki were PLZ 2,060,000 per person, whereas the average number for Poland was PLZ 2,513,000 (the approximate exchange rate in mid-1993 was PLZ 17,500 per U.S. dollar). Thus, the municipal revenues in Piecki can be estimated at $120 per person, which is 82 percent of the national average and corresponds to 6 percent of gross domestic product per capita (estimated at somewhat less than $2,000).

The composition of Piecki's budgetary revenues reflects the importance of the forestry as well as the relative importance of personal incomes *vis à vis* corporate profits. Despite low revenues per capita, Piecki was considered more self-sufficient than average, as reflected in the low "general subsidy" which serves a redistributive function and which is based on a complicated formula encompassing municipalities' socioeconomic characteristics.

Agriculture provides more jobs than any other sector in Piecki. There is a growing number of firms in the service sector, but their exact contribution to the local employment is not certain because of a reporting system that is far from perfect. Table 6–4 gives employment figures for sectors covered by regular reporting. The number of persons employed in agriculture, which is dominated by small family farms, is probably underestimated. In addition, of the 303 registered service firms, 78 operate in commerce, 45 in the tourism business, 34 in forestry, 33 run small restaurants, 30 operate in transport, and 28 are in the construction business. Most of them are one-person enterprises, and their contribution to the local employment yields to that of industry.

Arguments Against the Park

The primary local argument against the Mazurian National Park is the loss of the forestry tax, which accounts for 8.3 percent of budgetary revenues. The forestry tax, which is a flat rate payment based on the quality of the forest land rather than actual yields, was conceived as an instrument to stimulate an optimal use of the land. The tax, which is indexed by the price of timber, is collected by municipalities. The tax is waived if the forest is classified as protected. National park forests certainly belong in this category. However, the Minister of Environment can classify an area as protected if the forest plays an important role in controlling erosion, the water table, climate, local habitats, etc. In fact, a vast majority of protected forests are outside national parks.

No commercial hunting is allowed within national park boundaries. To the extent that some species may breed excessively while the local ecological system is not in a natural equilibrium (e.g., for historical reasons), hunting can be permitted, but only under direct supervision of park authorities. No foreign visitors are allowed to hunt. Even though the latter issue was never raised by park opponents openly, conservationists believe that the loss of incomes linked to the lack of a foreign hunting business is nevertheless the main cause of the opposition. However, only few families were involved in foreign hunting activities. Typical tips for assisting in a successful shooting of a deer range from DM 100 to 200 (in Deutshe Marks). Given the number of hunts, one can estimate the local income loss at no more than DM 10,000 per year. Under central planning, with an average monthly salary worth $20 at the black market exchange rate, a DM 100 tip was a fortune. Now that an average salary is worth $200, the same tip is a pleasing addition to households' incomes, but its value has decreased tenfold. Certainly it does not contribute to the municipal budget at all, as it never enters official records.

Other arguments against the park include expected denial of building permits, constraints on selling real estate, reduced attractiveness of the area for tourists, and no perspectives for the development of industry and agriculture. Under closer scrutiny, it can be demonstrated that all these concerns are inappropriately linked to the national park's presence.

Actually, regulations which affect building permit procedure and real estate markets are totally independent from the park's existence. A house or a summer cottage can be built if the lot was designated in the municipal spatial development plan for this purpose. Also, real estate can be bought and sold subject to regulations which have nothing to do with the national park. Perhaps a tacit assumption is often made that illegal construction or real estate transactions which were tolerated or "overlooked" in the past will be prosecuted when the national park officers are around, and the region is an object of general interest. Fortunately for conservationists, it can be demonstrated that enforcement improved dramatically after 1989, that is, not as a result of the national park's presence, but rather because of the change of the political system. For instance, it was almost impossible in the past to enforce regulations against illegal construction. Since 1989 more than a dozen buildings erected without a valid building permit have been torn down in Piecki.

Not all of the municipality's area is planned for inclusion in the Mazurian National Park—only 15,300 hectares is, which is slightly less than half. Only 1,112 inhabitants (one-seventh of the total number) would live within the park boundaries, and only 678 hectares of agricultural land (out of 9,500 hectares) would be included. Thus, licensing economic activities by the park director will affect only a fraction of the local economy. In particular, all the existing industries operating in the municipality have valid pollution permits, and their presence does not interfere with the national park objectives. Moreover, the local spatial development plan, which is the main constraint for bringing new industries into the region, designates a number of sites for potential (small scale) industrial plants outside the park. Establishing businesses on these sites will not be hindered by the park's existence.

To some extent, agriculture will be affected by the park's presence. Currently the use of chemical inputs is minimal and close to the country average of 60 kilograms NPK (nitrogen + phosphorus + potassium) per hectare in mineral fertilizers, and 0.4 kilograms per hectare for pesticide use. It is several times lower than in Western Europe and does not interfere with park objectives. Problems may arise if in the future farmers would wish to apply Western input levels. However, the potential income loss is difficult to assess, since alternative low input options may prove attractive as envisaged in the study of benefits from the national park's presence.

To sum up, the only demonstrable loss related to the establishment of the Mazurian National Park is a decreased municipal revenue from the forestry tax. Since not all the forest would be included in the park, the loss does not affect the entire tax, that is, the sum of PLZ 1,300 million, but only PLZ 900 million (approximately $50,000). The municipal budget will suffer a loss of 6 percent. Tips left by foreign hunters are another quantifiable loss. They do not exceed 10,000 DM (approximately $7,000). Since this is a loss of a nonreported income, it does not affect the municipal budget.

Benefits from the Park's Existence

It proved to be fairly easy to demonstrate immediate local benefits from the park's existence in the form of additional employment and contracts. Most of the planned 160 employees of the Mazurian National Park will be recruited either from the existing landscape park administration or from the state forestry service; none of the present employees in these organizations will lose a job as a result of establishing the national park. On the contrary, the park will offer seventeen new positions. This implies additional annual incomes on the order of PLZ 1,000 million (in 1993 prices) or $57,000, the sum exactly equivalent (by a pure coincidence) to financial losses identified in the section above entitled *Arguments Against the Park*. The park will also employ additional part-time workers, thus creating incomes on the order of PLZ 400 million, or $23,000. Investment expenditures of the Mazurian National Park on tourist infrastructure are planned at the level of PLZ 800 million, or $46,000, for the first year.

In the longer run, indirect benefits from the park's presence are expected to play an increasingly important role. They include three broad categories: (1) benefits from increased demand for high-quality tourist services; (2) benefits from a potential specialization in supplying "ecological farming" products; and (3) benefits from attracting attention to the existence value of assets protected by the park.

The region is attractive for various types of tourists. It provides excellent opportunities for backpacking, sailing, kayaking, rafting, swimming, and bird-watching, among other activities. Despite local concerns, the establishment of the national park will not reduce the attractiveness of the region. The interest in the region will almost surely increase. According to a recent assessment of the "carrying capacity" of Piecki, the number of tourists can increase without adversely affecting the local ecosystems. To have this increased demand translated into new jobs and additional incomes requires only the ability to provide tourists with the services they look for. In a few years, further growth of the number of visitors may become constrained by what can be accommodated without degrading the natural capital or losing it due to congestion. By licensing services offered, the national park will keep their supply within sustainable limits. This does not necessarily imply lower incomes (even in the short run). By controlling supply and promoting high quality services rather than those aimed at consumers who expect less and pay less, it is possible to earn more than under an open access regime (Lanza and Pigliaru 1993). The latter assertion, however, depends on demand elasticities and should be empirically validated in each particular case.

Farmers in Piecki—especially those operating in the national park or its buffer zone—may find it profitable to specialize in high quality "ecological" products and services. There is a growing number of "ecological" grocery stores that claim that their products are pesticide free. While the demand for such commodities is uncertain, there is no doubt that customers will be increasingly choosy in selecting stores, brands, and producers they trust. Hence products endorsed in one way or another by a national park will be trusted more than ordinary ones. Again, however, this is an empirical question, and no firm conclusions about the Piecki farmers' revenues can be made at this moment. Another interesting option is agro-ecotourism, a new type of service combining accommodation on an environment-friendly family farm with purchasing high quality farm products, perhaps hand-picked by tourists themselves. There is a European Association of Agro-Ecotourism which publishes catalogues of farms that offer such services. Location in a national park or its buffer zone is an additional asset a farm can demonstrate.

Both high-quality tourist services and "ecological" farming involve arguments which are hypothetical and may be not convincing for the local community. One indirect benefit from establishing a national park that is tangible and certain is attracting attention to the existence value of assets protected. Existence values can materialize in several ways, including wealth transfers to those who steward the natural capital supporting these assets. While some of such transfers are hypothetical as well, one can point

at concrete mechanisms or funding sources that are available for national parks.

In Poland, there are several institutions whose charter activities include providing support for national parks. The most important one is the National Fund for Environmental Protection, which finances almost 25 percent of the country's environmental investment expenditures. The Fund has formal project selection procedures which favor investors located in national parks or their buffering zones. Thus, establishing a park increases the likelihood of receiving support for an environment-related investment. Upgrading and expanding tourist infrastructure in Piecki will require investment in sewage treatment plants and environmentally friendly heating systems. With the National Fund support, these (mainly private) projects will be much easier to undertake. There are also other domestic and international sources of project financing which favor national park sites that Piecki can be referred to. In fact, the municipality was offered free services to prepare project proposals (addressed to banks or funding institutions) which are already now at the park planning stage.

Summary

The direct financial benefits provided by the Mazurian National Park, should it be established, outweigh any quantifiable losses by a wide margin. Nevertheless, two qualifications must be added here. First, despite a demonstrable net increase in local revenues, there will be a net loss to the municipal budget (caused by the forestry tax loss), since 85 percent of personal income taxes and 95 percent or corporate profit taxes are claimed by the state budget. One way of responding to the municipality's concern is to argue that the forestry tax would have been lost anyway, since ministerial decisions are already prepared to increase the area of protected forest in the Great Mazurian Lake District. Even though this is a valid argument, it does not serve conflict resolution well and should be avoided. Second, there will be several households definitely worse off because of the loss of foreign hunters. In order to weaken their opposition to the park idea, it is possible to offer them financial support (for example, from sources like the National Fund for Environmental Protection) for investment in infrastructure to capture expected benefits from the park's presence.

It turns out that enclaves of private property within the park boundaries or in its buffer zone should not pose serious management problems. On the contrary, it is expected that private entrepreneurship can be channeled into high-quality tourism and "ecological" farming, providing sustainable revenues for the municipality. The national park logo attached to products and services provided by businesses licensed by the park authorities is a source of advantage Piecki can enjoy over competitors located elsewhere.

Concluding Remarks

As Eggertsson (1993) points out, in designing institutions for the control of natural assets, one has to face the universal problem of *nonexclusivity*. This means that none of the parties involved, such as private owners, the local community, or the government, can ever enjoy full control of resources they own or care for. A socially optimal use of resources requires that a balance is kept between the cost of governance (that is, internal control) and the cost of exclusion (that is, control against encroachers). One extreme case is a party's attempt to completely control an asset by excluding all other potential users. On the other extreme there is a fully cooperative arrangement, allowing for controlled access for all potential users. There is no universal rule on how to optimally allocate effort between governance and exclusion, and the problem has to be solved in each particular case. Nevertheless, it is obvious that neither of the extremes is a good model for managing ecologically valuable resources such as those protected in national parks.

Comanagement seems to be the only viable strategy for integrating diversified interests of local communities and other social groups having stakes in protecting the natural capital in question. This capital entails not only traditional resources such as grazing land and fisheries, but entire ecosystems and their life-supporting functions, too. It is unlikely that the communities themselves would be able to arrive at optimal—let alone effective—models of local resource control in the case of assets of national or international importance. A mix of local management with external support in the form of standards, enforcement, and funding will serve nature conservation best.

New property right regimes in Poland mean reestablishing respect for private and communal interests and mutual trust in economic relations between private and public entities (which, by the way, is a long process rather than a one-time event). This new situation implies certain problems for a number of national parks which struggle with the conflicts inherited from the communist rule, which carelessly manipulated ownership titles and private rights. For new parks, this situation creates a level playing field, where interests of various groups can be articulated and taken into account in the institutional design phase.

The case of the Mazurian National Park provides an interesting example of an experiment in designing a model for effective cooperation between local communities and representatives of the "public interest." The study referred to in this paper identified opportunities for local sustainable economic development based on the natural capital protected by the park. As of January 1995, the conflict between conservationists and the municipality of Piecki had not been resolved. There is, however, a firm economic foundation for a compromise, since the net outcome of establishing the park is positive beyond any doubt. Hence there are no fundamental reasons precluding a mutually satisfactory agreement. If the park is finally established with local support, the question raised in the title of this chapter can be answered positively. Interim results from the negotiation process suggest that a comanagement regime has been emerging with a somewhat smaller park size accepted by both sides as a key element of the final compromise.

Bibliography

Andrzejewski, Roman, and others. 1992. *Krajowe studium bioróżnorodności. Raport polski dla UNEP.* Warsaw: National biodiversity study. Poland's report to UNEP.

Berkes, Fikret, and Carl Folke. 1992, "A Systems Perspective on the Interrelations Between Natural, Human-made and Cultural Capital." *Ecological Economics* 5:1–8.

Eggertsson, Thrainn. 1993. "Economic Perspectives on Property Rights and the Economics of Institutions." Beijer Discussion Paper Series (40). Stockholm: The Beijer International Institute of Ecological Economics.

Kaczanowski, Feliks, Ewa Łapińska, Joanna Spyrka, Zdzisław Szkiruć, and Tomasz Żylicz. 1994. "Bilans kosztów i korzyści gminy Piecki związanych z utworzeniem Mazurskiego Parku Narodowego." Mimeo, Warsaw Ecological Economics Center, Warsaw University.

Lanza, Alessandro, and Francesco Pigliaru. 1993. *Specialization in Tourism Based on Natural Resources in the Presence of a Trade-off Between Quality and Quantity*. Milan: Nota di lavoro della Fondazione ENI Enrico Mattei.

McCay, Bonnie J. 1993. "Management Regimes." Beijer Discussion Paper (38). Stock-holm: Beijer International Institute of Ecological Economics.

McKean, Margaret A. 1993. "Empirical Analysis of Local and National Property Rights Institutions." Beijer Discussion Paper (42). Stockholm: Beijer International Institute of Ecological Economics.

Nelson, J. Gordon, and Rafal Serafin. 1992. "Assessing Biodiversity: A Human Ecological Approach." *Ambio* 21(3) (May):212–18.

Nowicki, Maciej. 1993. *Environment in Poland: Issues and solutions*. Kluwer: Dordrecht.

Ochrona Środowiska 1989...1994. 1994. Warsaw: Główny Urząd Statystyczny [Environmental Protection Yearbook 1989...1994].

Żylicz, Tomasz. 1994. "In Poland, It's Time for Economics." *Environmental Impact Assessment Review* 14:79–94.

Table 6–1: National Parks in Poland

	1988	1989	1990	1991	1992	1993
Number of national parks	14	15	17	17	17	19
National park area, 1,000 hectares	127	141	166	177	179	244

Source: Ochrona (1989–1994).

Table 6–2: Land Ownership in National Parks in Poland (Status December 31, 1992)

Land-use category	Total area	Of which private or communal property	
		hectares	% of total*
All categories	178,764	12,955	7.2
of which:			
Forest	130,058	5,757	4.4
Agricultural land	13,014	6,485	49.8
Water	15,388	21	0.1
Other	20,304	692	3.4

*As percent of the total area of a given land-use category.
Source: Files of the National Parks Board.

*Table 6–3: Breakdown of Municipal Budgets: Poland's Average and Piecki (1993)**

Revenue category	Poland	Piecki
All categories	100.0	100.0
of which:		
Real estate tax	14.8	17.0
Agricultural taxes and fees	3.8	4.7
Forest tax	0.3	8.3
Share in personal income tax**	21.8	36.8
Share in corporate tax***	3.6	0.3
Administrative fees	5.0	2.0
Grants from the state budget	16.7	14.2
General subsidy from the state budget	11.4	2.9

* Main revenue items providing 86.2 percent of revenues for the Piecki municipal budget.
** Municipalities receive 15 percent of the personal income tax the rest being claimed by the state budget.
*** Municipalities receive 5 percent of the corporate income tax the rest being claimed by the state budget.
Source: Kaczanowski and others (1994).

Table 6–4: Employment in Piecki in Selected Sectors, 1993

Sector	Employment
Agriculture	800
Saw mills, wood processing, and furniture production	467
Forestry	190
Food industry	40

Source: Kaczanowski and others (1994).

7

Nonsustainable Use of Renewable Resources: Mangrove Deforestation and Mariculture in Ecuador

Peter J. Parks and Manuel Bonifaz

Abstract

The chapter provides a conceptual model that examines (a) open-access exploitation and (b) mangrove deforestation as two potential causes for the scarcity of post-larval shrimp inputs to shrimp mariculture in Ecuador. Results indicate that conversion of mangrove ecosystems to shrimp ponds may have obtained short-term profit at the expense of long-term productivity. Open-access collection of post-larval shrimp may also have contributed to dwindling stock levels. Specific policy recommendations are presented, and future empirical studies are proposed.

A longer version of this chapter appears in *Marine Resource Economics* 9(1):1–18.

Ecuador's shrimp industry grew rapidly from 1973–1988 to become the country's second largest earner of foreign currency. At that time, Ecuador was the largest supplier of shrimp to the United States and one of the largest mariculture producers in the world (Instituto de Estrategias Agropecuarias 1989). However, recent decline in the competitiveness of the industry has raised concerns about its future stability, and has focused national attention on how to develop policies to sustain the productivity and competitiveness of shrimp mariculture in Ecuador.

Important factors contributing to the decline of shrimp mariculture include (a) the reduced availability of post-larval shrimp (PLS) to stock shrimp ponds, (b) low productivity of mature shrimp per hectare of ponds, (c) fluctuations of international market prices for mature shrimp, and (d) growing competition from Asian producers. While general policy guidelines have been developed to address some of these factors (for example, Olsen and Arriaga 1989; Southgate and Whitaker 1994), there are relatively few analytical studies that can provide more specific policy recommendations.

This chapter examines two potential causes for scarcity of PLS inputs. Causes for PLS scarcity include open-access exploitation of the PLS fishery (for example, Thian-Eng and Kungvankij 1989) and the depletion of mangrove habitat for PLS (for example, Turner 1989). Alternative explanations for stock fluctuations, such as the El Niño phenomenon—a southward shift of warm ocean current into Ecuadorean waters—of 1982–83, are considered in the context of comparative statics. Economic policies to correct for open access and deforestation externalities are described.

Results indicate that if mangrove ecosystems influence PLS stock development, conversion of forests to ponds for shrimp production has obtained short-term profit at the expense of long-term productivity. If Ecuador's shrimp industry is to maintain its competitiveness in the world market, it must invest in mangrove habitat restoration and technological improvements to increase long-run productivity per hectare, rather than continue to mine the country's renewable mangrove resources for nonsustainable benefit.

Shrimp Mariculture in Ecuador

Shrimp Production

A shrimp producer enters the production cycle first by obtaining a concession to publicly owned coastal lands below the high-tide line. If mangroves are present, the producer determines how much of these lands must be cleared for ponds. Trees are typically removed by workers using chain saws, and the residual biomass is burned. Once the forest has been removed, a bulldozer is used to create a rectangular levee that encloses a flat, rectangular pond. Most ponds are between 2 and 3 meters deep and between 7 and 15 hectares in area. After the pond has been built, it is filled with water pumped from adjacent estuaries and stocked with PLS.

Pennaeus vannamei has proved to be the most robust species for use in stocking shrimp ponds. Stocking densities range from 30,000 to 50,000 PLS per hectare, depending on management intensity. Once the PLS are mature, they are collected by workers in canoes, who sweep nets through the pond until the mature shrimp are removed. The mature shrimp are sold by the shrimp producer to processors who ready them for final consumption. The pond is then pumped dry and filled with fresh water for the next production cycle.

Collection of Post-Larval Shrimp by Artesanos

Pennaeus vannamei PLS are obtained by shrimp producers from middlemen, who in turn purchase them from *artesano* fishermen. *Artesanos* collect PLS in an open-access fishery. In Ecuador, PLS are collected by a few thousand full-time and about 10,000 part-time *artesano* fishermen who make a living collecting PLS with hand-held nets in estuaries and beaches along the coast (Scott and Gaibor 1992). *Artesanos* collect PLS using nets, which are held in water roughly one meter deep. Once the net is full, the *artesano* fisherman returns to the beach, and typically discards species other than *Pennaeus vannamei*. A day's catch of *Pennaeus vannamei* PLS is stored in buckets, which are sold to middlemen. The middlemen, in turn, transport the buckets of PLS to shrimp producers' ponds in unrefrigerated trucks (LiPuma and Meltzoff 1985).

The Shrimp Life Cycle and Mangrove Ecosystems

Shrimp begin life in the open sea. After going through several maturation phases, including a larval phase, the post-larval shrimp move to estuarine waters. Post-larval shrimp remain in estuaries between three and five months before returning to the ocean. The estuarine habitat provides nutrient-rich substrates, such as mangrove roots; the mangroves' complex vegetative system may also provide protection from predators.

Several studies link PLS stocks to mangrove ecosystems. Data for Malaysia and the Philippines suggest that although estuarine salinity and water temperature changes affect the survival rate of PLS, in the long term yields are related to both quality and area of the mangrove habitat. Similar studies from the Gulf of Mexico, Louisiana, and Japan corroborate this hypothesis (Turner 1989).

Mangrove forests are among the most biologically productive marine ecosystems. These forests are essential habitat for many species in addition to PLS. Besides providing habitat, these ecosystems maintain water quality, and they function as "kidneys" for estuarine environments by purifying water and ensuring sufficient oxygen for marine species. Other nonmarket and market benefits provided by mangrove forests include sediment stabilization, bird habitat, and a renewable supply of forest products, such as edible fruits, bark for tanning, charcoal, and construction wood. These benefits are only examples of the types of benefits that can be provided by mangrove ecosystems. Dixon and Lal (1994) give a thorough overview of the functions, products, and attributes provided by eight globally important wetlands categories, including mangroves. Barbier (1994) describes how such environmental functions may be valued.

National Trends in Shrimp Mariculture

Shrimp mariculture has dramatically changed Ecuador's coastal land uses. By 1991, 146,000 hectares had been converted to shrimp ponds. The first shrimp ponds were placed on intertidal salt flats, where costs of pumping and PLS stocking were lower; however, since 1979 pond construction has expanded into estuarine ecosystems. This includes the conversion of 41,700 hectares of mangroves, one-fifth of Ecuador's coastal mangrove resources. Individual estuaries have lost as much as half the primary mangrove forest (Centro de Levantamientos Integrados de Recursos Naturales por Sensores Remotos 1992). Furthermore, some low-lying agricultural lands have also been converted to ponds; high residual salinity in the converted lands makes this change practically irreversible.

The shrimp industry expanded most rapidly between 1979 and 1984. In 1978 there were 5,416 hectares of legally authorized shrimp ponds in production. By 1984, the authorized pond area grew to 89,400 hectares. Meanwhile, annual shrimp production increased by more than 600 percent, from less than 5,000 tons (one ton equals 10^6 g) of shrimp in 1979 to over 33,000 tons by 1984. Currently the industry's pond area has expanded to 146,000 hectares, and production has grown to about 100,000 metric tons per year^{-1} (Centro de Levantamientos Integrados de Recursos Naturales por Sensores Remotos 1992).

International competition in shrimp production is growing. The entry of more efficient and productive producers into the market has caused international prices to fall. Ecuador's ability to compete with other countries is in jeopardy. Over half of Ecuador's shrimp industry is dominated by semi-extensive production technologies. These technologies depend primarily on large pond areas and PLS collected in the wild. Average productivity in Ecuador is 0.68 metric tons^{-1} per hectare. This productivity is lower than that found in Honduras and Mexico—Ecuador's closest Latin American competitors—and far lower than China and Thailand—Asian competitors that have made effective use of hatchery-produced PLS inputs (Rosenberry 1990).

The rapid growth of the industry during the early 1980s can be attributed to the abundance of PLS stock as a result of El Niño, low costs for establishing ponds on intertidal salt flats, and high demand and prices for shrimp in U.S. markets. In 1983, almost all authorized ponds were placed into production (93 percent). However, beginning in the mid-1980s, the PLS required to stock ponds became scarce (Instituto de Estrategias Agropecuarias 1989; Iverson, Darryl, and Jory 1986). Shortages have been severe enough that since 1985 only half the authorized pond area is in production. In addition to changes in water temperature, loss of habitat, and overfishing of PLS, stocks decreased the PLS available for pond production of shrimp.

Decreases in stock of a marine species are difficult to document. This is especially true with PLS, which are collected for subsistence income by *artesano* fishermen in an open-access fishery: few, if any, catch-effort studies exist. However, there is some preliminary economic evidence that scarcity has increased: prices paid for PLS inputs have increased (Sutinen, Broadus, and Spurrier 1989; Southgate and Whitaker 1994). If marginal extraction costs for a given stock of PLS are relatively constant—an assumption that seems reasonable given harvesting practices (see the discussion of *artesanos* above)—then the increasing gap between price and marginal cost may indicate a scarcer stock.

Economic Analytical Strategy

Parks and Bonifaz (1994) integrate the benefits provided by PLS collection, shrimp production, and mangrove ecosystems into an economic management problem. The problem faced by Ecuador is to determine how to sustain maximum joint benefits from the PLS fishery, shrimp production, and mangrove ecosystems.

The analytical strategy is to construct and solve a social planner's problem, and use the planner's solution to identify policy instruments. The social planner's problem is a partial equilibrium model that includes the shrimp production and *artesano* sectors, as well as environmental services provided by mangroves. The key connection between the economic and environmental systems is via the recruitment function for PLS stocks, which depends not only on existing stock, but also on available mangrove habitat. The planner's solution is compared with solutions for profit-maximizing shrimp producers and *artesanos*; the latter are assumed to collect PLS in an open access fishery.

Economic Policy Instruments

In order to reconcile the producers' profit-maximizing deforestation rate with the social planner's benefit-maximizing rate, discounted benefits provided by mangroves must be internalized by the producer. A tax that includes (a) discounted stock effects of additional mangrove habitat and (b) discounted non-PLS mangrove benefits would internalize the environmental opportunity costs currently omitted in the producer's problem. Making these costs internal to the producer's decisions would lead the individual producers to act to maximize their own benefits to accomplish the collective welfare-maximizing solution sought by the planner. A tax on mangrove-clearing would ultimately provide more PLS habitat, which could in turn help replenish the dwindling stock. However, this is only part of an integrated solution.

Individual choices by producers and *artesanos* also determine the level of PLS harvest. Producers determine demand for PLS inputs, which in turn are supplied by *artesanos*. The aggregate harvest by *artesanos* influences the development of PLS stock over time. The producer will demand PLS in order to maximize profits. In an open-access PLS fishery with minimal costs of entry (that is, the cost of a hand-held net), *artesanos* determine the supply of PLS by harvesting until all rents are dissipated. Shrimp producers and *artesanos* will interact to exploit the PLS stock at greater harvests than the social planner.

A tax in the amount of marginal cost minus average cost will correct for the open-access externality, and a tax in the amount of marginal scarcity rent for PLS will account for opportunity costs of decreases in stock. Making these costs internal to the *artesanos'* decisions would accomplish the collective welfare-maximizing solution sought by the planner. Although these taxes would enable the PLS stock to recover, such instruments may be costly to administer and enforce (see below). While licensing fees that approximate these costs are a possibility, other regulatory instruments to reduce catch, such as quotas or equipment restrictions, may be more feasible.

Discussion

If mangrove habitat effects PLS stock, then the increasing scarcity of PLS represents a growing opportunity cost for the industry and fishermen in the form of foregone future benefits. By selecting excessive deforestation rates, the industry may have purchased short-term profits at the expense of long-term sustainable productivity.

One of the most critical consequences of the crises of the mid-1980s was the generation of a vicious cycle between mature shrimp prices and PLS fishing rates. This occurs in the market for PLS as a factor input. The supply of PLS is determined by open-access collection by *artesanos*. The demand for PLS inputs is the derived demand of shrimp producers for a production input. The rapid expansion of the industry's pond hectarage precipitated increased demand for PLS inputs. This created excess rents in the PLS market, and encouraged *artesanos* to increase PLS harvest rates, ultimately leading to the overexploitation of the resource. Diminished PLS stocks leads producers to compete for smaller and smaller amounts of PLS inputs, while at the same time, *artesanos* must continue to increase their effort to support their families from a dwindling PLS stock.

Exogenous shocks to the PLS input market, such as El Niño, provide transitory windfalls to both producers and *artesanos*. The warmer temperatures may be favorable to recruitment, which increases stock and lowers extraction costs to *artesano* suppliers. (The abundant PLS are easier to catch.) This downward shift in PLS supply decreases the marginal factor cost to shrimp producers, leading to increased equilibrium demand for PLS inputs. Equilibrium extraction (after El Niño causes a downward shift in PLS supply) may be greater than under normal ocean temperatures; however, this can only be temporarily supported. If capacity expands to take advantage of these ephemeral conditions, overcapacity is a natural consequence when the ocean (and PLS stocks) return to normal conditions.

The economic interaction between shrimp farmers demanding PLS inputs and *artesano* fishermen collecting these inputs can be environmentally devastating. Their unregulated interaction may perpetuate the crisis that the shrimp industry suffers. There are no public agencies regulating the activities of the *artesano* fishermen and, in fact, there is a government decree clearly stating that all beaches, estuaries, and mangrove ecosystems of public access are open to PLS fishing (Instituto de Estrategias Agropecuarias 1989).

Much of the alteration of coastal ecosystems in Ecuador can be attributed to the legal standing of coastal resources. Although a legal and institutional framework has been in place to regulate the development of the industry, for all practical purposes, access to the resources has been completely free (LiPuma and Meltzoff 1985; Perez and Robadue 1989). According to Ecuadorean laws, all coastal land lying below the highest tide line belongs to the government (LiPuma and Meltzoff 1985; Instituto de Estrategias Agropecuarias 1989)—that is, coastal beaches, large portions of salt flats, and, of course, all mangrove forests and estuarine ecosystems. The most critical example of the weakness of laws and government institutions is the total failure to protect the mangrove forests.

A 1975 regulation and its 1985 amendment contain specific articles prohibiting the conversion of mangrove forests to shrimp ponds. In addition, a law concerned with forestry and conservation of flora and fauna enacted in 1978 prohibits the construction of ponds in mangrove areas. Moreover, there are other laws and decrees enacted by several government agencies that created protected areas and declared the conservation of mangrove forests as "in the public interest" (Instituto de Estrategias Agropecuarias 1989). In spite of these laws, the rate of mangrove deforestation between 1979 and 1991 averaged about 3,000 hectares per year, resulting in the loss of one-fifth of Ecuador's mangrove forests.

The laws and regulations governing the industry were not designed to encourage a sustainable relationship between economic objectives and ecosystem management. In 1975 the government issued a regulation allowing the construction and operation of shrimp ponds on public lands under a renewable ten-year concession. Although the system of concessions was well intentioned, it very quickly became an open source of corruption and a critical policy issue affecting resource management. A longer concession that allowed producers to reap the PLS stock benefits from mangrove conservation would make more economic sense. The short length of current concessions may contribute to incentives for the short-term mining of mangrove resources as a location for ponds. In addition, the government sells concessions for far below their value: the annual charge, equal to

11 percent of a minimum monthly wage per hectare, is generally less than $10. This captures less than one percent of the economic rent that can be obtained from placing these lands in ponds; this rent can exceed $2,000 per hectare per year (Southgate and Whitaker 1994).

Short-term concession arrangements and poorly-enforced laws are among the main causes for the excessive deforestation and degradation of Ecuador's coastal ecosystems. Although government agencies must take much of the blame for the problems that the industry faces, it is also possible that the failure of shrimp farmers to recognize the costs of environmental disturbance are critical components for understanding the industry's dilemma. One of the most dramatic consequences of the lack of planning and regulation of the industry is the excessive amount of land in ponds relative to the availability of PLS. The result of this imbalance is that the industry's installed capacity has been largely underused (Instituto de Estrategias Agropecuarias 1989), and the ratio of shrimp produced to area in ponds has fallen below those of competing countries.

Because of the lack of integrated planning, short-term rent-seeking behavior of the industry, and unenforced laws, Ecuador's mariculture industry has developed without considering environmental costs. This has cost the industry competitiveness, and has resulted in excessive deforestation and the uncontrolled collection of PLS. The industry's failure to recognize these opportunity costs is jeopardizing the long-term sustainability of the industry itself.

Conclusions and Policy Implications

The conceptual model explores the consequences of a relationship between mangrove habitat and PLS stocks and concludes that deforestation may have been excessive. The most important policy implication of these results is that command-and-control approaches have completely failed to regulate the industry's economic development. In addition, public policies have encouraged the overexploitation of PLS stocks through open-access collection by *artesanos*. If drastic policy measures are not implemented, ecosystem destruction will continue as long as there are profits to be made from mangrove forest conversion and PLS collection.

Had it been implemented and enforced before the expansion in the early 1980s, an incentive-based tax approach could have encouraged recognition of the full costs of deforestation. Although it is true that the industry has been subjected to a tax on shrimp exports (Sutinen, Broadus, and Spurrier 1989, p. 31), this has failed to slow conversion of mangroves. A tax that is more directly linked to pond construction would help internalize the opportunity costs of deforestation. The addition of these costs into the shrimp producers' decisions could prevent excessive conversion of mangroves to ponds.

In the long term, there may be opportunities for tax revenues to be recycled into profitable investments in mangrove reforestation. Incentives to supplement these public investments with private funds could be strengthened by increasing the length of the land concessions. Concession length should be sufficient to allow concession holders to benefit from reforestation activities that they undertake (for example, sufficiently long for PLS stocks to respond to increased habitat area).

If the effects of mangrove deforestation on PLS stocks are fairly localized (for example, within an estuary), it may be feasible to internalize the opportunity costs of deforestation to cooperatives of shrimp producers within an estuary. Cordell and McKean (1992) identify physical and technical attributes and decisionmaking arrangements that have led to sustainable management of fisheries commons in Bahia, Brazil. These commons have flourished with minimal reliance on government agencies or policies. Provided that similar conditions are present in Ecuador, private solutions to excess exploitation of mangrove stocks by shrimp producers—or of PLS stocks by *artesanos*—may be possible.

At the same time, if Ecuador is to maintain its competitiveness in the world shrimp market, it is also critical that the industry's productivity per hectare be increased. To accomplish this, investments in human capital and scientific research must be encouraged. The development of a sustainable and profitable hatchery industry is a viable short- and long-term alternative to the unreliable supply of PLS collected in the wild. By providing a larger, more stable supply of PLS inputs, hatcheries will increase the industry's productivity per hectare. Improving the ability of hatchery-produced PLS to survive the production cycle is essential.

This approach represents a shift from land-intensive shrimp technology to capital-intensive technology—a shift that has already succeeded in Asia. The change in inputs from land toward capital will also help prevent future conversion of mangrove forests and agricultural land. An expanded model of the shrimp mariculture sector that includes both wild and hatchery-produced PLS inputs could clarify the incentives necessary for these shifts. Producing more shrimp from a relatively stable land base is clearly a step toward restoring and sustaining Ecuador's competitive position in the global shrimp market.

Although PLS hatcheries may contribute to a sustainable shrimp industry for Ecuador, their economic viability is uncertain. For example, equilibrium demand for PLS produced in hatcheries may fluctuate with changes in ocean temperature. When the El Niño effect is present, wild PLS is abundant and cheap; profit-maximizing shrimp producers may displace PLS produced in hatcheries with cheaper, wild PLS. Therefore, quantifying and planning for temperature effects on the hatchery industry is essential before any program designed to support this industry can be developed.

Conceptual extensions of the model can help by examining the economic connection between ocean temperature fluctuations and the returns to hatchery investment. As a starting point, one can recognize that since temperature is exogenous, the supply of wild PLS and derived demand for PLS inputs will depend on temperature levels. If wild PLS and PLS produced in hatcheries are substitutable inputs, then comparative statics could subsequently be used to anticipate how shrimp producers would change demand in response to changes in the availability of both types of PLS.

Finally, it is important to point out that many of the policies encouraging the mismanagement of coastal ecosystems are similar to the policies stimulating tropical deforestation. For example, the lack of enforceability of laws that prevent the use of forests in an open access fashion and the failure to recognize the opportunity costs of tropical forest conversion are parallel issues to the case of coastal resource management. Therefore, this study's arguments and results could cautiously be extended to analyze some of the socioeconomic forces and policies behind rain forest conversion. Extension of these policy recommendations presumes a positive economic feedback for those who make conservation decisions (that is, increased PLS stocks and lower input costs for shrimp producers). In the case of tropical forests, conservation benefits directly accrue to decisionmakers in some contexts (for example, ecotourism revenues and marketed rain forest products), but not everywhere that deforestation is of concern.

Bibliography

Barbier, E. B. 1994. "Valuing Environmental Functions: Tropical Wetlands." *Land Economics* 70(2):155–73.

Centro de Levantamientos Integrados de Recursos Naturales por Sensores Remotos (CLIRSEN). 1992. *Estudio Multitemporal de los Manglares, Camaroneras y Areas Salinas de la Costa Ecuatoriana, Actualizado a 1991*. Quito, Ecuador.

Cordell, J., and M. A. McKean. 1992. "Sea Tenure in Bahia, Brazil." In D. Bromley, ed., *Making the Commons Work*. San Francisco: Institute for Contemporary Studies Press.

Dixon, J. A., and P. N. Lal. 1994. "The Management of Coastal Wetlands: Economic Analysis of Combined Ecologic-Economic Systems." In P. Dasgupta and K. G. Mäler, eds., *The Environment and Emerging Development Issues*. Clarendon: Oxford University Press.

Instituto de Estrategias Agropecuarias (IDEA). 1989. *Situación Actual de la Maricultura del Camarón en el Ecuador y Estrategias para su Desarrollo Sostenido*. Quito, Ecuador.

Iverson, I., S. Darryl, and E. Jory. 1986. "Farmers without Seed: Shrimp Culture in Ecuador." *Sea Frontiers* 32 (November–December):442–53.

LiPuma, E., and S. Meltzoff. 1985. "The Social Economy of Shrimp Mariculture in Ecuador." Rosenstiel School of Marine and Atmospheric Science, University of Miami, Miami, Florida.

Olsen, S., and L. Arriaga, eds. 1989. *A Sustainable Shrimp Industry for Ecuador*. Narragansett, Rhode Island: University of Rhode Island Coastal Resource Center.

Parks, P. J., and M. Bonifaz. 1994. "Nonsustainable Use of Renewable Resources: Mangrove Deforestation and Mariculture in Ecuador." *Marine Resource Economics* 9(1):1–18.

Perez, E., and D. Robadue, Jr. 1989. "Institutional Issues of Shrimp Mariculture in Ecuador." In S. Olsen and L. Arriaga, eds., 1989.

Rosenberry, B. 1990. "World Shrimp Farming: Can the Western Hemisphere Compete with the Eastern?" *Agriculture* 16(5):60–64.

Scott, I. and N. Gaibor. 1992. *A Review of the Fishery for Shrimp Larvae in Ecuador: Biological, Economic, and Social Factors.* Guayaquil, Ecuador: Instituto Nacional de Pesca.

Southgate, D., and M. Whitaker. 1994. *Economic Progress and the Environment: One Developing Country's Policy Crisis.* New York: Oxford University Press.

Sutinen, J. G., J. Broadus, and W. Spurrier. 1989. "An Economic Analysis of Trends in the Shrimp Cultivation Industry in Ecuador." In S. Olsen and L. Arriaga, eds., 1989.

Thian-Eng, C., and P. Kungvankij. 1989. *An Assessment of Shrimp Culture and Mariculture Diversification.* Guayaquil, Ecuador: U.S. Agency for International Development, Coastal Resources Management Project.

Turner, R. 1989. "Factors Affecting the Relative Abundance of Shrimp in Ecuador." In S. Olsen and L. Arriaga, eds., 1989.

Traditional Knowledge

8

Learning by Fishing:
Practical Science and Scientific Practice

Gísli Pálsson

Abstract

PROFESSIONAL RESOURCE MANAGERS often assume that the ecological knowledge obtained by fishing skippers during years of practical experience is of relatively little use. At the same time, recent research indicates that knowledge gained on the spot, in the course of production, is of fundamental importance. This chapter explores, with particular reference to the Icelandic context, how fishers' knowledge differs from that of professional biologists and to what extent the former could be brought more systematically into the process of resource management for the purpose of ensuring resilience and sustainability.

Parts of this article are also presented in "Property rights and practical knowledge: the Icelandic quota system" (co-authored with Agnar Helgason), published in *Fisheries Management in Crisis: A Social Science Perspective*, D. Symes and K. Crean, eds., Blackwell Scientific Publications, 1995. In addition to being a part of the Property Rights Program of the Beijer Institute of the Swedish Academy of Sciences, the study on which the article is based relates to a collaborative research project, "Common Property and Environmental Policy in Comparative Perspective," funded by the Nordic Environmental Research Programme. It has also received financial support from the Nordic Committee for Social Science Research, the Beijer Institute of the Swedish Academy of Sciences, the Research Center of the Vestman Islands and the University of Iceland, and the Icelandic Science Foundation. I thank Agnar Helgason, Örn D. Jónsson, Jónas Allansson, and Broddi Sigurðsson for their help with practical logistics in the Vestman Islands, as well as for interviews and data collection.

An important recent attempt at bridging the gap between Icelandic fishers and marine scientists is the so-called trawling rally—a procedure whereby a group of skippers regularly follow the same trawling paths identified by biologists for the purpose of supplying detailed ecological information. I argue that while the trawling rally is a useful and interesting experiment, it is important to look for alternative ways of engaging fishers, of using practical knowledge of fishing for the purpose of sustainable resource use and responsible management.

✧

In many fisheries, resource management is largely informed by professional scientists and public officials. Such management often assumes that the extensive knowledge that fishing skippers have achieved in the course of their work is relatively irrelevant and ineffectual as far as fisheries management is concerned. Indeed, in many cases there is little attempt to draw upon such knowledge in the process of ecological research and decisionmaking.

The current denigration of practical knowledge has been reinforced by a powerful "modernist" paradigm in bio-economics and resource management which assumes that ecosystems are characterized by linear relationships and that only a market approach, emphasizing private ownership of resources (usually privileging capital rather than labor), will ensure stewardship and responsible resource use. The estimate of total allowable catch and the allocation of transferable resource quotas, it is often argued, are the only feasible and efficient management strategies.

Increasing empirical evidence and a growing body of theoretical scholarship suggest, however, that there are good grounds for questioning the assumptions of modernist management. Recent research indicates that, given the significance of the learning context and situated enskillment, the current restrictive emphasis on disembedded knowledge needs to be revised (Lave 1988, Gergen and Semin 1990; Fischer and others 1993). Moreover, research emphasizing the uncertain nature of many marine ecosystems suggests that managers modify their hierarchical notion of linearity and expertise. Multispecies ecosystems, it is argued, are highly unpredictable, with constant fluctuations in interactions among species and between species and their habitat (Gomes 1993). Several scholars have suggested that fisheries are chaotic systems with too many uncertainties for any kind of modernist, "scientific" control (Smith 1991; Wilson and others 1994:296). This does not mean that governance is impossible; it suggests, however, increasing reliance on a finer spatial and temporal scale, a scale that only the skillful practitioner is able to apply. It is essential, therefore, to pay attention to practical knowledge, allowing for contingency and extreme fluctuations in the ecosystem. Some form of self-governance may be a practical necessity, strange as it may sound to those accustomed to the theory of the "tragedy of the commons," which assumes that overfishing is inevitable as long as access is "free" for everyone.[1]

Focusing on Icelandic fishing, in particular the Vestman Islands, this chapter discusses the similarities and differences between the knowledge of fishers and that of professional biologists and the extent to which the former could be brought more systematically into the process of public resource management. With the persistent threat of overexploitation, Icelandic fishing has been subject to increasingly stringent public regulations and scientific control. Generally, both marine scientists and resource economists have presented the coastal ecosystem as a predictable, domesticated domain. At the same time, there has been a tendency to assume that the practical knowledge of those who are engaged in fishing on a daily basis is of little or no value for resource management. Thus, there is little attempt to utilize the knowledge that skippers have achieved. Skippers frequently complain that marine biologists tend to treat them "as idiots," reducing practical knowledge and local discourse to mere "loose talk." Despite the occasional lip service in the reference to "collaboration" (*samráð*), there is little real dialogue between fishers and marine biologists. Those who have come to know the fishing grounds

---

1. In some fisheries, including the lobster fishery of Maine in the United States (Acheson 1988), fishers have an important role to play in fisheries management. The relations of power between local fishers and professional managers and scientific experts typical for many fisheries in the western world seem to be reversed.

around Iceland, during a lifelong career in fishing, fishers complain, must remain silent when the "wise men" (*spekingar*) announce their precise measurements of the stocks. Recently, attempts have been made at bridging the gap between fishers and scientists. An important example is the "trawling rally" (*togararall*)—a procedure whereby a group of skippers regularly follows the same trawling paths identified by biologists in order to supply detailed ecological information. While the trawling rally represents an interesting endeavor, it has its shortcomings. It is important, I argue, to look for alternative ways of engaging fishers, of using knowledge obtained in the course of production for the purpose of responsible resource use and sustainable management.

Practical and Theoretical Knowledge

For several centuries, since the Renaissance and the Enlightenment, Western discourse has tended to radically separate scientific understanding and everyday accounts. Scientists, it has often been assumed, are objective explorers of reality, proceeding by rational methods and detached observations, while the lay person is locked up in a particular natural or cultural world, driven by genetic makeup, ecological context, superstitious beliefs, or local concerns. Thus, orthodox functional theory of learning suggests a one-way hierarchical ordering of knowledge:

> In this theory, duality of the person translates into a division of (intellectual) labor between academics and "the rest" that puts primitive, lower class, (school) children's, female, and everyday thought in a single structural position *vis-à-vis* rational scientific thought. (Lave 1988:8)

One of the consequences of such a Cartesian scheme is the tendency to reduce local environmental knowledge to mere trivia and to assume that what people have to say about ecological matters and human-environmental interactions is pure ideology, of relevance only as cultural data. Accordingly, sustainable resource use and sensible management become the privileged business of outsiders formally trained in public institutions.

In recent years, however, the dualistic theory of knowledge has been challenged on a number of fronts. Not only is the notion of absolute objectivity, the idea of some scientific Archimedean standpoint outside history and culture, frequently subject to critical discussion, it is increasingly apparent that the local view makes much more sense than supposedly objective "observers" have often assumed. The community of modelers has been both expanded and redefined, empowering the local voice and relaxing modernist assumptions of privilege and hierarchy (Gudeman and Rivera 1990). This is evident from current interest in practical knowledge in development agencies on the international scene as well as in academic studies of learning and expertise (Williams and Baines 1993; Lave and Wenger 1991). It is not quite clear, on the other hand, what the empowering of the "local voice" entails.

One of the important issues involved concerns the concepts of "indigenous" and "traditional" knowledge. While it is true that an extensive body of local knowledge has often been set aside, if not eliminated, in the course of Western expansion and domination and while there are good grounds for attempting to recapture and preserve what remains of such knowledge (Chapin 1994), the reference to the "indigenous" and "traditional" in such contexts tends to reproduce and reinforce the boundaries of the colonial world, much like earlier notions of the "native" and the "primitive" did. Such terms are not only loaded with hidden transcripts—the value terms of colonial discourse—they are fraught with ambiguity. How old does a particular skill or body of knowledge have to be to count as "traditional"? Where does it have to be located to be classified as "indigenous"? We may try to relativize our answers to such questions, emphasizing that everything is indigenous and traditional from some point of view, but in the long run "natives" have a tendency to congregate in particular times and locations.

Another contested issue relates to the meaning of knowledge and learning. Orthodox theories tend to present the learning process in highly functional terms, presupposing a natural novice who gradually becomes a member of society by assimilating its cultural heritage. Knowledge becomes analogous to grammar or dictionaries, invested with the structural properties and the stability often attributed to language. Given such a perspective, indigenous knowledge is sometimes presented as a marketable commodity—a thing-like "cultural capital"—and at times with "missionary fervor" (DeWalt 1994:123). It may be useful and quite legitimate in some contexts to think of practical knowledge as a bounded, tradable object, for instance when encoding "indigenous" knowledge for the protection of "intellectual property rights" (Brush 1993) and defending legal claims about patents and royalties.[2] Much of the practitioner's knowledge, however, is tacit—dispositions acquired in the process of direct engagement with everyday tasks. In reifying practical knowledge, we fall into the trap of Cartesian dualism that we may be trying to avoid, separating body and mind.

The distinction between practical and scientific knowledge resolves such conceptual ambiguities and difficulties. It does not necessarily suggest a cultural or temporal boundary, the radical separation of producers and scientists, participants and observers, traditionalists and modernists. Rather, it draws attention to different ways of knowing, irrespective of time and space. Practical knowledge is not restricted to any particular group of people, for none of us (including practicing scientists) would manage to live without it; scientific knowledge, of course, involves some degree of practical knowledge obtained in the course of engagement and experimentation. Likewise, on some occasions most of us seek to formulate our tacit knowledge in general terms, by verbal or textual means.

"Having a Pee in the Salty Sea"

The theory of practice (see, for instance, Lave 1988) offers a view of learning and craftsmanship which is very different from that of orthodox learning theory. Informed by the notions of situated action and mutual enskillment, it emphasizes democratic collaboration and direct engagement with everyday tasks. Such a perspective not only provides a useful antidote to the project of modernist management, it resonates with some aspects of the discourse of Icelandic fishers (Pálsson 1994). For them, "real" schooling is supposed to take place in actual fishing, not in formal institutions. As one skipper put it, "Naturally, most of the knowledge one uses on a daily basis is obtained by experience. One learns primarily from the results of personal encounters; that is what stays with you." The emphasis on "outdoor" learning is emphasized in frequent derogatory remarks about the "academic" learning of people who have never "peed in salty sea" (*migið í saltan sjó*). Even a novice fisher, skippers say, with minimal experience of fishing, is likely to know more about the practicalities of fishing than the teachers at the Marine Academy. Therefore, there is little connection between school performance and fishing success. Questioned about the role of formal schooling, skippers often say that what takes place in the classroom (during lessons in astronomy, for instance) is more or less futile as far as fishing skills and differential success are concerned, although they readily admit that schooling has some good points, preventing accidents and promoting proper responses in critical circumstances involving the safety of boat and crew. Commenting on the competence of young men who nowadays graduate from the Marine Academy, one skipper said, "they know absolutely nothing!"

Skipper education recognizes the importance of situated learning. Earlier participation in fishing, as a deck hand (*háseti*), is a condition for formal training, built into the teaching program; this is to ensure minimum knowledge about the practice of fishing. Once the student in the Marine Academy has finished his formal studies and received his certificate, he must work temporarily as an apprentice—a mate (*stýrimaður*)—guided by a practicing skipper, if he is to receive the full license of skipperhood. The attitude toward the mate varies from one skipper to another; as one skipper remarked, "some skippers regard themselves as teachers trying to advise those who work with them, but others don't." While skippers differ from one another and there is no formal economic recognition of the their role in this respect in terms of a teaching salary, according to many skippers, the period of apprenticeship is a critical one.

2. When defending indigenous claims, anthropologists have often emphasized the boundedness of cultural units and the intellectual properties belonging to them: "Biological knowledge is among the most important types of information *possessed* by any culture, a fact long recognized and emphasized by anthropologists" (Brush 1993:657; italics added).

Reflecting on his mentor, with whom he had spent several years at sea, one skipper explained, "I acquired my knowledge by working with this skipper, learning his way of fishing. I grew up with this man." It is precisely here, in the role of an apprentice at sea, that the mate learns to attend to the environment *as a skipper*. Working as a mate under the guidance of an experienced skipper gives the novice the opportunity to develop attentiveness and self-confidence, and to establish skills at fishing and directing a boat and crew. The role of the mate, in fact, institutionalizes what Lave and Wenger (1991) term "legitimate peripheral participation," a form of apprenticeship that allows for protection, experimentation, and varying degrees of skill and responsibility. This is not a one-way transfer of knowledge as the skipper frequently learns from the cooperation of his mate; mate and skipper—in fact, the whole crew—educate each other. In the beginning, the mate is just like an ordinary deck-hand; in the end he is knowledgeable enough to have a boat of his own. At first he is of little help to his tutor; later on he can be trusted with just about anything. Occasionally, the skipper may even take a break and stay ashore, leaving the boat and the crew to his mate.

The folk account of fishing also emphasizes a particular pragmatic view of technology. For the skilled skipper, fishing technology—the boat, electronic equipment, and fishing gear—is not to be regarded as an "external" mediator between the person and the environment but rather as a bodily extension in quite a literal sense. Experienced skippers often speak of knowing the details and the patterns of the "landscape" of the sea bottom "as well as their fingers." Thanks to technological extensions, the experienced skipper is able to "see" the fish and "probe" the landscape of the sea bed. For many landlubbers, no doubt, the sea is primarily fishing *space*. For skippers, in contrast, it is a three-dimensional world, with variable bottom features, migrating fish, and stratified masses of water.

The skipper's knowledge is complex; a skipper must choose times and places to fish on the basis of a series of detailed environmental information. It is not surprising, therefore, that fishers often refer to the importance of "attentiveness" (*eftirtekt, athygli*) and "perceptiveness" (*glöggskyggni*), the ability to recognize and apply an array of minute but relevant details. Attentiveness is a complex ability and includes, for example, being able to "read" the sky and predict the weather, to participate in discussions within the local fleet, to understand the "sparks" of electronic instruments, and to be able to coordinate crew activities. In order, however, to have success in catching fish, the skipper must reside with his crew. Moreover, the crew, of course, is part of a larger context. Fishers often speak of the personnel (*mannskapur*) of a boat in an extended sense—including several people ashore, those who ensure efficient repairs of equipment between fishing trips, and those who bait lines and take care of nets, repairing old ones or supplying new ones. Indeed, folk accounts of fishing success often emphasize the importance of good fishing gear and the diligence of the people ashore responsible for its maintenance. "Having a good crew," therefore, means not only being able to rely on a good *fishing* crew, but also being provided with good "services" (*þjónusta*) on land.

The fleet is ever-present as well. While one may speak of the vessels temporarily associated with a particular landing port and nearby fishing grounds as a "local" fleet, such a fleet knows no clear boundaries (cf. Acheson 1988). The fleet is a changing constellation of boats that are registered in different towns and municipalities, and many of the skippers, crew, and boat owners involved are permanent residents of other localities. Moreover, the fleets of different ports are hard to separate; during fishing they merge on the boundless sea. Nevertheless, the communion at sea is a very important one. Inevitably the skipper's decisions while fishing are constrained by the decisions of other skippers and by the movements of the fleet. While deciding where to fish is largely guided by the readings of electronic equipment and by the skipper's experience of earlier fishing seasons, of no less importance is knowing what *other* skippers are doing, where they are likely to be, and how much they will catch.

An important issue in current discussions of practical knowledge is the extent to which technical and economic changes influence levels of practical skill, leading to reduced or increased levels of skills (Gallie 1994). Somewhat paradoxically, with the crisis in the world's fisheries, fishing technology has been revolutionized. While in some fisheries, for instance in Brazil (see Kottak 1992), technological changes seem to have resulted in rapid deskilling, there is little reason to believe that this has generally been the case. Some skills are inevitably lost; in Iceland, old and retired skippers sometimes point out that fishing has been radically transformed by electronic technology (including the computer) and artificial intelligence, emphasizing that "natural signs" are increasingly redundant. Attentiveness continues, however, to be one of the central assets of the good skipper and, just as before, it demands lengthy training. The skipper's universe is very different from that of his colleagues of earlier decades, but what shows on the screens of the radar, the computer, and the fish finder is no less a "natural sign," directly sensed, than birds in the air or natural landmarks.

Scientific Management

Nowadays, decisions on the scope of fishing operations are usually informed by marine sciences, setting the limit of the total allowable catch for a fishing season on the basis of measurements and estimates of stock sizes and fish recruitment. The science of resource economics, however, has played an even more important role in fisheries management than marine biology, providing the theoretical framework and the political rationale for a quota system, and, by extension, private property. In many ways, resource economics has *replaced* marine biology as the hegemonic discourse on Icelandic fishing. While the original, formal demand for the quota system came from within the fishing industry, it would hardly have been instituted if it had not been advocated by influential Icelandic economists. Not only did they play a leading role within the major political parties as well as on a series of important committees that designed and modified the management regime, their writings—in newspapers, specialized magazines, and scholarly journals—paved the way for the "scientific" discourse on efficiency and the "rational" management which the quota system represents. Some of the economists argued, with reference to the "tragedy of the commons," that the only realistic alternative—euphemistically defined as "rights based" fishing, as if rights were something new—was a system of individ-

ual transferable quotas. Assuming a sense of responsibility among the new "owners" of the resource (the quota holders) and a free transfer of quotas from less to more efficient producers, economists argued, a quota system would both encourage ecological stewardship and ensure maximum economic efficiency.

It seems difficult to separate such bio-economic theorizing from politics, culture, and rhetorics (see, for instance, McCloskey 1985, Gudeman 1992, Ferber and Nelson 1993). One example of the rhetorical content of theorizing on enclosure and privatization is the persistent inclination of advocates of systems of individual transferable quotas to privilege capital over labor. Icelandic fishing is a case in point. Here, a quota system was introduced in the cod fishery in 1983 to prevent the "collapse" of the major stocks and make fishing more economical (Pálsson 1991:Chapter 6). This system divided access to the resource among those who happened to be boat owners when the system was introduced, largely on the basis of their fishing record during the three years preceding the system. Each fishing vessel over ten tons was allotted a fixed proportion (*aflahlutdeild*) of future total allowable catches of cod and five other demersal fish species. Catch quotas (*aflamark*) for each species, measured in tons, were allotted annually on the basis of this permanent quota share. And the fortunate quota holders were the owners of vessels, not crews. This arrangement did not go uncontested, for there have been heated debates about what to allocate and to whom. The issues involved illustrate the discursive contest between different groups of "producers." Boat owners argued for "catch quotas," to be allocated to *their* boats. Some fishers, on the other hand, advocated an "*effort* quota," to be allocated to skippers or crews.

In the modern world, individual transferable quotas and similar market approaches are increasingly adopted in response to environmental problems. Their wider social and economic implications are hotly debated, however, as they raise central questions of ethics, politics, and social theory (Dewees 1989; McCay and Creed 1990; Pálsson and Helgason 1995). For many of the critics, market approaches to resource management are incompatible with egalitarian sensibilities and communitarian notions of responsibility. Social scientists—including anthropologists and economists—should attempt to examine what the rather loose reference to the "market" entails (Dilley 1992). How the narrative of privatization and economic efficiency is used in specific ethnographic contexts is an important topic for research.

Icelandic fishers continue to challenge the privileging of capital over labor. This is sometimes expressed in a critique of the notion of "fishing history" which defined the original quota allocations on the basis of previous catches. To quote from an interview with a fisher,

> It's a shame that quotas were only allocated to boat owners. Originally, allocations were based on 'fishing history,' but that history has nothing to do with companies and boat ownership. It's the men on board the boats who have created the right to fish.

The present debate on fisheries management is not so much concerned with the technical details of quota allocation as with the larger social and political consequences of the system. The most serious criticism of the current system is that it transfers immense resources into the hands of a relatively small group of people, comprised of the owners and managers of the biggest fishing companies. Many people have questioned the privileged access of the large quota holders, the "feudal lords" or the "princes of the sea" (sægreifar), as the latter are frequently called. In a popular phrase from recent political campaigns, the quota system represents "the biggest theft in Icelandic history."

Not only has the quota system given permanent rights of access to an exclusive group, but this right has been turned into a marketable commodity. With some companies holding more than they are capable or willing to fish and others with less than they actually need, some companies temporarily rent a part of their annual quota. In public discourse, this is frequently referred to by a loaded and somewhat fuzzy term, "quota-profiteering" (kvótabrask). The public is increasingly concerned with growing inequality due to the concentration of quotas. One skipper who had a bigger quota at his disposal than most of his colleagues claimed that the apparently increased concentration of quotas

in only a few hands was "totally unacceptable": "It scares me to think of the possibility that four or five companies might gain control of the entire national quota." Results obtained through interviews and ethnographic field work were strengthened by statistical conclusions regarding the distribution of quotas. Statistical results show that there have been radical changes in the total number of quota holders, a reduction from 535 to 391 (27 percent) from 1984 to 1994. Another measure is provided by examining the relative holdings belonging to different groups of quota holders, heuristically defined as "giants," "large" owners, "small" owners, and "dwarves" (see Pálsson and Helgason 1995). If quotas are changing hands, with full transferability, and the total number of quota owners is decreasing, where are the quotas going? To make a long story short, the proportion of the quota holdings of the "giants" has rapidly increased in only one decade, from 27.9 percent to 49.7 percent. During the same period, the proportion of the quota belonging to the "dwarves" has decreased from 12.5 percent to 8.7 percent. Thus, quotas are increasingly concentrated at the top.

After more than a decade of stringent quota management and redistribution of assets, the major Icelandic fishery (the cod fishery) is still in a critical phase and, even worse, there are no signs of ecological recovery. Stock sizes and recruitment rates continue to be far too low, given earlier estimates of maximum sustainable yield. The relative failure of the quota system and scientific management of recent years to deliver the goods they promised, and the severe social and ethical problems of inequality they have raised, suggest that it may be wise to look for alternative management schemes emphasizing the practical knowledge of the fishing industry, in particular the people who are directly engaged with the ecosystem.

Wilson and associates suggest that the "numerical" approach of current resource economics and marine biology, emphasizing linear relationships and states of equilibrium, fails to account for the chaotic aspects of many fisheries. Their empirical work shows that while fisheries are deterministic systems, because of their extreme sensitivity to initial conditions, even simple fish communities have no tendency toward equilibrium. As a result, management faces forbidding problems when trying to explain the noise in ecological relationships, for example, the relationship between recruitment and stock size, often a key issue for managers: "the degree of accuracy and the completeness of knowledge required for prediction are far beyond any capabilities we might expect to achieve in a fisheries environment" (Wilson and others 1994:296). Therefore, it becomes difficult, if not impossible, to know the outcomes of management actions such as quotas.

Bridging the Gap: The "Trawling Rally"

If marine ecosystems are chaotic and fluctuating regimes, those who are directly involved in resource use are likely to have the most reliable information as to what goes on in the system at any particular point in time. Often, however, scientists are reluctant to collaborate with fishers. One of the reasons for the lack of collaboration is the fundamental difference between the two groups in terms of the knowledge they seek; the knowledge of scientists is largely normative and textual, preoccupied with statistical methods and theoretical ways of knowing, while that of fishers, often tacit, is tuned to practical realities in the ever-changing sea.

In an attempt to encourage cooperation between scientists and fishers and to involve the latter in the collection of detailed ecological data on the state of the seas and the fishing stocks, the Marine Research Institute hires a group of skippers to regularly fish along the same pre-given trawling paths on their commercial vessels (see Pálsson and others 1989); this is the so-called "groundfish project"—in everyday language, the "trawling rally"—initiated in 1985:

> The cooperation with fishermen is based on the main objective of the project: to increase precision and reliability of stock size estimates of relevant fish stocks, especially cod, through the integration of fishermen's knowledge of fish behavior and migrations, as well as the topography of the fishing grounds. (Pálsson and others 1989:54)

Because mature cod sometimes migrate from Greenland to Icelandic fishing grounds, thereby making traditional stock assessment on the basis of fishing statistics relatively unreliable, a systematic fishery-independent survey was seen to be essential. Such a large-scale project was beyond the capabilities of Icelandic research vessels, and, therefore, commercial vessels were hired for the task. For two weeks in March every year, five vessels survey the same research stations (595 in the beginning, 600 later on), originally selected through a semi-randomly stratified process in cooperation with fishers (see Figure 8–1). The vessels (stern-trawlers) are identical in overall equipment and design, in terms of size, fishing gear, and engine power. This is seen to be important to ensure comparable data sets, allowing for reliable estimates of changes in the ecosystem from one year to another.

The trawling rally is an interesting experiment. While it is partly a diplomatic endeavor on behalf of the Marine Research Institute in order to reduce the tension that has developed between biologists and fishers in recent years as a result of stringent scientific management, and an attempt to improve the image of the Institute among the general public, there is obviously more to the story. No doubt the trawling rally yields extensive comparative information that the biologists could not possibly gain otherwise, given their limited funding.

Nevertheless, as an attempt to cultivate effective interactions between fishers and biologists for management purposes, the trawling rally has significant limitations. To begin with, while the design of controlled surveying has an obvious comparative rationale, it is also a straitjacket, preventing a more flexible and dynamic sensing of ecological interactions in the sea. Skippers fail to be impressed with the scientific design, criticizing the biologists for "isolating themselves temporarily on particular ships, pretending to practice great science," to paraphrase one of the skippers. Many skippers pointed out during interviews that, fixed to the same paths year after year, the rally fails to respond to fluctuations in the ecosystem, thus providing unreliable estimates. One skipper who had participated in the trawling rally remarked that knowing how the biologists worked had made him lose all faith in scientific procedures. "If these guys were skippers," another skipper remarked, "they would have been fired long ago."

Also, the reliance on trawling, skippers say, is likely to produce biased results. Often, those fishing with gill nets on nearby grounds offer a very different picture. From the skippers' point of view, a more intuitive and holistic approach, allowing for different kinds of fishing gear and greater flexibility in time and space, would make more sense. Indeed, skippers discuss their normal fishing strategies in such terms, emphasizing constant experimentation, the role of "perpetual engagement" (*ad vera í stanslausu sambandi*), and the importance of "hunches" (*stud*) and tacit knowledge.

Like their colleagues in other parts of the world, Icelandic biologists have often focused on one species at a time, modeling recruitment, growth rates, and stock sizes, although recently they have paid increasing attention to analyses of interactions in "multi-species" fisheries. While scientists may qualify their analyses and predictions with reference to some degree of uncertainty, the "margin of error," they often talk as if that margin is immaterial. Fishers question their basic assumptions, arguing that understanding of fish migrations and stock sizes is still limited. Knowledge of the ecosystem, they claim, is too imperfect for making reliable forecasts. "Erecting an ivory tower around themselves," one skipper argued, "biologists are somewhat removed from the field of action; they are too dependent on the book." While such comments have to be seen in the light of cultural and economic tension between social classes and between center and periphery, they should not be rejected on that basis alone, as they also have some grain of truth. Biological estimates and fisheries policy are often literal and rigid in form, unable to deal with variability and to respond to changes in the ecosystem. Skipper knowledge, in contrast—the result of situated learning, of direct engagement with the aquatic environment— is necessarily tuned to the flux and momentum of fishing. An important task on the management agenda is to look for ways in which that knowledge can be employed to a greater extent than at present for the purpose of responsible and democratic resource management, bridging the modernist gap between scientists and practitioners.

Conclusions and Policy Implications

There is a strange paradox in Western environmental discourse. On the one hand, there is a tendency to project an image of resource management as an apolitical enterprise, as the "rational" domination of nature independent of ethics and social discourse. Policy makers in fisheries often remain firmly committed to a modernist stance, curiously innocent of recent developments in social and ecological theory, presenting themselves as detached observers, as pure analysts of the economic and material world, independent of the "partial" viewpoints and the trivial, practical knowledge of the actors. On the other hand, current environmental discourse is characterized by the postmodern condition, emphasizing, much like medieval European discourse, the embedded nature of any kind of scholarship and the interrelatedness of nature and society (Pálsson 1996). The former view, which presents the pursuit of environmental knowledge as a relatively straightforward accumulation of "facts" and radically separates knowledge of nature and the social context in which it is produced, has come increasingly under attack in several fields of scholarship, including anthropology, economics, and environmental history. We may well be advised to search for alternative epistemologies and alternative management schemes, democratizing and decentralizing the policymaking process. It may simply be more effective. Below, I briefly discuss three related policy implications of the preceding discussion, emphasizing the issues of property rights, the nature and relevance of practical knowledge, and, finally, the need to develop institutional frameworks which allow for democratic participation.

Property Rights

Many scholars have raised serious doubts and criticisms with respect to the central assumptions of bio-economic theory. To begin with, the emphasis on privatization and the tragedy of the commons has been challenged on practical grounds. Some "commons" regimes function rather well (McCay and Acheson 1987, Durrenberger and Pálsson 1987) and, conversely, some privatized regimes are obvious failures. In some African pastoralist economies, for example, the argument about the tragedy of the commons has been forcefully used by governments and companies when pressing for privatization of communal grazing areas. In the process, earlier mechanisms for regulating access have sometimes been eliminated, with serious ecological consequences. Environmental degradation was not the consequence of the absence of property rights, but rather the result of the imposition of a privatized regime. There is some evidence that a similar erosion of responsibility is occurring in fisheries as a result of quota management. Discarding of small and immature fish during fishing operations and the "high-grading" of the catch (the dumping of species of relatively low economic value) seem to be major problems in many fisheries, including the Icelandic one. In addition, privatization sometimes causes severe social inequalities and ethical problems, which escalate the problem of irresponsible resource use. Before instituting programs of privatization and quota allocation, managers should be careful to examine the particularities of history and culture and the likely social and ecological consequences of their schemes.

Practical Knowledge

An important conceptual problem with current bio-economic theory relates to the tendency to separate systems and activities, experts and practitioners. Management is often presented and practiced as a hierarchical exercise, the business of privileged professionals (see Marglin 1990). As I have argued, learning by doing entails the development of detailed practical knowledge, the accumulation of personal wisdom potentially of crucial importance for any project of resource management that seeks to ensure resilience and sustainability. Standardized procedures such as the Icelandic trawling rally may prove to be quite useful in this respect. Science and practical knowledge should be seen as complimentary and interactive sources of wisdom, not mutually exclusive.

The fact, however, that skippers often fail to express what they know by verbal means, since much of what they have learned is tacit and intuitive, presents a formidable "translation" problem. One Icelandic skipper explained his approach in the following terms: "It's so strange: when I get there it's as if everything becomes clear. I may not be able to tell you exactly the location, but once I'm there it's as if everything opens up." Indeed, a frequent comment in interviews with skippers on their fishing tactics is

simply "I cannot quite explain." How can one elicit and reformulate such tacit knowledge in general terms, in order to incorporate it into biological models and decisionmaking? If much of the relevant knowledge that skippers obtain in the course of their work is the result of first-hand experience, embedded in the practical world of fishing, its mediation to landlubbers is obviously a difficult task.

Scientists and practitioners, after all, have somewhat different methods and motives. One of the problems entailed by their collaboration, to draw upon J. Kloppenburg and B. R. DeWalt, is to transform practical knowledge which produces "mutable immobiles"—that is, relatively flexible knowledge geared to the details of a given task of a particular locality—into "mutable mobiles" (see DeWalt 1994)—general, holistic knowledge that can be applied to similar phenomena in other contexts. This should not, however, be seen as an insurmountable hindrance. One possible avenue in this direction, in the context of fisheries management, is to have biologists observe practicing skippers on different kinds of commercial vessels during actual fishing trips, using a variety of fishing gear at different times of the year. This would allow them to learn by fishing, much like a novice mate learns from a skipper in the course of production. Biologists would thereby periodically become apprentices, guided by experienced skippers. Knowledge obtained in such practical encounters may later on become important for ecological assessment, for the estimation of stock sizes, recruitment, migrations, and carrying capacity.

Frameworks of Cooperation

While much of fishers' knowledge is tacit and nonverbal, one should not forget that they often discuss their observations and theories in fairly clear terms, verbalizing their personal knowledge, their decisionmaking, and their management goals. To draw upon this personal resource—indeed, upon local knowledge and concerns in general (including those of fishworkers)—it is important to establish a democratic institutional framework, a framework that avoids the hierarchy of modernist management, allowing for what Habermas has called "the ideal speech situation," a "speech situation that is immune to repression and inequality"

(Habermas 1990:85). Such an institutional context is particularly important today, given the mutual integration of many fishing societies and the importance of coordinated fisheries policy. Several studies of European fishing communities, informed by theorizing on the process of "globalization," have drawn attention to the ways in which local concerns are articulated within a larger regional, national, and international context, emphasizing that in order to understand recent developments and to act responsibly, it is necessary to move beyond the study of either "local" or "external" influences to the wider encompassment of the local community within larger contexts (see, for instance, LiPuma and Melzoff 1994). Often fishing associations act as mediating institutions in this process, coordinating individual concerns, local activities, and the political structures of the larger environment, looking both inside and outward.

Bibliography

Acheson, James M. 1988. *The Lobster Gangs of Maine.* Hanover and London: University Press of New England.

Brush, Stephen. 1993. "Indigenous Knowledge of Biological Resources as Intellectual Property Rights: The Role of Anthropology." *American Anthropologist* 95(3):653–86.

Chapin, Mac. 1994. "Recapturing the Old Ways: Traditional Knowledge and Western Science among the Kuna Indians of Panama." In C. D. Kleymeyer, ed., *Cultural Expression and Grassroots Development: Cases from Latin America.* Boulder and London: Lynne Rienner Publishers, pp. 83–101.

DeWalt, Billie R. 1994. "Using Indigenous Knowledge to Improve Agriculture and Natural Resource Management." *Human Organization* 53(2):123–31.

Dewees, Christopher M. 1989. "Assessment of the Implementation of Individual Transferable Quotas in New Zealand's Inshore Fishery." *North American Journal of Fisheries Management* 9:131–39.

Dilley, Roy, ed. 1992. *Contesting Markets: Analyses of Ideology, Discourse and Practice.* Edinburgh: Edinburgh University Press.

Durrenberger, E. Paul, and Gísli Pálsson. 1987. "Ownership at Sea: Fishing Territories and Access to Sea Resources." *American Ethnologist* 14(3):508–22.

Ferber, Marianne A., and Julie A. Nelson, eds. 1993. *Beyond Economic Man: Feminist Theory and Economics.* Chicago: University of Chicago Press.

Fischer, K. W., D. H. Bullock, E. J. Rotenberg, and P. Raya. 1993. "The Dynamics of Competence: How Context Contributes Directly to Skill." In R. H. Wozniak and K. W. Fischer, eds., *Development in Context: Acting and Thinking in Specific Environments.* Hillsdale, New Jersey: Lawrence Erlbaum Associates, Publishers, pp. 93–117.

Gallie, Duncan. 1994. "Patterns of Skill Change: Upskilling, Deskilling, or Polarization?" In R. Penn, M. Rose, and J. Rubery, eds. *Skill and Occupational Change.* Oxford: Oxford University Press, Oxford, pp. 41–75

Gergen, K. J., and G. R. Semin. 1990. "Everyday Understanding in Science and Daily Life." In K. J. Gergen, ed., *Everyday Understanding: Social and Scientific Implications.* London: Sage Publications, pp. 1–18.

Gomes, Manuel do Carmo. 1993. *Predictions under Uncertainty: Fish Assemblages and Food Webs on the Grand Banks of Newfoundland.* St. John's: Institute of Social and Economic Research.

Gudeman, Stephen. 1992. "Remodeling the House of Economics: Culture and Innovation." *American Ethnologist* 19(1):139–52.

Gudeman, Stephen, and Alberto Rivera. 1990. *Conversations in Colombia: The Domestic Economy in Life and Text.* Cambridge: Cambridge University Press.

Habermas, Jürgen. 1990. "Discourse Ethics: Notes on a Program of Philosophical Justification." In S. Benhabib and F. Dallmar, eds., *The Communicative Ethics Controversy.* Cambridge, Massachusetts: MIT Press, pp. 60–110.

Kottak, C. P. 1992. *Assault on Paradise: Social Change in a Brazilian Village.* Second Edition. New York: McGraw Hill.

Lave, J. 1988. *Cognition in Practice: Mind, Mathematics and Culture in Everyday Life.* Cambridge: Cambridge University Press.

Lave, J., and E. Wenger. 1991. *Situated Learning: Legitimate Peripheral Participation.* Cambridge: Cambridge University Press.

LiPuma, Edward, and Sarah Keene Melzoff. 1994. "Economic Mediation and the Power of Associations: Toward a Concept of Encompassment. *American Anthropologist* 96(1):31–51.

Marglin, S. 1990. "Towards the Decolonization of the Mind." In F. Apffel Marglin and S. Marglin, eds., *Dominating Knowledge: Development, Culture, and Resistance*. Oxford: Clarendon.

McCay, Bonnie M., and James M. Acheson, eds. 1987. *The Question of the Commons: The Culture and Ecology of Communal Resources*. Tucson, Arizona: University of Arizona Press.

McCay, Bonnie M., and C. F. Creed. 1990. "Social Structure and Debates on Fisheries Management in the Atlantic Surf Clam Fishery." *Ocean and Shoreline Management* 13:199–229.

McCloskey, Donald. 1985. *The Rhetoric of Economics*. Madison, Wisconsin: University of Wisconsin Press.

Neher, P. A., R. Arnason, and N. Mollett, eds. 1989. *Rights Based Fishing*. Dordrecht, Netherlands: Kluwer Academic Publishers.

Pálsson, Gísli. 1991. *Coastal Economies, Cultural Accounts: Human Ecology and Icelandic Discourse*. Manchester, U.K.: Manchester University Press.

———. 1994. "Enskilment at Sea." *Man* 29(4):901–28.

———. 1996. "Human-Environmental Relations: Orientalism, Paternalism, and Communalism." In P. Descola and G. Pálsson, eds., *Nature and Society: Anthropological Perspectives*. London and New York: Routledge, in press.

Pálsson, Gísli, and Agnar Helgason. 1995. "Figuring Fish and Measuring Men: The Quota System in the Icelandic Cod Fishery." *Ocean and Coastal Management*. Under review.

Pálsson, Ó., K. E. Jonsson, S. A. Schopka, G. Stefánsson, and B. A. E. Steinarsson. 1989. "Icelandic Groundfish Survey Data Used to Improve Precision in Stock Assessments." *Journal of Northwest Atlantic Fishery Science* 9:53–72.

Smith, M. Estellie. 1991. "Chaos in Fisheries Management." *Maritime Anthropological Studies* 3(2):1–13.

Williams, Nancy M., and Graham Baines, eds. 1993. *Traditional Ecological Knowledge: Wisdom for Sustainable Development*. Canberra: Centre for Resource and Environmental Studies.

Wilson, James A. 1990. "Fishing for Knowledge." *Land Economics* 66:12–29.

Wilson, James A., James M. Acheson, Mark Metcalfe, and Peter Kleban. 1994. "Chaos, Complexity and Community Management of Fisheries." *Marine Policy* 18(4):291–305.

Figure 8–1: Fishery Survey Data

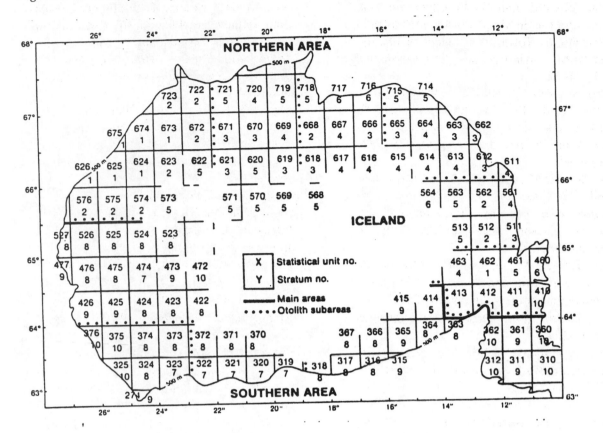

9

Indigenous Knowledge
and Resource Management Systems:
A Native Canadian Case Study from James Bay

Fikret Berkes

Abstract

THIS CHAPTER IS BASED ON A CASE STUDY of Cree Indians from the Canadian subarctic. It includes an analysis of the evidence regarding the distinctions of the local indigenous system from Euro-Canadian, science-based wildlife and fishery management systems. There is good evidence that the local system has incorporated certain Western scientific game conservation ideas since the 1800s. However, there is also good evidence that the indigenous system retains certain distinctive features in both thought and practice—core characteristics that could not have come from a Western source.

This chapter is based on a paper delivered at the Canadian Anthropology Society Annual Conference, Vancouver, May 1994. For the development of many of the ideas in this chapter, I owe much to colleagues Harvey Feit, Carl Folke, Madhav Gadgil, and Buzz Holling. The chapter is based on a long-term research project supported by the Social Sciences and Humanities Research Council of Canada (SSHRC).

Cree traditional management systems cannot be assessed by the criteria of conventional resource management science because they are based on a different system of knowledge. The Cree are not concerned, for example, with the population dynamics of wildlife and fish species, and how much can be taken. They are concerned with how people hunt or fish. Cree management systems can be assessed by the use of outcome measures (sustainability). Appropriate for cross-validation with Cree traditional practice is the emerging alternative resource management approaches of C. S. Holling, with its nonlinear, multi-equilibrium concept of an ecosystem and its focus on system resilience and feedback. It can be argued that there is a remarkable convergence between some indigenous views of the natural world and Holling's unpredictable ecosystems.

✧

Only recently have scholars and policymakers considered the possibility that systems of natural resource management based on indigenous practices may exist and may be considered alternatives to resource management and economic development based on Western scientific knowledge. This chapter explores the idea that indigenous knowledge systems can provide alternative frameworks for sustainable uses of the environment. Indigenous knowledge is used here to mean local knowledge held by indigenous peoples, or local knowledge unique to a given culture or society. Traditional ecological knowledge is defined as a cumulative body of knowledge and beliefs, handed down through generations by cultural transmission, about the relationship of living beings (including humans) with one another and with their environment; traditional ecological knowledge is used here as a subset of indigenous knowledge (Gadgil, Berkes, and Folke 1993).

The chapter is based on a case study of Cree Amerindians from the James Bay area in the Eastern Subarctic region of Canada. It has been known for some years that a number of Cree resource use practices provide potentially significant lessons in wildlife management (Feit 1973, 1986, 1987; Tanner 1979; Scott 1986). In the area of fisheries, community-based management systems of the Cree, with knowledgeable master

fishermen controlling access to resources, provide lessons on how common-property resources can be managed (Berkes 1987). Encoding ideals such as respect, reciprocity, and sharing simultaneously into religious tradition *and* hunting culture has powerful potential. Switching prey and fishing areas according to declining catch per effort shows how harvesters can respond to ecological feedback and conserve biodiversity (Berkes 1977). Rotational use of fishing areas improves both biological and economic returns. The thinning of fish populations by the use of a mix of gillnet mesh sizes helps conserve fish population resilience (Berkes and Gonenc 1982).

Resource management professionals have always been skeptical about claims of "native wisdom" in the use of resources, a view shared by other scholars as well, including anthropologists such as Smith (1983) and Alvard (1993), who have provided evidence from different groups of hunters that foragers tend to maximize their short-term harvests, and that apparent resource management is merely an artifact of optimal foraging strategies. Indigenous peoples may have a profound knowledge of their environments, but it does not follow that they use this knowledge for a conscious conservation of their resources (Hames 1987). In the case of contemporary Canadian subarctic hunting groups, conservation-oriented practices have been attributed to European, rather than indigenous, thought. Brightman (1993) has argued on the basis of ethnohistorical evidence that Central Canadian Subarctic Cree resource management practices for beaver were most likely learned from the Hudson Bay Company in the 1800s.

The questions raised by these authors touch upon a number of fundamental issues with indigenous knowledge and resource management systems: just what is "traditional" knowledge, and how "pure" is it? Can elements of an "indigenous" resource management system be segregated from that of a Western scientific resource management system? How do these two systems of knowledge interact? The chapter starts with a Cree hunter's narrative, a device to provide insight into a contemporary indigenous knowledge and resource management system, as described first-hand by a local expert. The chapter then proceeds to argue that:

- Western concepts of resource management available to the Hudson Bay Company (HBC) in the 1800s were too simplistic to be much use for the conservation of beaver or other game;

- The notions of resource management of the early and mid-1900s were utilitarian, useful for maximizing production but prejudicial to optimizing long-term use (that is, sustainability); and

- Indigenous systems of knowledge and practice which have the potential to result in sustainable outcomes are not uncommon. Some of these indigenous systems, including those of the Cree, are consistent with alternative resource management theories of C. S. Holling which focus on ecosystem processes and resilience.

There are a number of policy implications of the above arguments for development planners and development projects in areas inhabited by indigenous peoples. In fact, the very area of the case study has been affected by a large development project, the James Bay hydroelectric project, which has interfered with the use of local resources and which has rendered some of the major fish resources unusable (Berkes 1988). Indigenous knowledge could have been used to avoid some of the impacts but was not. Various issues in the development of indigenous and tribal lands have been debated for some time in the World Bank and other international circles (Goodland 1982; ICIHI 1987; Davis 1991). Warren (1991) argued that development agencies can take a leading role in promoting the use of indigenous knowledge for development by preserving indigenous knowledge, incorporating indigenous knowledge into education, conducting participatory research, and establishing networks.

A Cree Hunter's Narrative

"The tallyman takes care of a trapline so that the beaver continue to be productive. Taking care of a trapline means not killing too many. A trapper paces himself, killing only what he needs, and what can be prepared by the women, so that there is no wastage of meat and fur, and respect for the animals is maintained. He should also make sure that the area is rested. He divides up his area and concentrates on one part at a time during a trapping season. The remainder of his area is rested. Normally a trapper should rest parts of his trapline for two or three years but no longer than four years. If he leaves it, say, six or ten years, he is not properly using his area, and the beaver will not be plentiful.

"In an area which has not been trapped for a long time, there will be many empty lodges (that is, beaver houses made of mud and wood). This may be due to disease because of overcrowding; it may be due to beavers depleting their food supplies. The trapper knows that in an area which has not been trapped for a long time, various types of beaver food, such as aspen, would be in low supply. If there has been a fire, this also affects the beaver. Trappers know that three or four years after a fire, the beaver will again begin to inhabit an area. At first, however, they would be eating more of the root foods. The trapper may resume trapping again when the willows are half grown. This may be some eight to ten years after a fire.

"The tallyman makes an inventory of the lodges of the area where he intends to trap. He would normally prepare this inventory during the last time he was in that area. Before the James Bay Agreement, the Provincial Game Department (MLCP) used to assign beaver quotas to individual tallymen based on the tallyman's inventory of beaver lodges. More recently, the Cree Trappers Association (CTA) has taken over this function. The principle is that the yearly harvest of beaver be in line with the number of beaver lodges in a trapline.

"The tallyman went to trap a part of his trapline. He had not been there for several years, but he had given permission to another group to trap it a few years previously. These people had reported plenty of beaver at that time. But the trapper knew that there would not be many beaver in that area because these other people had killed too many. He knew this because when these people returned to the village that year, their furs had not been prepared properly. Many of the furs had to be thrown out. They had killed indiscriminately—young, old, every animal. Some of the beaver even may have been trapped out of season. The trapper visited, one after another, lakes and ponds which he knew to be good beaver lakes. There were beaver signs, but these were old signs from before that group's visit. Beaver had declined, had not produced because those trappers had not taken care of that spot. They had done wrong to the game. In such cases, game retaliates. Leave nothing behind—and it affects the later hunt. Bad management has repercussions for later years.

"The tallyman started his inventory in early fall when he arrived at his trapline. This was before freeze-up, so he was using his canoe to check for signs of beaver. He was looking for lodges and food piles. But beaver do not always make a food pile if there is in that lake a certain kind of water plant (a species of water lily) with roots used for food. He was also checking for teeth marks on nearby trees to figure out the numbers and age of the beaver in the lodge.

"The size and shape of the lodge also gave him clues as to what to expect: how many animals of different ages. He noted the distance between lodges and his camp by pacing himself. When he started trapping, he took care to leave some animals behind. Sometimes he would leave behind the younger beaver, sometimes he would kill them. Leaving an adult behind ensures quicker reproduction. The first-year beaver would not reproduce the following year. But leave one adult, and it will find a mate and reproduce the following year.

"By November, he was finished trapping around his base camp. He started setting up new camps in new areas. He would be gone from the base camp for one or two weeks at a time. Moving to a new area, he would check 'beaver lakes,' lakes where he knew from experience that he would expect to find beaver. Making an inventory of 'beaver lakes' told him what to expect in that new area as a whole. He also kept an eye open for other fur animals, mainly by checking for tracks. The beaver is not the only animal he is after, of course; he needs a bit of everything (for commercial sale and for food). It was now near Christmas. He built a cache (platform with legs) for his traps and gear in this new area. This way he would not have to haul everything back to main camp. By this time, he knew of the existing lodges in the new area.

"After Christmas, he went back to his main camp; this was a lodge built of sod (a traditional building style with split logs and blocks of *Sphagnum* moss on the outside for insulation).

Keeping in mind what he left behind at the other area just before Christmas, he checked some additional areas near the main camp. Now there was more daylight, and he had more time to check the lakes he did not have time to visit earlier. He found ten lakes in this new area with signs of beaver in them. He set new traps but did not check them immediately the next day. Instead, he broke trail to a new area and did an inventory. He also set a fish net in this new area. He would be making camp in one of those lakes later. The next day he checked his traps and brought in beaver. The wife had to work hard to keep up in cleaning skins.

"The next day, he left his traps in and went to the new area to actually set up camp this time. He checked his traps the following day, and brought beaver to be cleaned and to be stretched on frames. With the new camp already set up for the whole family, he proceeded there. The traps were still set, but he did not check them that day. Instead, he inventoried a different area again. Even if there were no beaver in this new area, he knew there would be no problem because he already had a set of traps in the previous area.

"From the new camp, he set out the next day with his traps. He was lucky to find beaver lodges, four or five of them, and he was quite happy about that. He sent his son to go even further east the next day. The son checked the traps set the previous day and brought in the beaver. The next day after that, the son checked the last set of traps set further east, but had no luck. With son and wife, he checked the first set of traps placed earlier. But he still had no luck with those traps set most recently. He took the traps out; 'let them be; they will increase for the next time,' he said. He was not catching anything there, and there was a meaning to that. The beaver did not want to be caught yet. Next fall, he would come back to this area, and maybe the beaver would then be ready to be caught."[1]

---

1. The above narrative was recorded in 1985 in the meetings of a working group organized by the CTA in Chisasibi, James Bay, Quebec. The speaker was Robbie Matthew, then the head of CTA, respected hunter and traditional leader, one time chief of Chisasibi First Nation, ten years later an elder and still an active hunter.

Indigenous System: Ideologically Pure?

Does the narrative indicate a European or an indigenous style of resource management, or perhaps a mixture of both? One striking feature of the narrative is that the speaker has a nondominant relationship with game, one based on respect, and on the assumption that the animals control the hunt, and that the role of humans in the natural system is characterized by a "community-of-beings" worldview (Gadgil and Berkes 1991). These are notions that have no counterparts in Western European thought, at least not since the Middle Ages (e.g., White 1967; Capra 1982). Thus, they characterize an indigenous, non-Western system of thought and attitude towards nature. The phrase "the beaver did not want to be caught yet" reveals a worldview in which it is the animals (and not the hunter or the resource manager) who control the success of the hunt; it is a notion that is still common among the older Cree hunters of the James Bay area (Tanner 1979).

Yet other phrases and descriptions reveal resource management thinking more closely associated with current Western practice. For example, "taking care of a trapline means not killing too many" shows a concern with numbers which, according to Brightman (1993), is not historically associated with the Cree and other subarctic hunting peoples. The speaker has an obvious quantitative understanding of animal conservation that is a characteristic of European thought and practice (Brightman 1993). Other parts of the narrative show evidence of mixing European and indigenous notions. For example, the previous group's misdeeds are assessed on a criterion likely to be non-Western: "their furs had not been prepared properly" and yet, they "may have trapped out of season," a notion that could only have come from the fur trade. The narrator speaks of "respect for the animals" in the same sentence with "no wastage of meat and fur." Brightman (1993) argues that the Cree hunters of the 1800s were not concerned with wastage at all, although the contemporary Cree hunter considers wastage taboo.

The notions of hunting territories and hunt leaders is a source of much debate in subarctic anthropology (Bishop and Morantz 1986). Thought by many to be a product of the fur trade, territories and leaders in fact characterize resources other than fur trade species and may well have indigenous origins in the James bay area (Scott 1986; Berkes 1987; Feit 1991). However, even if we were to accept that the master hunt leader or steward (Feit 1991) is an indigenous institution, the designation "tally-man" (one who keeps a tally of beaver lodges for the determination of harvest quotas) is clearly recent.

Thus, the speaker is describing neither a purely indigenous, non-Western resource management system, nor one which the Cree adopted from the Hudson Bay Company in the 1800s or later. There is strong evidence that it is a system that has a mixture of both European and indigenous styles of management, a system strongly influenced by Western resource management but one that retains the fundamentals of an ancient worldview and a locally-evolved system of practice.

Limits of Western Resource Management Science

The idea and practice of beaver conservation based on trapping seasons were introduced by the Hudson Bay Company into the Canadian subarctic in the 1800s (Brightman 1993). However, there are reasons to think that Western resource management was of limited use to the Cree, at least initially. The first scientific theories of overharvesting did not develop until the 1920s and the 1930s, starting in the field of fisheries. Prior to that, notions of depletion no doubt existed, but there was no scientific basis for resource management policy and no mathematical tools appropriate for analysis (Gause 1934; Lotka 1956). The conventional wisdom used by the Europeans in 1800s for game management seems to have been derived from experience with domestic animals. Much of this "management" thinking seems to be comprised of prescriptions against the killing of young animals and mothers, and against hunting in the reproductive season. Much of the available ethnohistorical material makes this clear (e.g., Brightman 1993).

As reasonable as these measures may be for the management of cows in the barn, they have little relevance or applicability to hunting strategies in complex ecosystems. The optimal hunting period for a given species may well be in the peak reproductive season, and as in the case of many fish species, harvesting may not even be possible in other seasons (Berkes 1987). There is good reason to be skeptical of the observations and impressions of the early Europeans. If the indigenous peoples of the Canadian subarctic had a management system, chances are that it would not have been recognizable to the personnel of the Hudson Bay Company. Further, as people coming from a country in which most of the wildlife had already disappeared, the Hudson Bay Company personnel, missionaries, and those others likely to observe indigenous hunters did not have a knowledge base that would have enabled them to evaluate indigenous hunting practices. The effectiveness of British conservation prescriptions exported to Canada by the Hudson Bay Company can be readily put to test: beaver had already been hunted to extinction in Britain by the 1500s.

When conventional scientific resource management did develop, it developed in the service of utilitarian, exploitative premises of a "dominion-over-nature" worldview. Reductionistic science, as used for example in the maximum sustained yield management of cod, is best geared to the efficient utilization of resources. Ecosystem interactions and environmental limits are not integral parts of management thinking. Resources are often treated as if they are boundless. This is a legacy of the *laissez-faire* ideology of Adam Smith and still persists in the neoclassical economic theory of today (Daly and Cobb 1989).

It is important to identify correctly the dominant ideology of conventional resource management: it is well suited by design for short-term exploitative development by means of maximizing production of a particular resource at a particular time and place. But it is not well suited for long-term sustainable use of resources in a complex ecosystem (Gadgil and Berkes 1991). Dominant resource management paradigms did not develop in an ideological vacuum, nor did they develop without scientific controversies. Worster (1985) has described in some detail the struggle between the more holistic, ecosystem management views of the ecologists, as opposed to the utilitarian approaches of conventional resource managers.

The ecological dimensions of resource management are closely linked to their social dimensions. Regier, Mason, and Berkes (1989) noted that "our experience with most 'successful' conventional exploitative development is that it is not ecologically sustainable, and often leads to the marginalization of local populations dependent on these resources." Single-minded concern with economic or biological maximization and lack of concern with equity or culture are among the characteristics of conventional resource management science. As such, these resource managers can hardly be expected to be sympathetic observers of indigenous resource management systems, in which the main concerns are precisely the opposite.

Systems of Knowledge

The expression "systems of knowledge" comes from an extensive body of literature in philosophy and anthropology, and is used here to signify that there are multiple ways of defining reality. As Banuri and Apffel Marglin (1993:9) put it, "...indigenous and modern communities are not just different political groups aiming to maximize their income or wealth, but embody different systems of knowledge, different ways of understanding, perceiving, experiencing, in sum, of defining reality, which includes the notions of one's relationship not only to the social milieu but also to the natural environment."

In sketching what they call modern and nonmodern knowledge as ideal types, Banuri and Apffel Marglin (1993) note that the distinguishing characteristics of modern knowledge are disembeddedness, universalism, individualism, objectivity, and instrumentalism. In contrast, nonmodern knowledge is characterized by embeddedness, locality, community, a lack of separation between subject and object, and a non-instrumental approach. The modern or scientific knowledge system, although not exclusively Western, is dominant because of certain unquestioned assumptions, such as individualism and instrumentalism, deeply rooted in Western civilization.

Conventional resource managers have usually seen indigenous peoples not as a source of solutions to resource and environmental problems; rather, they have often seen indigenous people themselves as a source of the problem (Freeman 1989). Indigenous peoples have often been blamed for resource depletion when, in reality, there were other forces at work. Examples include the depletion of beaver and caribou in the Canadian North, and deforestation in the tropics. Population growth rates of indigenous peoples have been seen as putting pressure on scarce resources, and their systems of collective resource management have been seen as being incapable of coping with the "tragedy of the commons." The solutions, according to this view, would include reducing population growth rates and instituting modern managerial systems of resource management or privatizing rights (Berkes 1989).

Modern management systems, however, have no room for respecting the wishes of the beaver and whether or not "it" wants to be captured. Nor have they any room for reciprocity between the hunter and the hunted. The very detailed contextual knowledge of the Cree hunter of beaver teeth marks, health of beaver feed, and signs of beaver abundance, are often respected by the field ecologist. However, as far as the conventional resource manager is concerned, such indigenous knowledge (or for that matter, detailed ecological knowledge) has no place in the disembodied population models that must be used.

Detailed local knowledge is the starting point of indigenous knowledge and management systems. Subarctic Indian hunters and fishermen are not unique in this regard (Berkes, Folke, and Gadgil 1994). The issue is not merely that indigenous peoples are conservationists but whether systems of knowledge other than Western resource management science can provide the capability to manage resources sustainably. The body of evidence accumulating especially in the last decade or so makes it difficult to reject the notion that some indigenous knowledge systems have this capability.

The growth of interest in indigenous knowledge in recent years is partly related to the failures of conventional resource management science. It is a paradox to many that modern managerial systems, with all their power, seem unable to halt or reverse the depletion of resources. Is this failure due to a systemic problem stemming from its ideology of utilitarianism

(Gadgil and Berkes 1991), or from its instrumental attitudes that undermine the larger social basis of conservation (Banuri and Apffel Marglin 1993)? The apparent convergence between indigenous ideologies and the nonlinear, multi-equilibrium ecosystem thinking of C. S. Holling provides an insight for the possible integration of Western science and indigenous knowledge.

Indigenous Knowledge and Ecosystem Resilience

Conventional resource management based on Western science often generates simplified ecosystems, as, for example, in modern agricultural systems. Resource management practices are often designed to lock out feedback from the environment and to avoid natural perturbations, as in fire management in forestry. Assuming away signals from the environment allows the conventional resource manager to carry on without having to worry about complications. Reductionism tends to rely on simplified views of natural systems. In contrast to the Cree hunter, who sees nature pulsating with life and meaning, and who regards it with awe and uncertainty, the resource manager is often self-confident in the belief that nature is an inanimate clockwork governed by simple, universal laws and "behaves as an automaton which, once programmed, continues to follow the rules inscribed in the program" (Prigogine and Stengers 1984:5).

Only in the last few years has there been a systematic critique of the view of science as consisting of linear, cause-and-effect, and predictive relationships. Holling is perhaps the best known proponent of an alternative view of ecosystem science and resource management. In Holling's view, ecosystems are characterized by changes that could not, on looking back, have been anticipated. These changes Holling calls "surprise," and their study "the science of surprise" (Holling 1986). The equilibrium-centered view of ecosystems ("ecosystem balance") is replaced by a multi-equilibrium view of stochastic uncertainties, as in chaos theory. Dynamic processes and ecosystem resilience (the ability of the system to maintain its structural integrity) become all-important (Holling 1986; Holling and Bocking 1990).

Holling observes that when ecosystems are managed for human benefit, perturbations are eliminated to increase the efficiency of management and hence the productivity of the resource, be it trees, wheat, or big game. But the very success of management freezes the ecosystem at a certain stage of dynamic change, making the ecosystem more fragile or more "brittle." Blocking out perturbations and feedback, efficient in the short term, tends to make the ecosystem brittle by inviting even larger and less predictable feedback from the environment. The feedback and surprises may be harder to deal with than the natural perturbations, and may have devastating effects on the ecosystem and societies dependent on it (Holling and Bocking 1990; Holling 1994). Examples include budworm control in Canadian forests (in which more and more control effort seem to result in larger infestations when they do occur), and forest fire suppression (following a century of fire suppression, half of Yellowstone Park burned down in one major fire in 1988).

Resource management characterized by indigenous knowledge and management systems allows perturbations to act on the system, instead of trying to lock them out. In indigenous cultures, a knowledge base has evolved to provide guidance on how to deal with perturbations and feedback, and how to respond to environmental change. For example, the Cree hunter's narrative provides recipes from the indigenous wisdom to deal with fire in a trapping area ("three or four years after a fire, the beaver will begin to inhabit an area"). Cultural practices are not only adapted to, but actively modify the environment by managing feedback. For example, the depletion of aspen signals possible overcrowding of beaver, warning the trapper that a new cycle of beaver trapping is necessary. Contrary to textbook wisdom, hunters can manipulate environmental feedback and manage habitat, as, for example, in the use of fire to rejuvenate wildlife habitat (Lewis and Ferguson 1988).

A detailed example of the interaction of indigenous knowledge and ecosystem resilience is provided by the fishery system in Chisasibi, James Bay. Studied and documented over an extended period, the case provides a detailed illustration of some of the fundamental differences between Western and indigenous systems and the role of the latter in conserving resilience.

The conventional scientific management systems for subarctic fisheries in Canada may employ the following tools: restrictions on gillnet mesh size and fishing gear used, minimum fish size, season closures, prohibition of fishing at times and places when fish are spawning. Catch quotas and maximum sustainable yield calculations based on population dynamics of the stock may also be used in larger-scale fisheries. However, many commercial fisheries based on whitefish (*Coregonus* species) in the Canadian North have proved to be nonsustainable (Berkes 1987). One explanation for observed stock failures is the reduction of reproductive resilience, by the selective removal of larger fish, in populations in which multiple reproductive year-classes provide an adaptation to an unpredictable environment whereby reproduction may fail in a given year (Berkes and Gonenc 1982).

Subsistence fisheries in many parts of Canada are exempt from government regulations. Cree subsistence fishermen in Chisasibi fish with the most effective gear available, using a mix of mesh sizes that gives the highest catch per unit of effort by area and season, and concentrate effort on aggregations of the most efficiently exploitable fish (Berkes 1977). In short, Cree fishermen violate just about every conservation or management practice used elsewhere by government managers. Yet records going back to the 1930s show that *Coregonus* fisheries in Chisasibi have been sustainable (Berkes 1987). How do the Cree do it?

The thinning of populations by the use of a mix of mesh sizes appears to help conserve population resilience, compared with the wholesale removal of the older age groups by single large mesh size (Berkes and Gonenc 1982). In addition, a number of other practices contribute to sustainability: Cree fishermen switch fishing areas according to falling catches per unit of effort; rotate the more remote fishing areas on a five- to ten-year cycle; key harvest to needs; have master fishermen or stewards who control access into harvest areas; and have a land use system with common-property institutions at the community level to ensure that resources are used under principles and ethics agreed upon by all (Berkes 1987). The viability of the Cree fishery shows that sustainability is possible under community-oriented economics and indigenous knowledge systems, whereby fishermen know how to respond to environmental feedback, such as declining catches per unit of effort, and maintain resilient fish populations.

Conclusions and Policy Implications

The question of indigenous conservation of resources (Hames 1987; Alvard 1993; Brightman 1993) cannot be assessed by the criteria of conventional resource management science because of the mismatch in systems of knowledge. Further, the appropriateness of criteria based on conventional resource management science is altogether suspect: it was not a system designed for sustainability—not even ecological sustainability. Hence, traditional knowledge and resource management systems can best be assessed in terms of their own long-term survival, as evidence (but not necessarily proof) of ecological sustainability.

Whether indigenous systems can conserve resources is not merely an academic question. It is a very practical matter for a group of people trying to survive on a resource. All groups of resource users have powerful, built-in incentives to conserve the resources on which they depend. In many cases they do conserve them, provided that they can control access to the resource and can work out rules for collective action, that is, solve the exclusion and jointness problems of common-property resource management (Berkes 1989). Indigenous management systems have provided adaptations for societies to cope with their environment; those which did not disappeared a long time ago.

In contrast to the beaver case, in which the existing local system has elements which may be attributed to Western scientific thinking, the fishery case is so fundamentally different from Western scientific practice that it could only have been based on an altogether different system of knowledge. In terms of its operation, the Cree system is characterized by much closer attention to, and much greater sensitivity of, environmental feedback, such as declining local catches. Detailed local knowledge is backed up by appropriate social institutions, and a "community-of-beings" worldview provides the ethical backdrop.

A number of principles illustrated by the Cree case study extrapolate to other situations. For Western observers looking for indigenous peoples to be "in equilibrium" with their resources, there is no such equilibrium—presumably because equilibrium in the ecosystem is an elusive notion. Instead, indigenous hunters may be harvesting opportunistically and maximizing short-term gains; this applies to the James Bay Cree as well as the Amazonian foragers of Hames (1987) and Alvard (1993). Unlike the foragers of Hames and Alvard, however, the Cree also safeguard long-term productivity by territorial behavior and prey-switching. Researchers steeped in the traditions of Western resource management, like the Hudson Bay Company workers of the 1800s, may be limited in their ability to identify those fundamentally different but nevertheless ecologically sustainable practices of indigenous peoples.

Many researchers in the area of fisheries management have been forced to question the wisdom of using catch quotas, an equilibrium-centered concept, in a highly fluctuating, multi-equilibrium environment. Are there any lessons that can be learned from the many long-surviving, indigenous fishery management systems? A recent review by Wilson and others (1994) concluded that traditional fisheries are managed by rules and practices limiting "how" people fish, as in the Cree case, rather than by attempting to regulate "how much" can be taken. In addition, many of the cases covered by Wilson and colleagues indicate systems highly adapted to respond to feedback from the environment.

The process by which indigenous knowledge accumulates and local management systems evolve is the natural process of adaptation. There is a great deal of learning-by-doing and "adaptive management" (Holling 1994) involved in the development of local resource management systems. The evolution of indigenous knowledge can be seen as part of a general process of self-organization arising from the necessity for a social group to deal with information from the environment (Berkes, Folke, and Gadgil 1994). It is a "cultural capital" of knowledge that contains not only the simpler, "is this good to eat?" type of information, but also the codified essential knowledge of how to respond, for example, to changes in abundance and behavior of animals. The indigenous ecological knowledge held by a social group contains the recipes for responding to and managing ecological feedback. This can be seen in the Cree case and in many of the cases summarized by Wilson and others (1994). We have hypothesized elsewhere that conserving resilience and diversity of the local ecosystem assures the resilience of the local social system (Berkes, Folke, and Gadgil 1994).

Western science is moving away from the positivist emphasis on objectivity towards a recognition that fundamental uncertainty is large, that certain processes are irreversible, and that qualitative judgments do matter. Traditional elders in groups such as the James Bay Cree would be quite comfortable with these ideas. In contrast, quantitative concerns of conventional resource managers, such as population dynamics of wildlife and fish, make limited sense to indigenous resource managers. Thus, their quantitative understanding of game populations, or lack thereof, cannot constitute appropriate evaluative criteria for assessing indigenous systems.

In the larger scheme of things, the gap between scientific knowledge and indigenous knowledge may be narrowing. Current Western science, with chaos theory, Prigogine's irreversible thermodynamic systems, and Holling's science of surprise, may be more akin to indigenous thought than many were willing to recognize. Some of these findings will be of interest for development planning which is sensitive to local needs and values. They may also be of use in minimizing social and environmental impacts of development, especially in indigenous and tribal areas. As Warren (1991) proposed, it makes sense to incorporate into development planning a process for understanding and using local knowledge systems and conducting participatory research to strengthen those systems.

Bibliography

Alvard, M. S. 1993. "Testing the 'Ecologically Noble Savage' Hypothesis: Interspecific Prey Choice by Piro Hunters of Amazonian Peru." *Human Ecology* 21:355–87.

Banuri, T. and F. Apffel Marglin. 1993. "A Systems-of-Knowledge Analysis of Deforestation." In T. Banuri and F. Apffel Marglin, eds., *Who Will Save the Forests?* London: The United Nations University/Zed Books, pp. 1–23

Berkes, F. 1977. "Fishery Resource Use in a Subarctic Indian Community." *Human Ecology* 5:289–307.

Berkes, F. 1987. "Common Property Resource Management and Cree Indian Fisheries in Subarctic Canada." In B. J. McCay and J. M. Acheson, eds., *The Question of the Commons*. Tucson: University of Arizona Press, pp. 66–91.

Berkes, F. 1988. "The Intrinsic Difficulty of Predicting Impacts: Lessons from the James Bay Hydro Project." *Environmental Impact Assessment Review* 8:201–20.

Berkes, F., ed. 1989. *Common Property Resources: Ecology and Community-Based Sustainable Development*. London: Belhaven.

Berkes, F., C. Folke, and M. Gadgil. 1994. "Traditional Ecological Knowledge, Biodiversity, Resilience and Sustainability." In C. A. Perrings, K. G. Mäler, C. Folke, C. S. Holling, and B.-O. Jansson, eds., *Biodiversity Conservation*. Kluwer Academic Publishers, pp. 269–87.

Berkes, F. and T. Gonenc. 1982. "A Mathematical Model on the Exploitation of Northern Lake Whitefish with Gillnets." *North American Journal of Fisheries Management* 2:176–83.

Bishop, C. A., and T. Morantz, eds. 1986. *Who Owns the Beaver? Northern Algonquian Land Tenure Reconsidered*. Special issue of *Anthropologica* NS 28(1–2).

Brightman, R. A. 1993. *Grateful Prey: Rock Cree Human-Animal Relationships*. Los Angeles: University of California Press.

Capra, F. 1982. *The Turning Point: Science, Society and the Rising Culture*. New York: Simon and Schuster.

Daly, H. E., and J. B. Cobb. 1989. *For the Common Good: Redirecting the Economy toward Community, the Environment, and a Sustainable Future*. Boston: Beacon Press.

Davis, S. D. 1991. *Indigenous views of land and the environment. A Report for the World Development Report 1992*. Washington, D.C.: World Bank.

Feit, H. A. 1973. "The Ethno-Ecology of the Waswanipi Cree, or How Hunters Can Manage Their Resources." In B. Cox, ed., *Cultural Ecology*. Toronto: McClelland and Stewart, pp. 115–25.

Feit, H. A. 1986. "James Bay Cree Indian Management and Moral Considerations of Furbearers." In *Native People and Resource Management*. Edmonton: Alberta Society of Professional Zoologists, pp. 49–65.

Feit, H. A. 1987. "North American Native Hunting and Management of Moose Populations." *Swedish Wildlife Research Vitlrevy* Suppl. 1:25–42.

Feit, H. A. 1991. "Gifts of the Land: Hunting Territories, Guaranteed Incomes and the Construction of Social Relations in James Bay Cree Society." *Senri Ethnological Studies* 30:223–68.

Freeman, M. M. R. 1989. "Graphs and Gaffs: a Cautionary Tale in the Common-Property Resources Debate. In F. Berkes, ed., *Common Property Resources*. London: Belhaven, pp. 92–109.

Gadgil, M., and F. Berkes. 1991. "Traditional Resource Management Systems." *Resource Management and Optimization* 18:127–141.

Gadgil, M., F. Berkes, and C. Folke. 1993. "Indigenous Knowledge for Biodiversity Conservation." *Ambio* 22:151–56.

Gause, C. F. 1934. *The Struggle for Existence*. Baltimore: Williams and Wilkins.

Goodland, R. J. A. 1982. *Tribal Peoples and Economic Development: Human Ecologic Considerations*. Washington, D.C.: World Bank.

Hames, R. 1987. "Game Conservation or Efficient Hunting?" In B. J. McCay and J. M. Acheson, eds., *The Question of the Commons*. Tucson: University of Arizona Press, pp. 97–102.

Holling, C. S. 1986. "The resilience of terrestrial ecosystems: Local surprise and global change." In W. C. Clarke and R. E. Munn, eds., *Sustainable Development of the Biosphere*. Cambridge: Cambridge University Press, pp. 292–317.

Holling, C. S. 1994. "New science and new investments for a sustainable biosphere. Pages" In A. M. Jansson, M. Hammer, C. Folke, and R. Costanza, eds., *Investing in Natural Capital*. Washington, D.C.: Island Press, pp. 57–73.

Holling, C. S., and S. Bocking. 1990. "Surprise and Opportunity: in Evolution, in Ecosystems, in Society." In R. McLaren, ed., *Planet under Stress*. Toronto: Oxford University Press, pp. 285–300.

ICIHI. 1987. *Indigenous Peoples: A Global Quest for Justice*. Secretariat of the Independent Commission on International Humanitarian Issues. London: Zed Books.

Lewis, H. T., and T. A. Ferguson. 1988. "Yards, Corridors and Mosaics: How to Burn a Boreal Forest." *Human Ecology* 16:57–77.

Lotka, A. J. 1956. *Elements of Mathematical Biology*. New York: Dover.

Prigogine, I., and I. Stengers. 1984. *Order Out of Chaos: Man's New Dialogue with Nature*. New York: Bantam.

Regier, H. A., R. V. Mason, and F. Berkes. 1989. "Reforming the Use of Natural Resources." In F. Berkes, ed., *Common Property Resources*. London: Belhaven Press. 110–26.

Scott, C. 1986. "Hunting Territories, Hunting Bosses and Communal Production among Coastal James Bay Cree." Anthropologica NS 28:163–73.

Smith, E. A. 1983. "Anthropological Applications of Optimal Foraging Theory: a Critical Theory." *Current Anthropology* 24: 625–651.

Tanner, A. 1979. *Bringing Home Animals*. London: Hurst.

Warren, D. M. 1991. *Using Indigenous Knowledge in Agricultural Development*. World Bank Discussion Papers 127.

White, L. 1967. "The Historical Roots of Our Ecologic Crisis." *Science* 155:1203–07.

Wilson, J. A., J. M. Acheson, M. Metcalfe, and P. Kleban. 1994. "Chaos, Complexity and Community Management of Fisheries." *Marine Policy* 18:291–305.

Worster, D. 1985. *Nature's Economy: A History of Ecological Ideas*. New Edition. Cambridge: Cambridge University Press.

10

The Role of Validated Local Knowledge
in the Restoration of Fisheries Property Rights:
The Example of the New Zealand Maori

Kenneth Ruddle

Abstract

SYSTEMATICALLY DOCUMENTED and validated local knowledge of resources and environments provides persuasive evidence of traditional property rights recognized by customary law. As demonstrated by the case of the New Zealand Maori, such bodies of local knowledge are acceptable as legal evidence in the process of restoring usurped rights. The simple and culturally sensitive methodology used is also directly relevant to the codification of existing rights and customary laws within a systems of statutory law in various cultural settings. This is a contemporary process in many nations in the Pacific Basin, and one which might provide useful precedents for application worldwide.

A travel grant from the Norwegian Ministry of Foreign Affairs enabled me to do research in the archives of the Waitangi Tribunal in February 1992. I am most grateful to former Prime Minister Sir Geoffrey Palmer, Professor, School of Law, Victoria University of Wellington, Sir Tipene O'Regan, Chairman, Treaty of Waitangi Fisheries Commission, and Hon. Mr. Justice John Wallace, Commissioner, Law Commission, Department of Justice, for valuable advice and discussions while in Wellington. I also greatly appreciate the assistance of Tessa Castree, Information Manager, Waitangi Tribunal Division, Department of Justice, for helping locate and copy documents.

Local knowledge of coastal marine environments is of direct practical importance for policy design, planning, and management (Ruddle 1994d).[1] It is also a system of actual or potential power. The way in which the rights of the marine fisheries of the New Zealand Maori were legally restored after 150 years, via a formal tribunal process that collected and then validated their local fisheries knowledge, provides a good example. The methodology used in New Zealand is an equally powerful example that merits replication wherever historical injustices remain to be corrected, and where minority rights are in jeopardy.

The colonial era had a major and lasting impact on indigenous systems for managing marine inshore fisheries (Ruddle 1994a; 1994b, 1994e). Impacts were particularly severe where large-scale and permanent European settlement occurred, and where indigenous property concepts and rights were either not recognized or, if recognized initially, as in New Zealand, were gradually overridden and forgotten. There, despite a vital and well-documented fisheries tradition and a treaty intended to protect Maori property, the rights of indigenous fisheries were gradually usurped. Initially, European settlers were only minor users of marine resources, but as the Maori population declined, their land rights diminished, and laws effectively dispossessed them of their fishing rights, Euro-New Zealanders gradually came to dominate fishing. By the late nineteenth Century, Maori fishing had declined to subsistence activities.

Causes of the Loss of Maori Property Rights

British settlement of New Zealand and recognition of Maori resource rights were based on

---

1. Several terms have been used to describe such knowledge systems. The main ones are *local knowledge, indigenous knowledge, traditional (ecological) knowledge, indigenous skill*, and *ethnoscience*. All have conceptual and semantic problems, but *local knowledge* is used here because it is the least problematical (Ruddle 1994c). Until very recently, local knowledge has been either summarily dismissed or denigrated. Thus to be acceptable as evidence for adjudicating claims, it requires validation by scientific and social scientific methods.

The Treaty of Waitangi (1840), which described the nature of the Crown's right to govern and the protection of Maori interests. In the English version of the Treaty, the Maori received full, exclusive, and undisturbed possession of their lands and estates, forests, and fisheries for as long as they wished to retain them.

Because the Treaty of Waitangi was neither ratified nor passed into law, it lacked legal standing, and has been treated as a legal nullity. That situation was exacerbated by interpretation problems of mutually incomprehensible property rights concepts. The existence of an English and a Maori version, neither of which is a translation of the other, has not helped matters.

Consequently, Maori rights were gradually eroded. This process was accelerated by legislation aimed at dispossession. Conspicuous were the destruction of traditional Maori authority by the Native Land Act (1862), which individualized titles to tribal lands (Kawhuru 1977), and land confiscation under the New Zealand Settlements Act (1863).

Fisheries laws followed. Although Maori fishing rights were provided for in law, in practice they were denied. Rights under the Treaty of Waitangi were acknowledged in general terms by the Fish Protection Act (1877) and by the Fisheries Conservation Act (1884). The Fisheries Amendment Act (1903) reintroduced a general and essentially meaningless provision (since it was left to administrators to interpretand thus was basically ignored in practice) that "Nothing in this Act shall affect any existing Maori fishing rights." Conflicting interpretations of that general statement led to many court cases. But it was invariably held that it did not provide for fishing rights. The Oyster Fisheries Act (1866), the first New Zealand fisheries legislation, was also the first statutory expression of erroneous assumptions regarding Maori fishing. By allowing only exclusive subsistence use of oyster beds near Maori villages, this Act implied that: (1) the Crown had an unencumbered right to dispose of foreshore fisheries because foreshore and the sea space beyond belonged to the Crown; (2) the Treaty of Waitangi could be ignored; (3) Maori fishing traditionally had no commercial component; (4) the Crown alone had the right to manage fisheries; and (5) only non-Maori had the right to commercially exploit traditionally Maori inshore fisheries (Waitangi Tribunal 1988). Thus, proof of customary entitlement was no longer acceptable as evidence of a fishing right, as confirmed by the Larceny Act (1869), which made it an offense to take fish from private waters or from an area governed by a fishery right. This effectively demonstrated that unless specifically provided for, traditional Maori fishery rights lacked any status.

The Fish Protection Act (1877) illustrates typical legislative window dressing by blithely assuming that Maori interests under the Treaty of Waitangi could be accommodated by a general statement "...that nothing in the Act was to affect any of the provisions of the Treaty of Waitangi, or to take away Maori rights to any fishery secured by it" (Section 8). This was stated even though everything else in the piece of legislation was clearly contrary to Treaty of Waitangi principles (Waitangi Tribunal 1988).

The social climate also changed drastically. In 1840 the intentions of the Crown were benign. Governors were directed "...to honourably and scrupulously fulfil" the treaty conditions "...as a question of honour and Justice no less than of policy" (Wards 1968:171). But policy changed as permanent settlers began to outnumber the Maori and the first Colonial parliament was formed, in 1855. Racial relations changed drastically as a consequence of the "Land Wars," in the 1860s.

But unlike the colonizers, the Maori never entirely forgot their treaty-enshrined fishing rights and management systems; they were embedded in and transmitted via a comprehensive system of local knowledge and a rich oral culture. Preserved in that way, and together with the enormous injustice of their dispossession, the legacy remained as an *aide memoire* for posterity, until conditions were suitable to seek redress. Although there were occasional appeals for justice, substantive action had to await the politicization of the 1960s.

The Waitangi Tribunal

In 1975 the Treaty of Waitangi Act established the Waitangi Tribunal, a permanent commission of enquiry, to investigate and "...make recommendations on [Maori] claims relating to the practical application of the principles of the Treaty [of Waitangi] and, for that purpose to determine its meaning and effect and whether matters are inconsistent with those principles" (GNZ 1975). Since the intentions of the signatories of 150 years ago can no longer be interpreted, the Tribunal is reconstructing the underlying Treaty principles (Levine 1989).

Initially jurisdiction of the Waitangi Tribunal included only Crown actions after the Treaty of Waitangi Act (October 10, 1975). But with the Treaty of Waitangi Amendment Act (1985), jurisdiction was extended to February 6, 1840, when the Treaty of Waitangi was signed. The Treaty of Waitangi Amendment Acts of 1986 and 1988 increased Tribunal membership to seven members, four of whom were to be Maori, provided a research and administrative staff, and granted authority for the Tribunal to appoint counsel for itself and for claimants.

The initial terms of the Waitangi Tribunal Act (1976) meant that fisheries claims took a "point position" in the resurgence of Maori ethnic politics. Whereas by 1976 they had long since lost most of their lands, the Maori retained a residual interest in marine waters. The official perspective was that marine fisheries remained common property under the Crown. Whereas versions of the Fisheries Act acknowledged some residual Maori fishing rights, nowhere were they ever specified. Thus fisheries issues were current (that is, ongoing in the post-1976 era), pertained to a vital resource, and, although acknowledged, had never been specified.

Making "Cultural Deprivation" Actionable

In the first three fisheries claims (Motonui, Kaituna, and Manukau), the Maori emphasized loss of reefs as a cultural resource. Since seafood and reef habitats are highly prized in Maori culture as *taonga katoa* ("treasures"), pollution damage is a cultural affront, by degrading the *mana* ("authority," "status," "prestige") of the tribes involved, and so protected by the Article 2 of the Treaty of Waitangi. In this way, Maori culture, demonstrated through local knowledge, became an instrument of empowerment. The Waitangi Tribunal hearings on the three water rights cases show that simple issues of effluent pollution to food sources have been expanded into far wider ethnic demands (Levine 1987; Oliver 1991).

The Motonui case (Waitangi Tribunal 1983) established the principle that Maori cultural deprivation was actionable under the Treaty. This aspect was examined in the pollution claims for the Kaituna River (Waitangi Tribunal 1984) and Manukau Harbour (Waitangi Tribunal 1985).

The Maori successfully demonstrated that traditional life was intimately shaped by the availability and sustainability of renewable natural resources. Water is regarded as so vital to life that it acquired a spirit (*wairua*). Traditionally, the Maori believed that life is derived from the waters of the womb of the Earthmother (*Papatuanuku*), and that water, the life-giving essence, must remain pure and unadulterated to ensure life for the following generations (Taylor and Patrick 1987). Thus to pollute seriously diminishes "...the life-force (*mauri*) of the water, demeans its *wairua* and thereby affects the *mana*, the prestige, of those who use it and its resources" (Taylor and Patrick 1987:22). The Maori relied heavily on marine and freshwater fish. Seafood (*kaimoana*) was of great cultural importance, since much prestige and social standing accrued to groups that could provide a lavish feast at social and cultural events. This remains important to the Maori (Sandrey 1987). On those bases, according to the principles of the Treaty of Waitangi, cultural deprivation is actionable.

The Tribunal Environment

The "business environment" of the Tribunal balances the strictly legalistic Euro-New Zealander interpretations of Maori interests characteristic of the last 150 years with a Maori understanding of Treaty intentions. The Tribunal conducts investigations and collects evidence in the field, at the traditional communal assembly site (*marae*) of the claimant group. At these hearings, Maori protocol and ceremonial are stressed. Thus what had become traditional ethnic roles are reversed. Hitherto the Maori were intimidated by European-style court proceedings and English legal language. But now the Euro-New Zealanders typically feel intimidated: "The 'court' comes to their [the Maoris'] home, as their guest, to respectfully hear them. It is the non-Maori lawyers, speakers for the

Crown and companies, who are in strange surroundings" (Levine 1987:429).

With cultural deprivation actionable, the Maori themselves are now expert witnesses in the cultural realm, on an equal footing with Euro-New Zealander technical specialists and lawyers. Whereas expert Maori witnesses in a court have their testimony translated into English property rights terms—which undermines the Maori claims—in the *marae* setting of Tribunal hearings, English property terms and other legalistic notions are deemphasized, and the concept of cultural damage correspondingly emphasized. Unlike a formal court setting, no cross-examination of witnesses is conducted, and no opposition witnesses are called.

Using Local Knowledge to Refute Erroneous Perceptions

That the New Zealand Maori were historically expert fishers with a profound fisheries tradition was recognized during the earliest European contacts, accounts of which commented briefly on the sizes and composition of catches, the gear employed, fisheries knowledge, long-distance fishing expeditions, large fishing fleet operations, trading in marine products, and traditional fisheries management systems.

Despite that documented tradition, through the social, economic, and legal processes described above, the heavy Maori involvement in fisheries characteristic of the early decades of the nineteenth Century had so declined in the twentieth Century that little credence of its former importance existed. Changed economic circumstances of the Maori as well as general acculturation took their inevitable toll on the old ways. Thus it is now widely believed that Maori fisheries never were commercial and always were a household subsistence activity done on a few local reefs and grounds (Waitangi Tribunal 1988).

The erroneous assumptions about Maori fishing embedded in early legislation became uncritically accepted. Maori fishing was assumed to traditionally have been (a) limited to few species; (b) confined to limited inshore areas; (c) for household subsistence; and (d) rightfully managed by the Crown.

The Waitangi Tribunal has demonstrated the falsehood of those perceptions by: (a) systematically collecting evidence from Maori fishers to establish empirically the existence of a local knowledge base; and (b) validating local knowledge bases from both historical records and scientific evidence of fisheries biologists and other specialists.

This process was used first for the Muriwhenua claim, in North Island (Waitangi Tribunal 1988) and then repeated for the Ngai Tahu claim of South Island (Waitangi Tribunal 1992). Here I refer just to the former.

Few Species

Maori Evidence

Maori informants listed ninety-four species of marine finfish, twenty-seven species of marine invertebrates, and four species of marine plants, along with thirty-five species of freshwater finfish and three species of freshwater invertebrates as having been harvested in traditional fishing areas. They named the grounds and pinpointed their locations precisely (Waitangi Tribunal 1988).

Literature Evidence

Over 120 species of fish were known to have been taken by the Maori of North Island (Firth 1929). In addition, the Maori were intimately familiar with spawning and maturing seasons as well as fish habitats and behavior. Fishing grounds far offshore were visited seasonally, when fish were known to be there.

Limited Inshore Areas

Maori Evidence

The depth of local knowledge of traditional fishing grounds is demonstrated by navigational bearings for locating traditional fishing grounds within a 40-kilometer band off the coast. Also demonstrated is a profound local knowledge of species caught on each ground and the seasonality of fishing each location. Individual fishers gave evidence. One identified nine grounds in the Karatia Estuary, twenty in the Waitiki Estuary, eight in the Waihuahau Channel, seventeen in open waters, fourteen in the Poroporo Estuary, twenty-seven along the coastline from Parengarenga Harbour entrance to Cape Reinga, and four at Te Oneroa-o-Tohe (Waitangi Tribunal 1988).

Scientific Verification

The visual triangulation coordinates for establishing navigational direction presented by Maori witnesses were plotted on topographic maps and marine charts. Those fishing grounds were found to locate precisely small areas of shallow water—the summits of seamounts—16–32 kilometers offshore and totally surrounded by very deep waters. These shallows were then confirmed by fisheries scientists to be known locations of fish aggregations. From the mass of evidence accumulated from witnesses and plotted onto maps and charts, it was apparent that traditional Maori fishers had explored all areas within workable depths of water (Waitangi Tribunal 1988).

Literature Evidence

Traditionally, Maori marine fishing was widespread and encompassed most of the coastline and offshore islands. However, it was mostly concentrated within 16 kilometers of the shore, although special fishing grounds much further away were also worked (Buller 1878; Waitangi Tribunal 1988).

Limited to Household Subsistence

Literature Evidence

Gear, especially large (900-meter) seine nets, was described by Anderson (1781) and Crozet (1891), based on observations made during a visit in 1772; Savage (1807), Thomson (1859), Buller (1878), Banks (1896), and Roux (1914), describing a 1772 voyage; and Best (1929). Polack (1840) described the very large Maori seines and expertly made lines. Colenso (1868), Taylor (1870), and Matthews (1910) described the fishing operations of large canoe fleets. These were hardly the gear types and vessel operations typically associated with household subsistence. Fish trade before and after contact with Europeans is summarized in Waitangi Tribunal (1988).

Rightfully Managed by the Crown

This assumes that either no indigenous system of marine resources management existed, or if it did, the only valid type of management system is one based on European concepts.

Literature Evidence

Examples of Maori fisheries property rights areas were mentioned by Nicholas (1817), Polack (1840), Taylor (1870), White (1889), and Best (1909). Traditional fisheries property rights were comprehensive.

Conclusions and Policy Implications

The example of the New Zealand Maori demonstrates how validated local knowledge can be applied to restore fisheries property rights, particularly in cases where a treaty exists, and especially at a time when resurgent ethnic pride coincides with a Western liberalist trend to right past wrongs. In particular, the example demonstrates a simple data collection and validation methodology and a culturally sensitive "business environment" that is replicable in other contexts. It is likely to be particularly effective, of course, in cases where historical documentary evidence exists, as it does usually in Western colonial archives.

The main policy implication goes far beyond local knowledge, *sensu strictu*. The imputation is that local knowledge, based on generations of praxis, demonstrates entitlement via prior established and continuous usage—"credentials of ownership," as in the case of the Torres Strait Islands (Nietschmann 1989)—and therefore a property right upheld in customary law. The prime policy issue then becomes that of accepting local knowledge *qua* customary law within the framework of Western-based legal systems.

The relationship between customary law that governs, or governed, traditional marine resource management and statutory law is highly varied and extremely complex. It is characterized basically by a strongly contradictory legal complexity, with Western-based statutory law that essentially regards all waters below the high tide mark as being state property and open to access, at odds with local, indigenous-based customary law, which recognizes some form of marine property right. Worse, it is generally accepted by Westerners and those with Western training that customary law, which locally legitimizes customary rights to resources, is invalid for upholding legal claims because it is unwritten, not made by either a sovereign or legally-constituted legislative body, and arises

from societies lacking any notion of "law." In contrast, in customary law, as exemplified by the Kiriwinan Islanders of the Trobriand Islands, Papua New Guinea, traditional claims are substantiated by records preserved in lore, legend, song, and dance. As observed by Williamson (1989:31–32), himself a Western-trained lawyer, "Traditions and customary usage are important in resolving disputes relating to maritime claims. Folklores, legends, songs, and dances to a Kiriwinan are like principles of the English Common Law to judges in Common law jurisdiction."

Contemporary, unsystematic, and *ad hoc* statutory frameworks relating to community-based marine resource management claims result from the absence of appropriate policy, itself partly a legacy of colonial neglect. Neglect was understandable, since the underlying philosophy of colonialism was to displace indigenous systems and institutions by metropolitan legal systems and to educate native peoples to use them.[2] To have encouraged resource management systems rooted in local systems of customary law would have been inimical to that objective. Rather, the objective would be attained by legislating directly against community-based systems and by allowing them to wither and become displaced during a gradual process of modernization and Westernization, as in New Zealand.

National independence has not changed the situation. This is partly because nations have been preoccupied with other development priorities, partly because devolution of power to local communities is an anathema in many nations still concerned with the fundamental task of "nation-building," and partly because, as in colonial times, the sheer logistical and practical complexity of attempting to incorporate customary rights into a system of legal norms is almost overwhelming. In an extraordinarily diverse society like Papua New Guinea, for example, it is all but impossible to devise an appropriate national system of laws and policies to embrace

---

2.   But traditional institutions for conflict resolution and such functions as land transactions, transfers and inheritance were permitted to operate, provided they did not conflict directly with colonial administrations and statutory law (Pulea 1993).

the specific customs of some 700 distinct cultural groups.

Tom'tavala (1990), a Trobriand Islander and a Western-trained legal scholar, observes of Papua New Guinea that neither the national government nor the provincial governments had a policy for traditional marine fishing rights, despite the official admission that conflicts over them are among the most prevalent contemporary disputes. This actually or potentially impedes economic development, leads to social and political instability, and contributes to an increase in criminality, since customary claimants tend to uphold their claims by physical violence, without regard either to the national good or to the validity of outsiders' claims. But violence or the threat of it to enforce claims, although customarily sanctioned in many parts of Papua New Guinea, is unacceptable according to modern criminal law. However, unless traditional claims are given some degree of recognition or protection, communities will continue to enforce their claims with violence, since they regard their actions as both culturally warranted and sanctioned.

In the context of economic and social change, during which rights to resources increase in value, groups may attempt to obtain codification of their customary rights. This has occurred in Papua New Guinea (Wright 1985). The most compelling reason for codification is to restore to local communities the authority to protect their rights. One principal reason why traditional community-based management systems have been undermined is that the quality and security of rights has been eroded: "Traditional [local] authority has been usurped, replaced by the ephemeral authority of central governments; the institutions in which [traditional management systems were] previously 'informally codified' have collapsed" (Graham 1992:36). Thus modern codification is required to re-institute local authority to protect rights.

This linkage between the preservation of systems of traditional authority and the preservation of traditional resource management systems has been recognized in the constitutions of some Pacific Island nations, particularly in Cook Islands, Samoa, Fiji, Vanuatu, Marshall Islands, the Federated States of Micronesia, and Palau (Pulea 1993). This enables traditional leaders to influence national and lower-level marine resource management, and in particular to assist in the reconciliation of the ambiguities between statutory and customary law.

Comanagement is the outcome of these approaches: national government sets rules and principles, simultaneously recognizing traditional rights and allowing local government to manage locally within this national legislative framework. It can be argued that local "title to" resources implies an obligation to manage them effectively. But this is problematical because it goes beyond fisheries legislation to include political issues of local autonomy, national policy, hereditary claims and rights, and other highly contentious factors.

Nevertheless, the reality is that in a great many nations in the Asia-Pacific Region, particularly in the far-flung archipelagic states where the central government lacks the capacity to manage fisheries comprehensively, that *de facto* comanagement has long existed in practice. It remains now for legislation to formalize this, and for central governments to shoulder a larger, complementary share of the task.

In many nations, despite an absence of clear-cut policy and the requisite statutes, the contemporary value and role of traditional community-based coastal-marine resource management systems is recognized. There has also been scattered and somewhat *ad hoc* attempts to implement this recognition. For example, the government of Papua New Guinea seeks to return enforcement to local "resource owners." In this effort, devolution of power to provincial and lower levels is fundamental (Chapeau, Lokani, and Tenakanai 1991). Similarly, based on the Provincial Government Act (1981), revisions to the Fisheries Act of Solomon Islands seek to transfer inshore fisheries management to the provinces, whereby they will have full jurisdiction over "Provincial Waters" for 3 nautical miles offshore, and will formulate their own by-laws. In this way it is hoped to achieve a better correspondence between provincial management and customary laws (Moore 1987). In Vanuatu, all reefs are owned by coastal communities. This is enshrined in the constitution: "All Land in the Republic belongs to the indigenous custom owners and their descendants" (Article 71, Chapter 12) (Amos 1993). In Fiji, the Native Lands Trusts Board is attempting to increase integration of the traditional community-based fisheries management system with state law by seeking more formal Fijian ownership of proposed Marine Parks. This planned devolution of management responsibility has recently received ministerial support (Adams 1993).

It is being increasingly accepted that many subsistence fisheries are governed by community-based management systems, and that such systems must be accounted for in evaluating potential development strategies (Lewis 1990). Further, the policies of many governments recognize that traditional systems are an integral part of a matrix that regulates social and political relationships and defines cultural identities and ways of life, rather than being concerned with just fishing rights and the organization of economic activities. Thus in many instances abandonment would entail severe social and cultural repercussions. In recognition of this, although generally not without considerable confusion and complications, in Papua New Guinea, Solomon Islands, and Vanuatu, where traditional marine resource management systems are recognized as a form of customary law, they have been embedded within statutory law. In those countries it is a tenet of policy that customary law may empower community-based management, as well as being a basis for comanagement of local marine resources.

Practical management considerations make it likely that this trend will continue worldwide. The New Zealand Maori case provides both a solid example of what can be achieved, given the political will, and a common-sense methodology for substantiating and upholding historical property rights claims grounded in non-Western legal concepts and systems of law.

Bibliography

Adams, T. 1993. "Forthcoming Changes in the Legal Status of Traditional Fishing Rights in Fiji." *Traditional Marine Resource Management and Knowledge Information Bulletin* 2:21–22.

Amos, M. 1993. "Traditionally Based Marine Management Systems in Vanuatu." *Traditional Marine Resource Management and Knowledge Information Bulletin* 2:14–17.

Anderson, G. W. 1781. *Account of Cook's Voyages*. London.

Banks, J. 1896. *Journal During Captain Cook's First Voyage*. London.

Best, E. 1909. "Maori Forest Law." *Transactions and Proceedings of the New Zealand Institute* 42:433.

Best, E. 1929. "Fishing Methods and Devices of the Maori." *Dominion Museum Bulletin* 12. Wellington: Government Printer.

Buller, J. 1878. *Forty Years in New Zealand*. London: Hodder and Stroughton.

Chapeau, M. R., P. M. Lokani, and C. D. Tenakanai. 1991. "Resource Owners as Implementing Agencies in Papua New Guinea Coastal Marine Resources Management Regulations." Paper presented to the South Pacific Commission 23rd Regional Technical Meeting on Fisheries. Noumea, New Caledonia, 5–9 August, 1991.

Colenso, W. M. 1868. "On the Maori Races of New Zealand." *Transactions and proceedings of the New Zealand Institute* 1.

Crozet, Lt. 1891. *Crozet's Voyage to Tasmania, New Zealand, the Ladrone Islands and the Philippines in the Years 1771-1772*. London: Truslove and Shirley.

Lewis, A. D. 1990. "Fisheries Research in the South Pacific: an Overview." In R. Herr, ed., *The Forum Fisheries Agency: Achievements, Challenges and Prospects*. Suva: Institute of Pacific Studies, University of the South Pacific, pp. 69–87.

Firth, R. 1929. *Economics of the New Zealand Maori*. Wellington: Government Printer.

GNZ (Government of New Zealand). 1975. *Treaty of Waitangi Act of 1975*. Wellington: Government Printer.

Graham, T. 1992. "The Application of Traditional Rights-Based Fishing Systems to Contemporary Problems in Fisheries Management: A Focus on the Pacific Basin." Master's thesis. Marine Resource Management Program, College of Oceanography, Oregon State University, Corvallis.

Kawhuru, I. K. 1977. *Maori Land Tenure*. Oxford: Clarendon Press.

Levine, H. B. 1987. "The Cultural Politics of Maori Fishing: an Anthropological Perspective on the First Three Significant Waitangi Tribunal Hearings." *Journal of the Polynesian Society* 96(4):421–443.

Levine, H. B. 1989. "Maori Fishing Rights: Ideological Developments and Practical Paradigms." *Maritime Anthropological Studies* 2(1):21–33.

Matthews, R. H. 1910. "Reminiscences of Maori Life Fifty Years Ago." *Transactions and Proceedings of the New Zealand Institute* 43.

Minhinnick, N. K. 1989. *Kaitiaki*. Auckland: The Print Centre.

Moore, G. 1987. *The Revision of the Fisheries Legislation in Solomon Islands: Draft Provincial Fisheries Ordinance, Central Province*. Fisheries Law Advisory Programme, Western Pacific and South China Sea Region. Rome: TCP/SOI/6601 (A) FI/WPs cs/87/14 Suppl. 1. FAO.

Nicholas, J. L. 1817. *Narrative of a Voyage to New Zealand*. London: James Black and Sons.

Nietschmann, B. 1989. "Traditional Sea Territories, Resources and Rights in Torres Strait." In J. C. Cordell, ed., *A Sea of Small Boats: Customary Law and Territoriality in the World of Inshore Fishing*. Report 62. Cultural Survival. Cambridge, pp. 60–93.

Oliver, W. H. 1991. *Claims to the Waitangi Tribunal*. Wellington: Department of Justice, Waitangi Tribunal Division.

Polack, J. S. 1840. *Manners and Customs of the New Zealanders*. London: R. Bentley.

Pulea, M. 1993. *An Overview of Constitutional and Legal Provisions Relevant to Customary Marine Tenure and Management Systems in the South Pacific*. Report 93/23. Honiara: Forum Fisheries Agency.

Roux, L. St. J. 1914. "Journal of the Voyage Made in the King's Ship 'Le Mascarin.'" In R. McNab, ed., *Historical Records of New Zealand*. Wellington.

Ruddle, K. 1994a. "External Forces and Change in Traditional Community-Based Fishery Management Systems in the Asia-Pacific Region." *Maritime Anthropological Studies* 6(1–2):1–37.

Ruddle, K. 1994b. *A Guide to the Literature on Traditional Community-Based Fishery Management in the Asia-Pacific Tropics*. Fisheries Circular 869. Rome: Food and Agriculture Organization.

Ruddle, K. 1994c. "Local Knowledge in the Folk Management of Fisheries and Coastal Marine Environments." In C. L. Dyer and J. R. McGoodwin, eds., *Folk Management in the World's Fisheries: Lessons for Modern Fisheries Management*. Niwot: University Press of Colorado, pp. 161–206.

Ruddle, K. 1994d. "Local Knowledge in the Future Management of Inshore Tropical Marine Resources and Environments." *Nature and Resources* 30(1):28–37.

Ruddle, K. 1994e. "Marine Tenure in the 90s." In G. R. South, D. Goulet, S. Tuqiri, and M. Church, eds., *Traditional Marine Tenure and Sustainable Management of Marine Resources in Asia and the Pacific: Proceedings of the International Workshop 4th-8th July, 1994*. Suva: The International Ocean Institute, South Pacific and Marine Studies Programme, University of the South Pacific. 6–45.

Sandrey, R. A. 1987. "Maori Fishing Rights in New Zealand: An Economic Perspective." In Anonymous, eds., *Proceedings, International Conference on Fisheries*, August 10–15, 1986. Rimouski: Universite du Quebec a Rimouski, pp. 499–503.

Savage, J. 1807. *Some Account of New Zealand*. London: Union Printing Office.

Taylor, R. 1870. *Te Ika a Maui, or, New Zealand and Its Inhabitants*. London: W. Macintosh.

Taylor, A., and M. Patrick. 1987. "Looking At Water Through Different Eyes—The Maori Perspective." *Soil and Water* (summer):22–24.

Thomson, A. S. 1859. *The Story of New Zealand*. London.

Tom'tavala, D. Y. 1990. *National Law, International Law and Traditional Marine Claims: A Case Study of the Trobriand Islands, Papua New Guinea*. Master's thesis. Halifax, Nova Scotia: Dalhousie University, Department of Law.

Waitangi Tribunal. 1983. *Motunui-Waitara Report* (WAI 6). Wellington: Department of Justice.

Waitangi Tribunal. 1984. *Kaituna River Report* (WAI 4). Wellington: Department of Justice.

Waitangi Tribunal. 1985. *Manukau Report* (WAI 8). Wellington: Department of Justice.

Waitangi Tribunal. 1988. *Muriwhenua Fishing Report* (WAI 22). Wellington: Department of Justice.

Waitangi Tribunal. 1992. *Ngai Tahu Sea Fisheries Report* (WAI 27). Wellington: Brooker and Friend, Ltd.

Wards, I. 1968. *The Shadow of the Land: a Study of British Policy and Racial Conflict in New Zealand*. Wellington: Government Printer.

White, J. 1889. *Ancient History of the Maori*. Six vols. Wellington: Government Printer.

Williamson, H. R. 1989. "Conflicting Claims to the Gardens of the Sea: The Traditional Ownership of Resources in the Trobriand Islands of Papua New Guinea." *Melanesian Law Journal* 17:26–42.

Wright, A. 1985. "Marine Resource Use in Papua New Guinea: Can Traditional Concepts and Contemporary Development Be Inte- grated?" In K. Ruddle and R. E. Johannes, eds., *The Traditional Knowledge and Management of Coastal Systems in Asia and the Pacific*. Jakarta: UNESCO-ROSTSEA, pp. 79–99.

Linking Mechanisms

The Role of Tenurial Shells
in Ecological Sustainability:
Property Rights
and Natural Resource Management
in Mexico

Janis B. Alcorn and Victor M. Toledo

Abstract

PROPERTY RIGHTS OPTIONS SHOULD BE ASSESSED for their
performance in supporting ecologically sustainable development. Tenurial systems function as "shells" in the sense that
they provide the superstructure within which activities are
developed and operate. They are constraining and enabling
structures with particular characteristics linked in very
specific ways to the larger operating system in which the
shell is embedded. Mexico has tested a mixture of private
and community-based tenurial shells for over fifty years.

This chapter is based on research undertaken in collaboration with the Property Rights
and Performance of Natural Resource Systems Program of the Beijer International
Institute of Ecological Economics, Swedish Royal Academy of Sciences, Stockholm.

We offer evidence from Mexican case studies that the best course of action for designing property rights shells to enable ecologically sustainable resource management is to support existing structures that have served this function. National recognition and policy support for existing, community-based property rights systems is a design principle that can be used to enable farmers to orchestrate natural processes, social processes, and multiple species to create sustainable agro-ecosystems that maintain forests and high levels of biodiversity while generating economic benefits and social services that complement those generated by urban development.

✧

In assessing the options as one sets out to design or reform a property rights system, one should consider the ecological and social impacts of the property rights regimes being considered, as well as the impacts of the property rights options on market function and national economic growth. Property rights systems do not just define and grant rights to property; rather they establish the rights and responsibilities of system participants vis-à-vis each other (Crocombe 1971). Property rights over land have generally been assessed in terms of trends in annual agricultural production as they relate to progress in formal titling to individuals because individual titling has been viewed as the property rights design to free the market to determine investments in land use.

The property of concern in this chapter, however, is broader than land considered as an agricultural input or real estate for sale. It is property comprised of ecosystems and their component parts and processes; that is, land, forest, water, and other associated resources of economic interest. The long-term value of these assets depends on their ecologically sustainable management. Using annual commercial crop production and its monetary value as a lens to assess the appropriateness of property rights alternatives ignores ecological impacts and thereby produces a shortsighted and narrow focus (for example, Porter, Allen, and Thompson 1991).

Sustainable economic development requires a proper balance between urban economic growth and ecologically sustainable management of rural natural resources. Rural property rights options should be assessed for how well they support the economically and ecologically sustainable development of both urban and rural sectors, including their performance in provision of essential safety net features for the poor (World Bank 1990).

Sometimes the best design is to seek ways to support an existing structure. Designing ways to allow the market to work efficiently is an example of designing support for an existing structure (in this case, the market). In this chapter we offer an insight into designing property rights to support an existing socio-ecological structure. We consider property rights where land use patterns exhibit ecologically sustainable adaptations to changing sets of opportunities and constraints. We conclude that national support for corporate, community-based property rights systems offers a design principle that can enable farmers to orchestrate natural processes, social processes, and multiple species to create complex, sustainable agro-ecosystems that maintain a high level of biodiversity while generating economic benefits and providing social services that complement those generated by urban development.

We focus on Mexico, a country that has tested a mixture of private individual and community-based property rights[1] within a modern capitalist environment for decades. Although sustainable resource management was not the objective[2] of

---

1. The mix includes corporate community-based landholdings (66.3 percent of the production units and covering 59 percent of the land area of Mexico); private individual holdings (comprised of 30.8 percent of the production units and covering 40.9 percent of the land area); and mixed systems (including 2.9 percent of the production units and covering 0.1 percent of the land area) (National Census 1990).

2. The political purposes and difficulties of Mexico's land reform program are evident in the unusually slow and sporadic way in which it was implemented. The process "fostered dependency on the apparatus of the state" (Powelson and Stock 1987, p. 29). Programs ostensibly established to support agriculture and marketing services were also designed to build political patronage and power bases for the ruling party rather than to assist communities to develop and market their products. These factors affected the productive performance of the ejidos and *comunidades* (indigenous communities), as well as the

Mexico's land reform legislation enacted some 80 years ago, Mexican recognition of community-based tenure has enabled locally adapted agro-ecosystems to continue to develop and adapt in the face of changes, while at the same time allowing maintenance of the biological and cultural patrimony that provides the inputs and means for future adaptations. For the past twenty years, Mexico has supported the largest experiment with community-based forestry in the world (Bray 1995).

The Mexican experience offers lessons for other countries. Group property rights are not legally recognized in most countries, although vestiges of pre-existing, customary property rights systems persist in many biodiverse areas. Legal support for community-based, corporate tenure is a policy option that is particularly attractive for sustainable management of forests and biodiversity in situations where indigenous peoples and other rural communities use locally adapted resource management systems.

Conceiving of Property Rights as Shells

Property rights systems provide the basic structure from which spring the opportunities and avenues for exploiting and managing resources. We propose that property rights systems function as "shells" in the computer jargon sense, in that they provide the superstructure, or inner environment, within which activities are developed and operate. In other words, a shell is a constraining and enabling structure with particular characteristics linked in very specific ways to the larger "operating system" in which the shell is embedded. This aspect of the shell responds to local cultural, ecological, and social factors, including those arising from externally generated stresses or opportunities. Such shells are generally nested within a hierarchy of shells—each outermost shell forming the operating environment in which the next level of inner shell operates. Shells are created within nations by special recognition of local systems that function within a particular national framework. In turn, national shells operate within the global

economy—the ultimate operating system in the computer jargon sense.

Recognition of existing local property rights regimes by powerful outside entities creates a shell around local systems, a protective border around subsystems that could not remain viable if fully exposed to the outer environment in which they are embedded. Communities, however, do need to interact with economies and organizations outside their shell. Therefore, the tenurial shell has, in addition to its protective dimensions, a facilitating dimension that enables selected interactions across the boundaries of the shell—rather like a cell membrane inside a living organism that separates one environment from another, yet at the same time facilitates essential transfers across the border between environments.

During colonial and neocolonial times, the shells of many local communities were disrupted, and the more common interface became isolated local shells abutting an outside global community and state property regimes (Alcorn 1995; Alcorn and Molnar 1995). The historical trend has been increasing loss of local tenurial shells and the locally based resource management systems they contain. Communities inside different local shells forge organizational links between themselves and with other national support organizations and networks in order to resist legal and illegal efforts to dismantle shells.

Each community-based tenurial shell is constructed of linkages into institutions that pervade the lives of community members. The term "institution" is used here to mean the invisible bodies of rules, regulations, and processes that guide decisionmaking (Ostrom 1990; Ostrom, Walker, and Gardner 1992). Such decisionmaking is often carried out within organizational structures—organizations being groups of people acting in relationships governed by and legitimized by institutions. Examples of organizations include families, clans, cooperative societies, community organizations, the church, local government councils, unions, and state agencies. Organizations are frequently linked in hierarchical relationships.

Local organizations often manage community members' access to forest or other natural resources based on local common property institutions (Berkes and others 1989; Bromley and Cernea 1989). Such institutions include rules

---

judicial process for recourse when laws were violated.

about use and acceptable distribution of benefits, means by which tenure is determined, and conflict resolution mechanisms. These institutions contribute to the structure of the tenurial shells. Tenurial shells are created at the interface between competing social and political systems and their associated institutions. Hence, the tenurial shell includes gateways for political intercourse between the inside and the outside.

Tenurial shells and systems are invisible to those who don't participate in local political activity or directly manage local resources. For this reason, few natural resource managers, economists, or ecologists have recognized or assessed the role of tenurial systems in ecological sustainability. Instead, they have uncritically accepted fee simple titling to individuals as a necessary step to facilitate development.

Our discussion focuses on old, local subsystems within the national and global economies where local feedback loops within local subsystems can lead to recognition of overexploitation of a resource and failure of ecosystem functions. When communities extract distant resources, recognition of overexploitation and follow-on harvest adjustment rarely occur. If ecosystem-level damage is registered by an extractor with long-term interest in maintaining his assets, alteration in exploitation or shifts in livelihood strategies are more likely to occur. In response to feedback and tensions between individuals seeking access to resources, local institutions have arisen to ensure community members' continued access to resources while restricting access by outsiders, as well as to manage the differentiated access rights of insiders. These institutions result from a political process of trade-offs between members of a community who must work together because of their interdependence in many other spheres.

Traditional shells are weakened by the lack of state support. The community's traditional resource management systems and related institutions are often slowly undermined by new laws. Unsustainable resource use increases as the old shell is weakened and replaced by a new operating shell—often an aberrant version of the legally-specified shell as it is interpreted and locally implemented by the politically powerful, including the military. In remote areas, traditional tenurial shells often continue to operate without legitimization by the government.

Alternatively, communities in remote areas may have rights that have been legitimized by the government, but these communities may be uninformed of their rights and therefore fail to seek state assistance in the face of illegal extraction of their resources (for example, Cortez Ruiz 1992). Design for support of local shells should be based on an assessment of factors undermining those shells.

In the remainder of this chapter, we briefly describe the tenurial shells in Mexico, summarize the attributes of sustainable tropical forest management, and demonstrate how sustainable forest management is related to design principles that support the protective, enabling shells of community-based tenurial systems.

The Mexican Case: National Support for Tenurial Shells

In Mexico, unlike most other countries rich in tropical forests, resource users gained the state's protection for community-based management of resources. The Mexican state formally recognized tenurial shells for communities after the Mexican Revolution, which was born, fought, and won on the demand for the return and redistribution of land to peasant communities (Sanderson 1984). The 1917 Constitution supported land reform and recognized community ownership of land under Article 27. Constitutional recognition of community-based tenure has provided a protective shell for the functioning and evolution of resource management systems responsive to local ecological conditions.

Community land rights in Mexico are typical of community-based tenure systems elsewhere in the world. Tenurial rights and responsibilities within the shell are defined by local communities within the basic framework established by the state. We refer to these systems as community-based because the primary legitimacy of community-based tenure systems is drawn from the community and not from the nation state which recognizes them (Lynch and Alcorn 1994). In other words, the local community, not the national government, is the primary allocator and enforcer of rights to resources within the boundaries of the community. Responsibilities to the land and to the community are defined by the community, and the national government defends a community's rights to its resources against the claims of noncommunity members. At the same time, however, the Mexican state retains ultimate rights over the resources and places restrictions on rights to sell, lease, or rent community properties.

In Mexico, two forms of community-based corporate ownership are currently recognized and supported by law: ejidos and *comunidades* (indigenous communities). The ejido is a creation of the Mexican revolution that enables groups of people to petition for access to resources to which they have no prior claim. The *comunidad*, on the other hand, is a pre-existing corporate entity whose rights are recognized if its members can demonstrate prior, longstanding, community-based use of the land and waters. The stated objective of legally establishing the post-Revolution *comunidad* was to return to the earlier corporate tenurial system originally recognized by Spanish colonial administrators based on similar European traditions of corporate land use (Sanderson 1984; Sheridan 1988). Traditional corporate systems derive strength from a cultural and social integrity which, on the one hand, reinforces a unified approach to management decisions and yet, on the other hand, offers individual households the freedom to benefit from differential, individual access to specific resources held within the community.[3]

During the Porfirian period (1876–1910) prior to the Revolution, the state withdrew its earlier support for the communities' tenurial shells. Federal laws eliminated communal property rights and claimed as state property all lands without official titles (Barthas 1994; Sanderson 1984; Stresser-Péan 1967). The state in turn gave rights to those same lands to capitalists and owners of haciendas, leaving communities to depend on wages for their survival. The impact of these policies varied in different regions of Mexico, but nationwide, by 1910, nearly half the rural population had become debt peons on haciendas and ranches, 82 percent of all communities were located on haciendas and ranches, and free agricultural villages held very little land (Sanderson 1984, p. 16–18). As a result of the

export-oriented policies, prices for food rose significantly, while profits from growth in the export sector primarily accrued to foreign investors. Wages remained low, "verging on slavery" in some areas (Sanderson 1984). These conditions gave rise to the Mexican Revolution. Under the post-Revolution land reforms, despite the legally specified difference between *comunidades* and ejidos, most pre-existing communities were not recognized as *comunidades* on the basis of documented prior claims, but were instead granted rights as ejidos for political reasons.[4]

Under both ejido and *comunidad* systems, each household in the community has the right to exploit the community's natural resources necessary for livelihood. The household cannot sell or rent community lands to anyone outside the community (but see 1992 revisions below). Inheritance and membership is regulated by communities. The household is, in effect, a user-manager of a set of resources that belongs to everyone in the community. Resources are allocated to members of the community who exploit and manage these resources on an individual basis within the limits set by the community. Communities are heterogeneous, dynamic entities containing subunits that form shifting alliances within shared institutions and that are guided by shared ethics. Their tenurial shells form crucibles within which local conflicts and differing strategies can bubble together without being destabilized by external factors. Land disputes within communities are common, but they are generally resolved at the community

---

3. Landholdings of individual farm families may be fragmented in order to provide each family with access to available soil types and microhabitats. This acts to strengthen in situ conservation of traditional crop varieties (Oldfield and Alcorn 1987, Brush and Bellon 1994).

---

4. The rights of ejidos are spelled out more clearly than those of *comunidades* in the agrarian reform legislation (Reyes Osorio and others 1974). The process of forming an ejido is much simpler than the tortuous process required to receive recognition as a *comunidad*. In addition, the state strongly favored the option of granting land to ejidos rather than recognizing pre-existing rights to *comunidades*; the former option placed the state in a more powerful position (Powelson and Stock 1987; Sanderson 1984). In practice, there are greater operational differences within the range of ejidos than there are between ejidos and *comunidades*. Communities that purchased their own lands when threatened with eviction at various times in past centuries have enjoyed stronger state support for their tenurial security when threatened by invasions. As of 1995, however, all ejidos and *comunidades* are functioning as longstanding communities with prior rights.

level and do not become a burden for state agencies (DeWalt and Rees 1994). Land disputes between communities are also common, but they are settled through state agencies and the state's judicial apparatus.[5] Land disputes between communities and ranchers are also common, particularly in forested areas (for example, Sandoval 1994), and the state apparatus offers the only peaceful recourse for justice in situations where ranchers have enormous political influence, and sometimes private armies.

The extent and impact of community-based resource management in Mexico are significant. Approximately 3 million households belong to the nearly 30,000 ejidos and *comunidades*[6] that manage 59 percent of Mexico's land area (103 million hectares) and 66 percent of the total rural production units. Most indigenous communities operate ejidos, and long-established mestizo ejidos often retain the pre-Hispanic traditions of their indigenous ancestors. For these reasons, it is appropriate to assess ejidos and *comunidades* as a group. Most of the land operated by ejidos and *comunidades* is marginal for agriculture due to poor climatic and soil conditions. Of the *comunidad* and ejido lands, only 22 percent is agricultural (arable), and the remainder is under pasture or forest. Highly productive lands (particularly those that are irrigated) are privately owned under individual title. Mexican rural communities, whether indigenous or mestizo, are similar to peasant communities in other parts of the world in that, while they produce goods for their own consumption, they also rely on outside jobs and the sale of cash crops to meet their subsistence needs and purchase other consumer goods.

Within the protective and enabling shells created by ejidos and *comunidades* in Mexico, communities apply an incredible range of innovative, sustainable, locally adapted natural resource management systems in a wide variety of ecosystems ranging from desert to rain forest (for example, Gómez-Pompa and Kaus 1990; Mora López and Medellín-Morales 1992; Wilken 1987; Nahmad, González, and Vásquez 1994; Toledo and Barrera-Bassols 1984; Toledo and others 1985; Zizumbo Villarreal and Colunga García-Marín 1982). Indigenous peoples live within the borders of 80 percent of Mexico's protected areas, an indication of the level of biodiversity maintained by their land use patterns. An archipelago of communities linked as a network of *campesino* (peasant) ecological reserves could effectively cover Mexico's biodiversity (Toledo 1992b, 1994b).

Every ecological zone in Mexico supports rich reserves of biodiversity, but the forested areas are especially rich (Ramamoorthy and others 1993). Between 70 percent and 80 percent of Mexico's forests are under management by some 7,000 to 9,000 ejidos and *comunidades* (Molnar 1995).[7] From a cultural perspective, it is also noteworthy that 4.8 million indigenous people[8] reside in ejidos and *comunidades* in forested areas (National Census 1990).

In the next section, we summarize the attributes of sustainable tropical forest management. Then we briefly explore community-based property rights and resource management by long-established communities in two of Mexico's forest ecosystems—the lowland humid tropical forest and the subhumid temperate forest—some 15 million hectares of which remain under the management of *comunidades* and ejidos (National Census 1990). Over the past few decades, ranchers have converted 20 million hectares of lowland and temperate forests into pasture (Toledo 1992a), and they continue to press on the edges of forested ejidos (for exam-

---

5.   Inefficiencies, rent-seeking behavior of bureaucrats, and political intrigues have often made settlement difficult. Nonetheless, despite analysts' focus on specific local cases where the government failed to resolve the problems (for example, Powelson and Stock 1987; DeWalt and Rees 1994), from a national perspective the majority of ejidos and *comunidades* have continued to function successfully without seeking government intervention in border disputes.

6.   Although the *comunidad* was expressly created for indigenous communities, due to the reasons described above there are only 1,231 *comunidades* covering some 9 million hectares (Sheridan 1988).

7.   A recent World Bank sector review found wide variation in published estimates of forest held by ejidos and *comunidades* and in the numbers of ejidos and *comunidades* who hold forest.

8.   Mexico's total indigenous population is 10.5 million (National Census 1990). There are 54 major indigenous groups speaking 240 languages.

ple, Sandoval 1994), putting external stress on their tenurial shells and their forests. Given the high percentage of indigenous communities living in these two zones and the importance of these two forest zones, it is appropriate to select case study examples from indigenous communities from these two forest zones.

Attributes of Sustainable Tropical Forest Management Systems

Patterns from tropical forests around the world suggest that the key elements of a sustainable management strategy are (a) patchy disturbance, (b) controls over placement of disturbance, and (c) active development of crops and crop varieties adapted to the local agro-ecosystem patches within the forest matrix. These elements are found in indigenous resource management systems. Patchy disturbance (spatial and/or temporal) creates patches of different types of habitat. For ecosystem integrity to be maintained by patchy disturbance, patches must include undisturbed areas of sufficient size and coverage, and of appropriate distribution and composition to (a) ensure regeneration of the species and the communities, and (b) maintain ecosystem services essential for habitat maintenance of the entire matrix and adjacent ecosystems. The management system's ability to create and maintain patches that meet these criteria is challenged by changes in population size, political organization, market values, in-migration, intensity of resource mining and other nonbiological factors.

Although most case studies contain insufficient information to ascertain the key factors that determine whether a society can create or adapt a resource management system to meet the ecological criteria for forest maintenance, existing evidence suggests it is important that several things are shared within the user group, including (a) cultural values, traditions, and sociopolitical organizations; (b) controls and incentives; and (c) attention to monitoring for negative changes.

Strong cultural traditions, social organizations, and institutions have evolved in many forest-dwelling societies which have experienced forest loss and then reacted in an effort to manage or reverse the change. Values and institutions (such as *milpa* described below) evolved to

support agricultural management systems adapted to the tropical forest ecosystem's limits. Controls (including tenurial rights and responsibilities defined by a community) and incentives to encourage community members to respond to evidence that forest is being damaged are also important. Finally, monitoring to recognize that the forest is being harmed or helped by certain changes may be a group or individual activity, but it must be linked through a feedback mechanism into an institution that can bring the community together to wrestle with a problem if it is detected. If loss of forest is not perceived or is not recognized as a problem, then no conscious choice is made to keep or lose the forest, and the process proceeds as an accident. If it is perceived and recognized as a problem, then choices are made to hold losses to an acceptable level or arrest and reverse the process. The successful implementation of choices (whether individual or group) depends on the societies' shared values, appropriate organizations, and political power vis-à-vis outsiders who may be causing the changes.

Inside the Shell: Resource Management in a Changing Environment

Introduction

The cases from Mexico summarized below include (a) strong tenurial rights held by individual families within a strong communal tenurial shell recognized and supported by the state; (b) some resources under communally shared tenure; (c) evidence that potential negative impacts of land use options are considered in making choices; and (d) shared cultural values, institutions, and organizations developed over centuries of changes in situ.

The in situ changes have included shifts from subsistence production to involvement with cash crop production, resistance to outside efforts to eradicate their cultural traditions, and efforts to counter increasing marginalization within the political economy. The specific resource management practices in the two eco-regions differ. In both zones, individual households and communitywide land use patterns are constructed from core elements that include forest, fallow cycled fields, corridors of wild vegetation within agricultural areas, bodies of water, house gardens, and permanent fields, including plantations and pastures (Toledo and others 1995b). A survey of forest use by indigenous people in the lowland humid tropical zone revealed that 1,052 forest species are used for a wide variety of products for consumption and sale, ranging from medicines and food to construction and fuel materials (Toledo and others 1995a). This study emphasizes the economic value of Mexico's forests beyond their value as standing timber for paper or plywood production.

The specific type of tenurial rights within a community is probably less important for ecological success than are the legitimacy of the tenurial shell and the strength of the institutions that reinforce tenurial responsibilities and provide the capacity to take action on the basis of feedback from monitoring. In both cases, community institutions influence local property rights interpretation and resource management. These include state-imposed institutions and cultural institutions. The local institutions created by the state to regulate activities on *comunidad* and ejido lands in accordance with state law include the General Assembly to which all households are represented by one person, and two important elected three-person committees: the *comisariado* (which represents the community to outside authorities and settles land disputes) and the *consejo de vigilancia* (which monitors the activities of the first committee). Community decisions are made in General Assembly meetings or special meetings by majority vote; representatives of all households must attend these meetings, or they are fined. To varying degrees, elders and traditional leaders influence the functioning of these institutions.

Case One: Lowland Tropical Moist Forest

The 1990 National Census identified twenty-two indigenous groups operating ejidos and *comunidades* (population 1.56 million) in the tropical humid zones of Mexico. The case study site is a representative example located in northeastern Mexico on the Gulf coastal slopes of the Sierra Madre Oriental in the states of San Luis Potosí and Veracruz where rain forests reach their northernmost range in the Americas (Rzedowski 1978). Prior to the arrival of the Spanish, the area was occupied for thousands of years and supported complex civilizations. From the time of the earliest written documents, the tropical moist forest region has been characterized as a "hell" or a "paradise," depending on the viewer (for example, Vetancourt 1689; Tapia Centeno 1960). If this ecosystem is managed properly, it is a paradise because it provides a wealth of short- and long-term benefits. If its special resources created under hot, humid conditions are misused for short-term extractive gains, or if conversion is attempted, then this ecosystem degenerates into a less valuable ecosystem requiring external inputs to maintain production.

We focus on two user groups located in contiguous areas (southeastern San Luis Potosí and northern Veracruz) of this ecosystem who use similar resource management systems: the Huastec Maya (population 121,000; National Census 1990 Table 10, Cuadro 8) and the Totonac (population 208,000; National Census 1990 Table 10, Cuadro 8). Totonac and Huastec both retain their language and strong cultural traditions, but at the same time have participated in economies linked to the global economy for several centuries.

Economic differences do exist between families, but only a few families in any given community hold significantly greater resources than the rest. Huastec and Totonac communities occupy *comunidad* and ejido lands where population densities average around 100 persons per square kilometer. Communities vary in size from 500 to several thousand hectares.

While there are no significantly distinct subgroups of resource users within their communities, Huastec and Totonac communities are spatially distributed as islands in a sea of lands operated by a different group of resource users—mestizos, the Spanish-speaking people who claim Mexican national identity. Mestizos' political power and domination of the economy influence the technical and organizational options available to indigenous resource users. Mestizos occupy towns, ranches, and citrus and sugarcane plantations in the more level lands and areas along roadways, while the islands of indigenous territories tend to be aggregates of communities grouped on steeper, less desirable agricultural lands. There is continued tension over borders between mestizo and indigenous lands and forests. Occasionally, powerful mestizos still assert their rights over these resources without any legal basis to back their claims (for example, Briseño Guerrero 1994).

The land use patterns of the indigenous people and the mestizos who own private lands are quite different. Mestizos manage the majority of the land in the region. Mestizo households operate a wider range of land sizes than do indigenous households—from large ranches to the small garden plots of landless laborers. On the margins of the Huastec and Totonac areas, mestizo ejidos also exist, and their land use varies from indigenous-like mosaic patterns to monocultures. Mestizo land use outside ejidos generally tends to follow the standard Eurocentric model of monocrops and pastures with intensive herbicide and pesticide use. Mestizos in this region dedicate most of their lands to cattle, although pastures are largely degraded and unproductive. This general pattern has been in place for several hundred years (Barthas 1994), but forest in mestizo areas decreased dramatically after World War II when mestizos gained access to machinery for clearing forest and used it to increase the area dedicated to cattle pasture (Aguilar-Robledo 1994).

Property within the borders of the *comunidad* or ejido is recognized, used, and inherited according to local institutions. Almost all forested land is under family ownership—a situation in which the family, not others, make management decisions. Families are responsible for making management decisions that are appropriate to the context and rules shared by the community. The small patches of communally shared forest are used to generate income to pay school expenses and maintenance of other buildings required by the state, as well as to provide materials for poorer community members who do not have access to forest resources on their own family lands. Decisions about community lands and forests are discussed at assemblies in which representatives of every family participate.

The specific lands that belong to each family are well defined, but border disputes do occur. Under the state-sponsored *comunidad* and ejido systems, a community-elected official adjudicates over land disputes and inheritance decisions in consultation with other community members. Community members understand the state's legal apparatus establishing ejidos and *comunidades* as an extension of traditional institutions that control human behavior in order to protect the community and the land and resources for which the community is collectively responsible. Middle American cultural concepts of ownership extend beyond the usual Western legal considerations. The real owners of the land and forest are divine beings and spirits (including ancestors). Another way of expressing this relationship is that the earth (with its resources) is a member of the community, and the community has the obligation to treat the earth and all other community members with respect and concern for their continued well-being (Briseño Guerrero 1994). In other words, ownership means that the human community has a moral responsibility to maintain the land, its resources, and society in good condition. Hence, despite the apparent clear-cut borders between Huastec families' lands, members of one family have the right to ask another family to borrow land or harvest forest products to meet their subsistence needs. This system provides a social safety net for the poorer members of the community.

Disputes over land borders and harvest rights are common and can disrupt congenial relationships between families within a community. Accusations of witchcraft are made against those who attempt to appropriate resources for private gain. A belief in witchcraft provides a strong social sanction against actions that go against conservative use of resources and a commitment to the corporate group. Traditional curers reinforce socially appropriate behavior during their interactions with patients, looking for causes of the illness in the patient's or others' misuse of resources. Here the importance of the relationship between the divine powers and the land comes into play, as well as the relationship between people. Clearing a private forest along a community watershed, for example, would result in strong pressure (including accusations of witchcraft) against the family, as well as in interpretations by the curer as causing illness or misfortune because the person went against religious sanctions about protecting water (ecologically unwise). Hence, ecologically sound land use is supported by cultural values and belief in the ethical commitments made between people and spiritual powers when people make land use decisions. The tenurial shell created by the state supports the traditional belief structure, which in turn supports ecologically sustainable land use.

The effects of these moral commitments and beliefs are visible in the stark contrast between land use on either side of the border where indigenous ejidos/*comunidades* abut mestizo lands. The tenurial shell that reinforces community and cultural values is physically visible at the border. At the border, people tell stories of how their way of life and forests were threatened before the Revolution, and how they were unable to reclaim parts of their territory (now outside the border). They say that the Revolution was terrible, but they acknowledge that the Revolution saved their forests and their way of life. Without the ejido and *comunidad*, there would be no borders and no islands, only a sea of pasture.

Within the borders of their territories, both Huastec and Totonac apply a high level of knowledge about species and ecosystems (Alcorn 1984, 1989a; Barrera-Bassols, Medellín, and Espejel 1991; Toledo and Medellín-Morales 1986). Huastec use 679 plant species and specifically manage 349 of those species. Totonacs use and manage 355 species of plants and animals. Useful species are harvested from lands managed by risk-spreading strategies to make multiple use of available resources while maintaining the natural processes on which agricultural and forest-based systems rely.

The Huastec and Totonac agro-ecosystem is a fluid mosaic of various resource zones: permanent planted fields, periodically planted fields, fallows, dooryards, orchards, forests, and streams. People use and manage the natural ecosystem for human benefits—crops, wild plants, wild animals, and ecological services. Simply put, the two systems create a shifting mosaic of replicates of three standard pieces: forest patches, swidden *milpa* patches, and cash crop patches.

In this shifting mosaic, the *milpa* cycled fields are the most "mobile" and the managed forests the least mobile part of the shifting mosaic. Managed forests, especially along streams and on ridges and steep slopes, have never been cleared in living memory. Approximately 25 percent of an average Huastec community's land will be under forest, 50 percent in *milpa*-fallow cycled land, and 25 percent in sugarcane. In a typical Totonac community, 30 percent of the land was under forest, 36 percent under *milpa*, 10 percent under cash crops (aside from vanilla), and 23 percent was in pasture (Toledo, Ortiz, and Medellín-Morales 1994). The Huastec and Totonac system is generally similar to that of other Mesoamerican *milpa* agriculturalists (Alcorn 1990). *Milpa* is the Mesoamerican version of integral swidden agriculture (Warner 1991) applied in most tropical areas of the world. *Milpa* is a central institution from which other institutions draw strength. From a property rights point of view, *milpa* is an institution which reinforces reciprocity and community-based control of natural resources. Making *milpa* requires reciprocal labor exchange and decisions made by following a specific regime associated with rituals and culturally appropriate rules of proper behavior. One analyst has argued that the *milpa* system requires corporate ownership (Rees 1974).

Farmers manage their forest patches through selective removal of unwanted individuals and selective encouragement of desirable species. In many cases, the high-value crops coffee (Huastec) or cacao (Totonac) are planted in the understory and then allowed to reproduce themselves naturally there where they are treated like any other useful wild species. These systems have been detailed extensively elsewhere (Alcorn 1981, 1983; Medellín-Morales 1986).

An economic assessment of costs and benefits of operating a typical Huastec community's lands yielded a net benefit of cash and subsistence goods valued at US$598 per hectare per year (Alcorn 1989b). This number compares favorably with the benefits generated by other systems (for example, Godoy, Lubowski, and Markandaya 1993). Despite the relatively high population density, approximately 25 percent of the area is still forested although it could have been cleared. People chose not to clear it. The reasons they give for their decision to maintain biologically diverse managed forests include (a) commercially valuable products; (b) direct access to products (firewood, fruits, medicine, construction materials, and other items having use values); (c) the option value of unknown products they may find useful in the future; (d) the superior quality of life offered by fresh breezes, shade, clean water, and clean air; (e) protection of the earth; and (f) ecological services, such as soil quality protection, prevention of erosion, and site improvement for swidden agriculture (Alcorn 1989b). Instead of clearing more forest, the *milpa* system was modified to use short fallow periods before all high forest was cleared, and people have chosen to increase cash crops and take outside jobs instead of increasing staple production by clearing more forest. This has enabled people to meet increasing needs by means other than clearing forest. In fact, increased dependence on cash from outside jobs is associated with increased area under forest.

Case Two: Subhumid Temperate Forest

Community-based systems in the subhumid temperate forest ecosystem (a zone that covers 33 million hectares and is occupied by 1.55 million indigenous people) are also adapting to changes. The case study covers two areas managed by Purépechan people (Tarascans) in the state of Michoacán. The first site is located in the Lake Pátzcuaro basin, which includes lake islands, shore, hillsides, mountains, and intermontane valleys. The second site is the community of San Juan Nuevo in pine-oak foreston the high plateau of western Michoacán. The pine-oak forests and the intervening grass and shrubland areas support the flora of an estimated 1,000 species. Archaeological research indicates human settlements in the area from approximately 3500 BP, and Spanish records indicate that the area supported a large population during the 1500s. Hence, these forests have also been disturbed for thousands of years, and local communities have adapted to a series of stresses and changes over time.

Purépechan communities and many of the mixed mestizo settlements around Lake Pátzcuaro retain their language and a strong Purépecha cultural heritage, including tenure systems, resource management systems, and social organization. All major basin settlements were in place and occupied by Purépechan people at the time of the Spanish Conquest around 1500. Purépechans recognize and name 400 plant species and 138 animal species. Two hundred twenty-four plant and mushroom species have multiple uses for food, medicine, and utilitarian values. The Purépechan economy is based on a combination of seed, tree, and vegetable agriculture, as well as hunting, fishing, gathering, cattle-raising, forest management, handicrafts (including weaving based on aquatic plants, wheat, and palms), bakeries, and textile weaving. Purépechans recognize fourteen different management systems and agricultural landscapes: three rainfed, one dryland, and six irrigated agricultural types; two silvicultural systems; and two home garden types. They use ten different types of fishing systems. Many of the products from these systems are sold in local markets.

In contrast to the Lake Pátzcuaro communities, San Juan Nuevo Parangaricutiro (population 10,000) has used its forest resources and organizational connections to acquire modern machinery for a vertically integrated forest products industry, including factories for moldings, parquet, furniture, packing crates, charcoal, and sawn wood for export markets (Alvarez Icaza 1993). Although forestry is the main activity at San Juan, families also rely on *milpa* fields, home gardens, gathering of forest products (firewood, resin, medicines, and foods, including mushrooms), and cattle raising. While nationally some 65 percent of forested ejidos and *comunidades* exploit their forests for commercial sales, San Juan Nuevo is among the few internationally recognized for its successful and profitable forest management. Since 1983, San Juan Nuevo's forestry enterprise has grown in both size and scope. In the last ten years, profits have increased 2,000 percent, and the personnel have increased from 100 to 1,000, with salaries well above the minimum wages for the region. Part of this administrative and economic success lies in the community decision to continue reinvesting all profits, rather than distribute them.

San Juan Nuevo illustrates a process of entrepreneurial efficiency and modernization within the traditional tenurial shell. Tenurial rights create a delicate balance between family rights, communal responsibility, and enterprise efficiency. Family rights to land and natural resources have been respected, since the exploitation of tracts of forests (for wood and resin extraction) by the communal enterprise affects portions of household parcels.

Purépechan communities, like the Huastec and Totonac, have communal ownership of their lands and resources, but individual households exercise ownership over their own agricultural lands. Community members may rent or mortgage their lands to other community members. Forest, pasture, and lake resources are considered community property with rules regulating their access and use. Different communities have managed their communal resources in different ways. In Pichataro, for example, 4,000 hectares of pine-oak forests have been divided evenly between eight subdivisions of the community, thereby giving each of the 559 households equal access to forest resources for resin, wood, firewood, and food. The lake is used by 700 fisherman from 21 settlements, 19 of which are Purépechan. The lake territory has been divided into sections to be exploited by each community. Each community, in turn, has divided the lake into fishing grounds and shore areas for each fisherman through collectively established rules. Shore areas are physically divided into territories by artificial channels lined by tules (reed plants).

In San Juan Nuevo, forests were divided into family patches for exploitation on an individual basis for resin extraction and small-scale woodworking shops. Until 1970, marketing was controlled by middlemen, and much of the forest eventually became degraded from overextraction. During the 1970s, however, the *comunidad* joined the Union of Forest Ejidos and Comunidades and worked for government authorization of community-based forest management and production. By 1981, the community's General Assembly approved the formation of a community enterprise that successfully competed with middlemen by offering a better price. Sale to the community mill requires sharing rights with the enterprise; the participants have entered into comanagement arrangements so that the community's forest has slowly come under stronger community control. Forest recovery has occurred because of the tenurial authority exerted by the community. The community as a whole moved to reduce individual rights in order to sustain the forest. It is unlikely that similar state-level action could have prevented clear-cutting through zoning or harvest regulations, given the poor record of state-level interventions.

The San Juan Nuevo Purépechans have developed a new local institution associated with the operation of the community's forestry enterprises and the forest comanagement rules linked to sustainable extraction for the enterprises. A Communal Council was established, which includes ten representatives from San Juan Nuevo's six subunits, the enterprise directors, property administrators, and a technical committee (Alvarez Icaza 1993). This group oversees and directs the community's projects, and serves as a forum for developing consensus. The *comunidad* has agreed to reinvest all profits into the enterprise, rather than distributing the profits.

As among the Huastec and Totonac, Purépechan culture supports values placed on reproduction of the community, conservative use of resources, protection of natural processes, economic equity among community members, consensus building, and collective resistance to intrusion by outsiders. Equitable distribution of the communities' resources among individual families prevents overuse by any one family, while communally shared values and institutions maintain resource use within acceptable bounds.

Discussion

Experiences from other areas of Mexico indicate that community-based tenure by itself is not a recipe for ecologically sustainable resource management.[9] Knowledge of and commitment to ecologically sustainable management regimes, strong organizations, and state implementation of supportive policies are required elements of the recipe. For example, newly founded "communal" ejidos of people resettled into tropical moist forest areas from other ecological zones during the 1960s and 1970s were encouraged by Mexican government policy to use capital-intensive inputs and heavy machinery for commercial agriculture (Ewell and Poleman 1980, DeWalt and Rees 1994). These ill-advised agricultural schemes failed and resulted in massive deforestation followed by unproductive cattle ranching. On the other hand, in some cases, spontaneous migrants into forests have attempted (with no government support) to

---

9. We are not claiming that the ejido and *comunidad* system, as it has been administered in the past, is a perfect system. It has, however, been proven to allow ecologically sustainable management in a subset of cases with shared characteristics described in this chapter. Much could be done to improve the economic performance of resource management under ejidos and *comunidades*, but assessments of options also need to consider the need for ecologically sustainable management for long-term maintenance of the natural resource assets.

apply the locally adapted, low-input agricultural systems found in long-established communities, and have successfully established new communities that recreated the land use patterns of the older communities (Ewell and Poleman 1980). Past policy support was sufficient to enable ecologically sustainable systems to persist, but support was insufficient to enable those systems to spread and prosper.

New Challenges to Shell Integrity and Function

Challenges to tenurial shell integrity affect ecological sustainability. Over the past several thousand years, community-based management of forest ecosystems has faced a variety of stresses, from colonization, massive depopulation, incorporation of tribute, and then from cash cropping, forced concentration of populations, introduction of foreign crops and livestock, and loss of land rights. Yet the system has proven resilient under the protection of the state's authority; indigenous resource management systems continued to adapt to their changing context within the space provided by the protective shells of ejidos and *comunidades*. Today, however, there is a new threat to community-based management as the ejido shell is being altered.

In 1992, in preparation for the North American Free Trade Agreement (NAFTA), President Salinas revised Article 27 of the Constitution to change the tenurial shells of communities, and Congress passed enabling legislation in the form of the new Agrarian Law, using haunting echoes of the reasoning used during the Porfirian period when the government moved to eliminate the "unproductive" community-based landholdings (Briseño Guerrero 1994, p. 45) in order to make land available to politically powerful elites. Salinas' actions created sweeping changes in the rules regulating ejidos, although *comunidades* were technically exempted from these changes. Among the changes are the following: ejido members can now rent, sell, or mortgage their lands; ejido members no longer have to work the land to retain rights to it; and ejido members can enter into joint ventures with outside entrepreneurs to exploit their resources (DeWalt and Rees 1994). Although they offer opportunities for communities to gain much-needed capital

and marketing services, these recent changes also have great potential to undermine the community-based sector and expand the rights of private individual property to mine resources in ecologically fragile areas instead of supporting ecologically sustainable agricultural systems (Toledo 1995). In effect, the new Agrarian Law tacitly recognizes the existing illegal large holdings (*latifundios*) of politically powerful ranchers (supporting the nationally infamous political bosses—*caciques*—of the Huasteca and other primarily indigenous areas) (Briseño Guerrero 1994) and supports expansion of an inefficient and ecologically damaging land use.

These changes may weaken the recent strength shown by communities that are using traditional communal values to compete in the marketplace. New peasant movements during the past decade have been using collective organization based on traditional values of reciprocity, communal property, and voluntary labor to create business corporations that provide quality products at competitive prices in the open market, despite resistance from local elites (Briseño Guerrero 1994; Nigh 1995).

Given the agriculturally marginal nature of the ejido lands, capital-intensive agriculture is unlikely to result in ecologically sustainable uses. Ecological analysis did not accompany the economic analysis that led to reform of the Agrarian Law. Furthermore, economic analyses did not consider recent studies that have demonstrated that many of the small-scale, labor-intensive systems operated by peasants achieve higher yields than large-scale agriculture in the same areas (Gómez-Pompa and others 1993; Toledo 1993).

It is too early to evaluate the impact of these changes on community-based resource management practices, but negative ecological and social impacts can be predicted. Economically marginal people will be dispossessed of secure access to resources, and long-term local ecological costs will be ignored in favor of short-term gains for outsiders. One can expect an expansion of the situation on the borders of the Lacandon Forest today where big ranches expand and drive landless poor to clear forest in nature reserves. Outside entrepreneurs are putting pressure on communities to cut their forests for immediate sale, or replace standing forests with eucalyptus plantations. It will be difficult for politically weak communities and weak community members to resist pressure from politically powerful people who seek personal gain from such deals.

Political movements in rural Mexico are seeking a route that includes control of productive processes, including marketing, and ecologically sustainable use of their natural resources as a means to maintain their social and ecological systems (for example, Bray 1991, 1992, 1995; Declaración del Foro Nacional sobre el Sector Social Forestal 1992; Merino 1992). A shell of community-based property rights is critical for the ecological and socioeconomic success of this fledgling strategy. Without strong organizations to protect communities' rights and develop supportive policies under NAFTA reforms, the Mexican experiment with community-based tenurial shells will be terminated, and an opportunity for ecologically sustainable development will be lost.

Conclusions and Policy Implications

Conclusions

Tenurial shells, in and of themselves, do not guarantee ecologically sustainable development. Tenurial shells can shelter unsustainable use, as well as promote sustainable management. For example, shells offered private corporations in order to attact foreign investment often result in unsustainable use of resources. Community-based tenurial shells, however, are a necessary condition for ecological sustainability in certain situations. Specifically, tenurial shells offer a way to protect existing indigenous and other traditional community-based resource management systems in biologically diverse and ecologically fragile areas. The state's interface with local shells, and the community-based legitimacy of the shell are critical elements determining the shell's contribution to ecological sustainability. In addition, many communities depend on outside jobs because they are unable to derive sufficient income from their lands. Rural populations continue to grow and many young people migrate to cities to seek work. Policies that support economic growth in urban areas are also necessary to support sustainable resource use by communities, because they support the absorption of excess labor. Without more nonfarm employment opportunities, people

will eventually be driven to nonsustainable resource use in order to survive (Thiesenhusen 1991), despite their reluctance to mine their resources.

In sum, despite the erosion, invasion, and disruption of old tenurial shells, the remnants that are in place today are associated with natural resource management systems that are much more ecologically sustainable than land use patterns outside these shells. Not all community-based tenurial shells contain ecologically sustainable systems, although ecologically sustainable systems are most frequently found inside shells. While the results of our analysis can be used to support proposals to engineer new community-based shells where none exist, success in such an endeavor is less likely than success through recognition and bolstering of existing shells. Furthermore, because most of the remaining bastions of natural areas overlap with remnant shells of customary tenure systems, salvaging those shells will contribute more to the long-term global ecological sustainability than will struggles to reconstitute shells in degraded areas bereft of biodiversity. If one accepts that biodiversity represents invaluable future options for development, then the value of conserving these shells should be obvious. Local, dynamic subsystems are essential for sustainability of the larger global system. Actions taken to sustain these local shells are actions taken to sustain earth's larger ecological and economic systems for future generations.

Policy Recommendations

1. Priority should be given to supporting community-based tenure in areas rich in biodiversity and forests.[10] Steps for such a program include (a) locating existing community-based tenurial shells that shelter locally adapted resource management systems; (b) assessing

---

10. Common property forest management systems are widespread globally (Messerschmidt 1993). Other countries also offer examples of successful corporate tenure systems and other tenurial options (for example, Davis and Wali 1993; Fox 1993; Herlihy 1990), and the basic elements of strategies for supporting community-based forest management have been offered from experiences in many countries (Legal Rights Center and Natural Resources Center 1994; Lynch and Talbott 1995; Poole 1995).

how such shells can be best supported within the existing state framework; (c) assessing how current policies are hurting these systems; and (d) enacting supportive policies, including those that support generation of off-farm jobs. Lynch and Talbot (1995) offer some basic, practical legal steps toward supporting community-based tenurial shells.

2. Assessments of options for group titling for indigenous peoples and other long-established communities should be done before a single strategy of individual titling is pursued. Around the world, multilateral development banks are encouraging governments to enact private titling programs that focus on individual titles.[11] Too often private titling enables powerful individuals to capture titles and then mine forests and other natural resources for short-term private gains—resulting in negative, long-term ecological, social and economic costs. In the Mexican case, this is an immediate concern as a new national individual titling program is being developed (DeWalt and Rees 1994; Goldring 1995).

3. Under the assumption that the reinforcement of community-based systems will promote and facilitate sustainable management of natural resources, policies should be implemented in order to (a) reinforce community-based organizations, local and regional self-reliance; (b) create economic incentives derived from ecological economics; (c) provide social recognition to the efforts of community-based units; (d) provide incentives for commercialization of organic products (including direct links with urban "green" markets), (e) promulgate programs for appropriate technical assistance and loans to support forest management by indigenous peoples in forested areas and assist them with market research for potential community-based ventures, and (f) vigorously prosecute those who trespass on and mine communities' forests. The World Bank and the Government of Mexico's current collaborative Resource Conservation and Forest Sector Review has produced similar policy recommendations specifically for Mexico.

4. National and global environmental laws and donors' internal regulations should recognize the force of traditional community-based rules that govern the use of natural resources and should seek to articulate with them as appropriate. Environmental assessments for development projects should require that development agents meet the communities' rules for forest, land, and water use.

5. Opportunities to support existing, corporate tenurial structures should be sought in sectoral policy reform. For example, the recent creation of a new Mexican Ministry of Environment, Natural Resources and Fisheries, and the opportunity for senior policy dialogue at cross-sectoral levels within the context of the Environmental Action plan offer unique opportunities to initiate a set of policies directed to convert natural resources management to a more ecologically sustainable pattern. The small-scale, community-based sector is positioned to play a central role in both ecologically sound rural production and biodiversity conservation. In situations where agricultural conditions are marginal, it is unrealistic to apply the agro-industrial model of rural development based on private individual control of medium- and large-scale properties because returns from marginal lands increase under management by smallholders. Instead, a strategy inspired by both indigenous and modern traditions should be applied (Toledo 1992b, 1994a). A revised agrarian law is needed to reverse the recent trend away from ecologically sustainable resource management. It should be inspired by the principles of ecological theory and the goals of sustainable development, and it should be developed with the broad participation of producers, scientists, conservationists, nongovernmental organizations (NGOs), and government sectors.

Bibliography

Aguilar-Robledo, M. 1994. "Reses y ecosistemas: Notas para una evaluación del impacto ambiental de la ganadería bovina en la Huasteca Potosina." *Cuadrante* 11/12:134–61.

Alcorn, J. B. 1981. "Huastec Noncrop Resource Management: Implications for Prehistoric Rainforest Management." *Human Ecology* 9:395–417.

---

11. In Mexico, for example, the World Bank has been considering post-NAFTA individual titling, and part of that project preparation work is considering options for an "ejido and communal land regularization and titling project."

————. 1983. "El te'lom huasteco: Presente, pasado, y futuro de un sistema de silvicultura indígena." *Biótica* 8:315–31.

————. 1984. *Huastec Mayan Ethnobotany.* Austin, Texas: University of Texas Press.

————. 1989a. "Process as Resource: The Traditional Agricultural Ideology of Bora and Huastec Resource Management and Its Implications for Research." In D. A. Posey and W. Balée (eds.), *Resource Management in Amazonia: Indigenous and Folk Strategies.* Bronx: New York Botanical Garden, pp. 63–77.

————. 1989b. "An Economic Analysis of Huastec Mayan Forest Management." In J. O. Browder (ed.), *Fragile Lands of Latin America: Strategies for Sustainable Development.* Boulder: Westview Press, pp. 182–203.

————. 1990. "Indigenous Agroforestry Systems in the Latin American Tropics." In M. A. Altieri and S. B. Hecht (eds.), *Agroecology and Small Farm Development.* Boca Raton, Florida: CRC Press, pp. 203–220.

————. 1995. "Economic Botany, Conservation, and Development: What's the Connection?" *Annals of the Missouri Botanical Garden* 82.

————. and A. Molnar. 1995. "Deforestation and Human-Forest Relationships: What Can We Learn from India?" In L. Sponsel, T. Headland, and R. Bailey (eds.), *Tropical Deforestation: The Human Dimension.* New York: Columbia University Press.

Alvarez Icaza, P. 1993. "Forestry as Social Enterprise." *Cultural Survival Quarterly,* Spring 1993:45–47.

Barrera-Bassols, N., S. Medellín, and B. Ortiz Espejel. 1991. "Un reducto de la abundancia: El caso excepcional de la milpa en Plan de Hidalgo, Veracruz. In C. Hewitt de Alcántara (ed.), *Reestructuración Económica y Subsistencia Rural.* United Nations Research Institute for Social Development (UNRISD), Centro Tepoztlán, and El Colegio de México, Mexico City, pp. 163–82.

Barthas, B. 1994. "Sistemas de producción y conflictos agrarios en la Huasteca Potosina (1870–1910)." *Cuadrante* 11/12:30–42.

Berkes, Fikret, D. Feeny, B. J. McCay, and J. M. Acheson. 1989. "The Benefits of the Commons." *Nature* 340:91–93.

Bray, D. 1991. "The Forests of Mexico: Moving from Concessions to Communities." *Grassroots Development* 15(3):16–17.

Bray, D. 1992. "La lucha por el bosque: Conservación y desarrollo en la Sierra Juárez." *El Cotidiano* 48 (June):21–27.

Bray, D. 1995. "Peasant Organizations and 'the Permanent Reconstruction of Nature': Grassroots Sustainable Development in Rural Mexico." *Journal for Environment and Development.*

Briseño Guerrero, J. 1994. "Tapabocas dos: El control del acceso a la tierra comunal ante el 'nuevo' Artículo 27 constitucional." *Cuadrante* 11/12:43–52.

Bromley, David, and Michael Cernea. 1989. "The Management of Common Property Resources: Some Conceptual and Operational Fallacies." Discussion Paper no. 57. Washington, DC.: World Bank.

Brush, S. B., and M. R. Bellon. 1994. "Keepers of Maize in Chiapas, Mexico." *Economic Botany* 48:196–209.

Cortez Ruiz, C. 1992. "El sector forestal mexicano ante el TLC [NAFTA]." *El Cotidiano* 48 (June):79–85.

Crocombe, R. 1971. "An Approach to the Analysis of Land Tenure Systems." In R. Crocombe (ed.), *Land Tenure in the Pacific.* Melbourne: Oxford University Press, pp. 1–17.

Davis, S. H., and A. Wali. 1993. "Indigenous Territories and Tropical Forest Management in Latin America." Policy Research Working Paper, WPS 1100. Washington D.C.: World Bank.

Declaración del foro nacional sobre el sector social forestal. 1992. *El Cotidiano* 48 (June):49–52.

DeWalt, B. R., and M. W. Rees. 1994. *The End of Agrarian Reform in Mexico: Past Lessons, Future Prospects.* San Diego: Center for U.S.-Mexican Studies, University of California at San Diego.

Ewell, P. T., and T. T. Poleman. 1980. *Uxpanapa: Agricultural Development in the Mexican Tropics.* New York: Pergamon Press.

Fox, J. (ed.). 1993. "Legal Frameworks in Forest Management in Asia." Occasional Papers, Program on Environment, Paper no. 16. Honolulu: East-West Center.

Godoy, R. A., R. Lubowski, and A. Markandaya. 1993. "A Method for the Economic Valuation of Non-timber Forest Products." *Economic Botany* 47(3):220–33.

Goldring, L. 1995. "State Sponsored Land Certification and Titling Programs and Changing State-Producer Relations: Ejido Reform in Mexico." *Common Property Resources Digest* 33:2–5.

Gómez-Pompa, A., and A. Kaus. 1990. "Traditional Management of Tropical Forests in Mexico." In A. B. Anderson (ed.), *Alternatives to Deforestation*. New York: Columbia University Press, pp. 45–64.

Gómez-Pompa, A., A. Kaus, J. Jiménez-Osornio, D. Bainbridge, and V. M. Rorive. 1993. "Mexico." In National Research Council, *Sustainable Agriculture and the Environment in the Humid Tropics*. Washington D.C.: National Academy Press, pp. 483–547.

Herlihy, P. 1990. "Panama's Quiet Revolution: Comarca Homelands and Indian Rights." *Cultural Survival Quarterly* 13(3):17–24.

Legal Rights and Natural Resources Center/Kasama sa Kalikasan. 1994. "Baguio Declaration." NGO Policy Workshop on Strategies for Effectively Promoting Community-Based Management of Tropical Forest Resources. Legal Rights and Natural Resources Center (LRC)/Kasama sa Kalikasan (KSK), Manila.

Lynch, O. J., and J. B. Alcorn. 1994. "Tenurial Rights and Community-Based Conservation." In D. Western, M. Wright, and S. Strum (eds.), *Natural Connections: Community-Based Conservation*. Washington, D.C.: Island Press, pp. 373–92.

Lynch, O. J., and K. Talbott. 1995. *Balancing Acts: Community-Based Forest Management and National Law in Asia and the Pacific*. Washington, D.C.: World Resources Institute.

Medellín-Morales, S. G. 1986. *Uso y Manejo de las Especies Vegetales Comestibles, Medicinales, para Construcción y Combustibles en una Comunidad Totonaca de la Costa (Plan de Hidalgo, Papantla, Veracruz, México)*. Xalapa, Veracruz, Mexico: Programa Formación de Recursos Humanos, INIREB.

Merino, L. 1992. "La experiencia de la Organización Forestal de la Zona Maya." *El Cotidiano* 48 (June):40–43.

Messerschmidt, D. A. (ed.). 1993. *Common Forest Resource Management: Annotated Bibliography of Asia, Africa, and Latin America*. Rome: Food and Agriculture Organization of the United Nations (FAO).

Molnar, A. 1995. Personal communication.

Mora López, J. L., and S. Medellín-Morales. 1992. "Los núcleos campesinos de la Reserva de la Biosfera 'El Cielo': Aliados en la conservación?" *BIOTAM* 4(2):13–40.

Nahmad, S., A. González, and M. A. Vásquez. 1994. *Medio Ambiente y Tecnologías Indígenas en el Sur del Oaxaca*. Mexico City: Centro de Ecología y Desarrollo.

National Census. 1990. *Estados Unidos Mexicanos, Resumen General XI Censo General de Poblacioón y Vivienda*. Mexico City: Instituto Nacional de Estadística, Geografía e Informática.

Nigh, R. 1995. "Associative Corporations, Organic Agriculture and Peasant Strategies in Post-Modern Mexico." *American Anthropologist* (in press).

Oldfield, M. L., and J. B. Alcorn. 1987. "Conservation of Traditional Agro-Ecosystems." *BioScience* 37:199–208.

Ostrom, Elinor. 1990. *Governing the Commons: The Evolution of Institutions for Collective Action*. New York: Cambridge University Press.

Ostrom, E., J. Walker, and Roy Gardner. 1992. "Covenants with and without a Sword: Self-Governance Is Possible." *American Political Science Review* 86:404–17.

Poole, P. 1995. "Indigenous Peoples, Mapping and Biodiversity Conservation: A Survey of Current Activities." Biodiversity Support Program (BSP) Peoples and Forests Discussion Paper Series, no. 1. BSP, World Wildlife Fund, Washington, D.C.

Porter, D., B. Allen, and G. Thompson. 1991. *Development in Practice: Paved With Good Intentions*. London: Routledge.

Powelson, J. P., and R. Stock. 1987. *The Peasant Betrayed: Agriculture and Land Reform in the Third World*. Boston: Lincoln Institute of Land Policy, Oelgeschlager, Gunn and Hain.

Ramamoorthy, T. P., R. Bye, A. Lot, and J. Fa (eds.). 1993. *Biological Diversity of Mexico: Origins and Distribution*. New York: Oxford University Press.

Rees, M. J. 1974. "Law, Land and Religion: an Analysis of Milpa Ownership." *Human Mosaic* 7:21–30.

Reyes Osorio, S., R. Stavenhagen, S. Eckstein, and J. Ballesteros. 1974. *Estructura Agraria y Desarrollo Agrícola en México.* Mexico City: Fondo de Cultura Económica.

Rzedowski, R. 1978. *Vegetación de México.* Mexico City: Editorial Limusa.

Sanderson, S. R. W. 1984. *Land Reform in Mexico: 1910–1980.* New York: Academic Press.

Sandoval, J. R. 1994. "Paraíso ascoliado." *Revista Epoca* no. 170 (September 5):4–11.

Sheridan, T. E. 1988. *Where the Dove Calls: The Political Ecology of a Peasant Corporate Community in Northwestern Mexico.* Tucson: University of Arizona Press.

Stresser-Péan, G. 1967. Problemes agraires de la Huasteca ou région de Tampico (Mexique). In *Les Problemes Agraires des Amériques Latines.* Colloques Internationaux de Centre Nacional de la Recherche Scientifique, Paris, pp. 201–214.

Tapia Centeno, C. 1960. "Paradigma Apologético (1725)." In R. Aguinaga y Montejano, *Notas de Bibliografía Linguistica Huasteca* 6, pp. 50–103.

Thiesenhusen, W. C. 1991. "Implications of the Rural Land Tenure System for the Environmental Debate: Three Scenarios." *The Journal of Developing Areas* 26:1–24.

Toledo, V. M. 1992a. "Biodiversidad y campesinado: La modernización en conflicto." *La Jornada del Campo* (November 10):1–3.

———. 1992b. "Campesinos, modernización rural y ecología política: Una mirada al caso de México." In J. A. González Alcantud and M. Gonzalez de Molina (eds.), *La Tierra: Mitos, Ritos y Realidades.* Granada, Spain: Anthropos, pp. 351–65.

———. 1993. "Ecología y nueva ley agraria en México: Preludio y fuga de una modernización obsoleta." In J. L. Calva (ed.), *Alternativas para el Campo Mexicano, Tomo II.* Mexico City: Universidad Nacional Autónoma de México (UNAM), pp. 31–43.

———. 1994a. *La Ecología, Chiapas y el Artículo 27.* Mexico City: Ediciones Quinto Sol.

———. 1994b. "Biodiversity and Cultural Diversity in Mexico." *Different Drummer* (summer):16–19.

———. 1995. "La ley agraria: Un obstáculo para la paz y el desarrollo sustentable." *La Jornada del Campo* (March 7).

Toledo, V. M., A. I. Batis, R. Becerra, E. Martínez, and C. H. Ramos. 1995a. "La selva útil: Etnobotánica cuantitativa de los grupos indígenas del trópica húmedo de México." *Interciencia* (in press).

Toledo, V. M., and N. Barrera-Bassols. 1984. *Ecología y Desarrollo Rural en Pátzcuaro.* Instituto de Biología, Universidad Nacional Autónoma de México, Mexico City.

Toledo, V. M., J. Carabias, C. Mapes, and C. Toledo. 1985. *Ecología y Autosuficiencia Alimentaria.* Mexico City: Siglo Veintiuno Editores.

Toledo, V. M., B. Ortiz, L. Cortés, P. Moguel, and M. J. Ordoñez. 1995b. "The Indigenous Management of Tropical Rain Forests in Mexico: Ecological and Economic Implications." *Agroforestry Systems* (in press).

Toledo, V. M., B. Ortiz, and S. Medellin-Morales. 1994. "Biodiversity Islands in a Sea of Pastureland: Indigenous Resource Management in the Humid Tropics of Mexico." *Etnoecológica* 3:37–50.

Vetancourt, A. de. 1689. *Teatro Mexicano.* Mexico. 4 a. p., trat. 30, c. I, pp. 91–92.

Warner, K. 1991. *Shifting Cultivators: Local Technical Knowledge and Natural Resource Management in the Humid Tropics.* Rome: Food and Agriculture Organization of the United Nations (FAO).

Wilken, G. 1987. *Good Farmers: Traditional Agricultural Resource Management in Mexico and Central America.* Berkeley: University of California Press.

World Bank. 1990. *Poverty: World Development Report, 1990.* Washington, D.C.: Oxford University Press.

Zizumbo Villarreal, D., and P. Colunga García-Marín. 1982. *Los Huaves: La Apropiación de los Recursos Naturales.* Universidad Autónoma Chapingo, Departamento de Sociología Rural, Chapingo, Mexico.

12

Integrating Ecological and Socioeconomic Feedbacks for Sustainable Fisheries

Monica Hammer

Abstract

THIS CASE STUDY FOCUSES ON THE LINKS between ecological and social systems in Swedish fisheries, especially in the Baltic Sea. By defining privileges and duties in the use of natural resources, property rights systems act as a coordinating mechanism between humans and the natural environment. From an ecosystem perspective, sustainability in fisheries lies in balancing the use and impacts of fisheries on the resilience of the marine ecosystem and so on the ability of the ecosystem to continue to provide valued fish resources and ecological services. Thus, an important aspect of future fisheries is the degree to which fisheries management can build property rights systems that reflect the ecological and socioeconomic context and sustain or improve the resilience of the life-supporting ecosystem.

The Baltic Sea hosts a significant offshore commercial fishery, as well as different local fisheries acting in nested institutional settings and in different ecosystem environments. In this study, traditional and current management systems are discussed in terms of selected indicators of resilience, especially spatial and temporal diversity. The current dominating management system, which blocks out ecosystem feedback, has led to unsustainable resource use. The importance of learning how potential new principles derived from local studies can be used to redirect resource use systems towards generating a sustainable flow of ecological services is discussed in the context of fisheries.

✧

Sweden's development in fisheries in recent decades has followed that of many other western countries, resulting in overexploitation problems and overcapitalization of the fishing industry. The proximate causes, such as overexploitation by fisheries and destruction of habitat due to environmental degradation, are widely documented. It is now also becoming increasingly recognized that successful strategies for curbing unsustainable resource use patterns in fisheries need to encompass a broader ecosystem approach to fisheries as well as address the underlying causes in the economic system. From an ecosystem perspective, sustainability in fisheries lies in balancing the use and impacts of fisheries on the resilience of the marine ecosystem and thus on the ability of the ecosystem to continue to provide valued fish resources and ecological services.

By defining privileges and duties in the use of natural resources, property rights systems act as a coordinating mechanism and a structuring factor between humans and the natural environment. Thus, an important aspect of future fisheries is the degree to which fisheries management can build property rights systems that reflect the ecological and socioeconomic context and sustain or improve the resilience of the life-supporting ecosystem. A growing body of literature points to numerous examples in various regions of the world where local communities have independently developed dynamic, self-regulating patterns for a sustainable use of a resource held as a common property that they depend on. This capacity of self-regulation in the community builds on a capability to adapt to the natural resource variabilities and to construct and enforce rules that restrict the behavior of the individual to the benefit of the community (Berkes 1989; Dyer and McGoodwin 1994; McCay and Acheson 1987; Ostrom 1990).

There is, however, still little understanding of how such traditional knowledge of ecological and social systems have been translated into resource use systems that promote sustainable use of biological resources and ecosystem resilience. The loss of this knowledge in the transformation of local systems has been attributed to a number of factors, including commercialization, population growth, breakdown of traditional land, and marine tenure systems (Berkes et al., in press). The failure of the specialization-focused western management systems in Sweden as well as in other countries is now redirecting the focus towards smaller-scale coastal fishing practices. There are two important questions to be answered in restoring sustainable resource use in fisheries: (a) what can we learn from traditional systems? and (b) what is inherent in the world view of today's fishers that is not manifested as a result of institutional incentives?

In this chapter, examples of traditional and current knowledge, world views and fisheries management systems in Swedish fisheries, especially in the Baltic Sea, are described—in particular with respect to adaptiveness and understanding of the ecosystem. How these institutions and practices have evolved and how they have been impacted by a number of other aspects of the socioeconomic/political system are also discussed.

Resource Rights and Management in Swedish Marine Fisheries

Sweden has a long coast line with large archipelago areas, and fishing is, by tradition, an important part of the livelihood in the coastal zones (Figure 12–1). Fisheries have been managed by a combination of local rules, customs, and written law, and Sweden obtained its first general Fisheries Law in 1766 (Anon. 1992a). Fishing rights are dependent on whether the fishing takes place in private or common waters. One important feature in Sweden's history of fishing rights was that on common waters, fisheries were declared free for all Swedish citizens in the 1766 Fisheries Law. In private waters, there is always a fishing right which is tied to land ownership. Traditionally, in the nineteenth Century, coastal and archipelago fisheries were highly integrated with agriculture in Sweden as well as in many other countries in the Baltic and North Atlantic regions (Granlund 1956; Löfgren 1977).

Since the sea represented a common property resource, many of the landless established themselves as small-scale fishers and combined their coastal fishing with several other subsistence activities. Examples from the Bua fishing community in the district of Halland on the Swedish west coast show that a majority of the landless households had to make a living fishing in the periphery of the agrarian community of landowning peasants and settled on the barren common land close to the sea (Löfgren 1977).

The fishers also had to lease fishing rights from the landowning farmers. For example, in the Skeppsmalen fishing community in the Västernorrland district in the northern parts of the Baltic coast, the fishing rights (or formally, access to the port property) were divided into shares ("halvnot"). The fishers collectively leased these fishing rights from the landowning farmers via a port council, which was then leased to the fishers. In addition to these rights, special lots for fishing with fixed gear were divided by auction or by lot to the fishers one fishing season at a time (Scotte 1981).

With the development of the industrialized fisheries in the twentieth Century, the integration between fisheries and agriculture diminished. One example described by Arén (1989) is the Koster Islands in the Bohuslän district archipelago on the Swedish west coast, where agriculture constituted the basis for human settlements. The relatively poor soils contributed to making fisheries an important subsidiary to agriculture, and a community of fishing farmers had existed on the islands since at least the fourteenth Century. The basic catch species was herring, which also periodically appeared in the nearshore waters in large abundances. Due primarily to these "herring periods" (the two last were 1747–1808 and 1882–1920), the population on the Koster Islands increased five times between the years 1800 and 1900. Farming,

however, could not sustain this growing population, and an occupational group of commercial fishers developed. One prerequisiste for this development was the open access conditions in offshore waters. The abandonment of the fishing-farming culture on the Koster Islands was intensified after World War II primarily for two reasons. The first was the Swedish agricultural policy, where the government actively supported the creation of large production units by controlling land sales. However, on the Koster Islands, the soil was considered to be too poor for profitable farming, and the land was split and sold more or less freely; as a result, summer tourists started to acquire land on the islands. This policy contributed to the disappearance of the type of small-scale subsidiary farms that had existed on the Koster Islands in one form or another for the last 600 years. The second reason was the capitalization of fisheries, where the development of larger, more technically advanced fishing vessels necessitated fishing year-round, mainly in order to cover costs for loans (Arén 1989).

By tradition, there are differences between the Baltic coast fisheries and those of the west coast. Sweden's fisheries along the Baltic coast are less industrialized and have a larger proportion of the coastal and part-time fishers (over 80 percent in 1990). However, in the last two decades, Sweden's fisheries have shifted their geographical focus from the western sea areas and the North Sea towards the Baltic Sea. In 1978, the Baltic Sea became essentially fully divided among, at that time, seven coastal states into fishing zones. The littoral states agreed to consider Baltic fish stocks as common property, to be managed jointly. Fisheries are most intense in the southern parts of the Baltic Sea, which have more abundant fish stocks. Sweden, with its long coastline in the Baltic Sea, gained the rights to 40 percent of the sea area and harvests around 10 percent of the total Baltic Sea catches.

The Swedish commercial fishing fleet in the Baltic Sea consists of boats of varying capacity and size, harvesting in total 100,000–150,000 tons of fish per year, which corresponds to some 50 percent of Sweden's total catches. However, only about 25 percent (1991) is landed on the Swedish Baltic coast, reflecting the increased activity of west coast-based vessels in the Baltic Sea. In contrast to the offshore fisheries on the Swedish west coast, there is little tradition of distant water fishing among the Baltic coast fishers, and most of them remain within the Baltic Sea.

In the Baltic Sea, the fisheries' policy on the international level has in practice been close to laissez faire, and fishing mortality rates have been allowed to increase with minimal intervention from management bodies (Hildén 1992), creating a "tragedy of the commons" situation (Hardin 1968). The recent development of the Baltic fisheries, especially concerning cod and salmon, points to severe management problems, with overcapitalized fleets and overexploited fish stocks close to the point of extinction.

Figure 12–2 depicts some of the major factors in Sweden's development of modern fisheries during industrialization. Important factors driving the development in Sweden's fisheries could be summarized as a combination of changes within and outside fisheries where the main driving forces for development have been initiated outside fisheries, postponing ecosystem signals of overexploitation until the situation became very severe.

In light of the difficulties of managing fish stocks in the Baltic Sea, new interest is taken in coastal fisheries. One important question is what features of traditional fisheries and institutional constructions would be useful in reemerging fisheries systems.

Ecosystem Dynamics and Local Knowledge

Even though humans aim for stability, both changes and stability occur in natural systems, and pulsing is a characteristic of many ecosystems. Pulsing is established by basic processes of production and respiration, or consumption, in natural ecosystems. Holling (1986) has described this world of pulses as four sequential phases: exploitation (a buildup using released resources), conservation (increasing complexity and size), creative destruction (for example, fire storms and pests), resulting in release of basic material used in reorganization, which prepares for the next round of pulses.

The pattern of exploitation of natural resources is determined and modified by cultural traditions, an underlying view of nature, state of knowledge, and institutions. Western fisheries management, in large part built on a frontier conception of nature as inexhaustible, has commonly acted as if the ecosystem supporting fish production existed in a constant conservation phase with no functioning, built-in mechanisms for responding to feedback from the ecosystem. For a resource use to be sustainable, there should be feedback between the regime, the resource user, and the ecological system supporting the resource exploited. When this stabilizing feedback is absent, one is left with a runaway positive feedback loop, and the integrated social-natural system cannot be sustainable. The dynamics of the supporting ecosystem, such as the Baltic Sea, provide the platform from which a sustainable resource use pattern can be built.

Spatial and Temporal Variability in the Baltic Sea Ecosystem

The Baltic Sea is the world's largest brackish sea, with a low number of species which individually, however, exist in great numbers. In a low-diversity system like the Baltic Sea, focus on the ecosystem level is particularly important. Its semi-enclosed conditions and low salinity make it difficult for marine species to enter the Baltic from the North Sea and establish sustainable populations. Because there are few species that can fill the functional niche of a key species like the Baltic cod, large, indirect changes can be expected in lower trophic levels, such as increased algal blooms, because of less predation by zooplankton effectively consumed by expanding stocks of sprat and herring as a result of depleted cod stocks.

The total life-support system and the life-support area differ in size and quantity for the different species of fish. The dependence of fish on both offshore and coastal areas for life support, resulting in annual migrations between the two, is a world phenomenon. Fish migration and reproduction are considered to be triggered by the pulsing behavior of the support system due to the seasonal variations in light, temperature, and water quality, a pattern which is clearly exemplified by the two most important commercial fish species in the Baltic Sea, cod and herring (Zijlstra 1988).

The Baltic cod perform annual migrations between the coastal and offshore areas. The major spawning takes place in March through April in the Bornholm deep in the southwestern part of the Baltic Sea. The larvae, hatched in spring at deeper water layers, spend their first months offshore, feeding on zooplankton before becoming bottom-living in shallow areas (Aro 1988). In contrast, the adult spring spawning herring feed largely in the offshore during summer, utilizing the zooplankton maximum in July. When plankton becomes scarce in late autumn, the herring switches to opossum shrimps congregating near the bottom. Towards the end of the year, they stop feeding almost completely and form a few large schools in the archipelago, where they remain until the spawning in spring (Aneer, Lindquist, and Westin 1978; Smetacek 1984). The wild spawning results in large bottom areas covered with a layer of roe. The geographically wide spreading of the herring roe probably ensures optimal hatching conditions and sufficient food for the larvae at least somewhere in the large, patchy environment. This is essential for the young herring larvae that spend their first month in shallow waters before migrating further out from the coast.

Spatial and Temporal Variability in Fisheries

A typical feature of the traditional coastal fisheries is the marked time periodicity. The yearly cycle combining fishing and farming was possible thanks to the large variability in harvesting methods and fishing periods. The household rather than the individual made up the primary economic unit and determined how time and resources should be divided between the diverse set of occupations and members of the family (Löfgren 1977).

This natural variation is illustrated in the interchanges between agriculture and fishing in the summer season on Hasslö Island in the southwestern Baltic Sea: after midsummer, during the intensive hay harvest period, the herring fishery stopped, an event which was well coordinated with the migration of herring to offshore waters due to the rise in water temperature, where the herring were out of reach for the small coastal vessels (Rosén 1987). The harvest of different fish species is thus decided by their migration patterns and spawning periods. The fishing year on Hasslö Island in the nineteenth Century, with its large variety of species and gear, also reveals the profound ecological knowledge developed in the fishing community (Figure 12–3).

Since the smaller-scale fisheries are more constrained by weather conditions, especially in the northern Baltic with maybe six to seven months of ice cover, the combination of fishing during the summer season with land-based activities in the winter became a natural pattern. Many lived in the coastal fishing village only during the fishing season, which began in spring when the ice cover began to disappear and the fisher-farmers moved inland during the winter period (Scotte 1981).

In the Västernorrland district in the northern Baltic, herring provided the primary means of subsistence to the fishery. The fishing season began when the ice cover started to break up in spring. This early fishery was performed with herring nets with a larger mesh size, since the herring caught at this time of the year were mainly older age classes, relatively big in size. However, the harvests in this fishery were not very large. The fishery that yielded the larger catches was the beach seine fishery that started in May when the herring moved towards the shore in larger quantities. This fishery required calm weather, since fishing was performed in the shore area at dawn and dusk and the fishing teams were normally out during the whole night waiting for the herring shoals to approach. Their arrival was revealed by small bubbles on the sea surface. This fishery continued until around mid July. When the catches decreased, the local port council, jointly with the rest of the fishers, decided whether it was time to switch to the net fishery on the banks. This fishery continued until September or until the herring had migrated away from the banks. After that, a net fishery followed, with nets positioned on suitable depths, depending on weather and location. When the catches decreased in this fishery and the ice came back, it marked the end of the fishing year, and the fishers moved back inland over winter.

Also in the Västernorrland trawl fishery, the fishing season was divided into periods determined by the movement and abundance of the targeted fish and the variability in the ecosystem. A fishing year at Lörudden fishing community in Västernorrland district in the 1970s is an example (Scotte 1981). During the winter time, a bottom trawling within a relatively small area was performed. There was competition for the best spots, but once positioned, the trawler captains cooperated with continuous radio contact. Towards the end of the winter (March–April), the catches in the bottom trawling usually decreased, and the fishing teams gradually shifted to pelagic trawls. As these are substantially larger, they fish in pairs of two vessels. Unlike bottom trawling, the pelagic trawling is performed at night, since the herring are scattered close to the bottom during the day. When it gets dark, the herring gather in shoals and move towards the surface. As the summer season approaches, the nights become shorter, as does the period when herring can be caught with the pelagic trawl. However, this is partly compensated by the increased abundance of herring as it gathers in the archipelago areas to spawn. Eventually, the herring moves closer to the shore, where pelagic trawling is not possible (and prohibited to secure the coastal net fishery). During early summer, the trawling stops, to be taken up again later in the summer and continued until the water temperature starts to drop. The fishing year ends with another period of bottom trawling, but this time further out at sea on the banks (Scotte 1981).

Even though fishers in the Baltic are a heterogenous group in terms of fishing practices, they seem more homogenous in terms of concern for their resource base. In a survey among Baltic fishers, the results indicated that the majority of the respondents, irrespective of the type of fishing they engaged in, recognize that their resource base is limited and that fishing needs to be restricted. The Baltic fishers gave details of the type of environmental changes they had observed in the Baltic Sea. This is evidence of the knowledge capital of the ecosystem-supporting fish production that fishers accumulate by spending time at sea and which is transferred from generation to generation by kinship relations to other fishers (Hammer 1994a). This awareness of the long-term collective effects of the actions of the individual fishers has been described for various community-based resource management systems (for example, McCay and Acheson 1987; Ruddle 1989), but also for open access trawling (Hanna and Smith 1993). However, even if they know what is good for the resource, this knowledge may not be reflected in their actions, so long as the incentive structure discourages such actions.

The technical and economic development in fisheries that has taken place during the last century has broadened the gap between the archipelago and coastal and the offshore. With the increased pressure on fish stocks and the danger of overfishing that may result from large investments in fishing technology, the important constraint for fisheries lies in the marine production system—the natural capital—rather than in the actual capacity to fish. The functioning of the ecological life-support system and its capacity to sustain the production of fish species valued as human food therefore determines the value of the natural capital to fisheries.

In the Baltic fisheries, there is a difference between coastal and offshore fishers in terms of the size of the fishing area. In the survey conducted among Swedish Baltic fishers, the offshore fishery moved over areas on average four times as large as the coastal fishery (Hammer 1994a). As common waters within Sweden's territory are in principal open to all Swedish fishers, there is a risk of overfishing on regional and local levels, even if catches are successfully regulated on an international level. For example, the migrating cod and salmon, where the large harvests in the offshore fishery occur, have resulted in a decrease in some local fisheries (Anon. 1992b). The critical effects of treating the fish resources as homogenous is especially obvious in the case of the Baltic salmon. Salmon spawn in the rivers, and the young salmon migrate out to the open sea for a couple of years, before returning to the river, where they were born, to spawn. Some of the salmon stocks in the Baltic Sea are more threatened than others. However, in the open sea, the stocks mix, and there is no possibility of being selective towards certain stocks in the offshore fisheries, resulting in danger of depleting the weakest stocks.

Government bureaucracies have a limited capacity to oversee the many local and seasonal variations among different regions and sectors of the fishery. Regulations need to be considered as fair in order to be efficiently carried out, and to be fair, this local, ecological, and socioeconomic patchiness needs to be taken into account. This requires a large amount of detailed knowledge of local circumstances in the fishing industry and the ecological conditions which exist in various fisheries.

It has been argued that the "diachronic" knowledge capital based on a long series of local observations by local resource users could be of great value as a complement to scientific "synchronic" monitoring (Gadgil, Berkes, and Folke 1993). Tapping fishers' knowledge capital on ecological systems could help to increase the feedback between the ecosystem and the resource use system. This two-way feedback management would be one way to speed up the introduction of more proactive environmental management based on an integrated ecosystem perspective.

Conclusions and Policy Implications

In the traditional Swedish fisheries, agriculture and fisheries were highly integrated, explicitly building on the variability of the natural systems, rather than trying to block out variability. The interdependencies between cultural and biological diversities are most clearly visible in the coastal fishing communities by cultural tradition coevolving with the fluctuations of a patchy coastal ecosystem. Management policies focused on single species tend to ignore the associations of limited species to other species in the landed mix, which may create incentives to structure fishing activities against natural fluctuations.

Offshore and coastal fisheries are part of two different but coupled ecological, economic, as well as cultural systems, and they have to respond to cycling changes of quite different frequencies and order of magnitude. The particular feature of natural settings that might effectively be used by local fishers in selecting rules cannot be included in general models. The different life-support areas of fish species during their life cycle—especially for migrating fish—rarely coincides with the boundaries of the fish exploiters. The more that fishers exploit local nonmigratory stocks the more useful indigenous knowledge will be for stock management. When fish species migrate—as demonstrated in the example of the Baltic salmon, where stocks of varying strength mix at certain stages in their life-cycle—management efforts that can coordinate fishing practices and pinpoint the vulnerable stages are crucial. Attempts by localized community members to assert control over fisheries close to their communities will usually be unsuccessful if those fisheries are already experiencing intense competition from outsiders and a severe depletion of important marine resources. This emphasizes the cross-scale nature of fisheries management and the importance of developing different but well-coordinated fishery policies for different exploitation situations.

The choice of indicator or focus will be critical to the social construction of the problem, maintaining diversity and resilience of ecosystems for sustainable fisheries. The life-support system, that is, the organisms, processes (such as food production, water recycling, waste assimilation, and air purification), and resources interacting to provide the physical necessities for society, constitute a natural capital. The value of the natural capital to fisheries is largely determined by the functioning of the ecological life-support system and its possibility to sustain the production of fish species valued as human food. It is not primarily the species number, but the quality of species in concert with the functioning of the whole community which makes the species important and which constitutes biodiversity (Hammer, Jansson, and Jansson 1993; Schulze and Mooney 1993; Perrings and others, forthcoming).

Enhancing diversity in fisheries management for maintaining the resilience in the supporting ecosystem is also largely determined by the surrounding land use and sociopolitical factors, since biological diversity and ecosystem patchiness is an interdependent part of a cluster of diversities in society and in the ecological system. In order to assure ecological and economic sustainability in fisheries, matching human activities with the natural pulses of the ecosystem should be particularly stressed in management practices rather than basing such practice on an unrealistic expectation that fish populations will provide a steady source for exploitation. Fishing communities should be treated as unique dynamic ecosystems, with a fundamental management goal being to sustain their economic and social viability. One major challenge for the future is to create and match ecological and economic boundaries in a hierarchical set of nested ecological economic systems.

Bibliography

Aneer, G., A. Lindquist, and L. Westin. 1978. "Winter Concentrations of Baltic Herring (Clupea harengus var. membras L.)." *Contr. Askö Lab.* 21. Stockholm: Stockholm University.

Anonymous. 1992a. "Enklare fiskebestämmelser." Ds 1992:70. Stockholm: Jordbruksdepartementet.

Anonymous. 1992b. "Blekinge Kust-och Skärgårdsförenings synpunkter på det svenska fisket i Östersjön och förslag till åtgärder." Blekinge Kust- Skärgårdsförening (mimeo in Swedish).

Arén, H. 1989. "Markägoförhållanden och utvecklingsmöjligheter i Göteborgs och Bohus läns skärgård—exempel från Käringön och Koster." *Nordenskiöldsamfundets tidskrift* 49 suppl: 191–209.

Aro, E. 1988. "A Review of Fish Migration Patterns in the Baltic Sea." *Ices Bal.*, no. 13.

Berkes F., ed. 1989. *Common Property Resources: Ecology and Community-Based Sustainable Development.* London: Belhaven Press.

Berkes, F., C. Folke, and M. Gadgil. Forthcoming. "Traditional Ecological Knowledge, Biodiversity, Resilience and Sustainability." In C. A. Perrings and others. Dordrecht: Biodiversity Conservation, Kluwer Academic Publishers.

Dyer, C. L., and J. R. McGoodwin, eds. 1994. *Folk Management in the World's Fisheries: Lessons for Modern Fisheries Management.* Niwot, Colorado: University Press of Colorado.

Gadgil, M., F. Berkes, and C. Folke. 1993. "Indigenous Knowledge for Biodiversity Conservation." *Ambio* 22:151–56.

Granlund, J. 1956. "Runnö i Kalmarsund. Stranda härads hembygdsförening." *Årsskrift* 331/32:3-113.

Hammer, M. 1994a. *Natural and Human-Made Capital Interactions in Fisheries Examples from the Baltic Sea.* Dissertation. Stockholm: Stockholm University.

Hammer, M. 1994b. "Resource Demands and Management Approaches for Multiscale Fisheries." In M. Hammer, *Natural and Human-Made Capital Interactions in Fisher-*ies Examples From the Baltic Sea. Dissertation. Stockholm: Stockholm University.

Hammer, M., A. M. Jansson, and B.-O. Jansson. 1993. "Diversity, Change, and Sustainability: Implications for Fisheries." *Ambio* 22:97–105.

Hanna, S., and C. Smith. 1993. "Attitudes of Trawl Vessel Captains about Work, Resource Use, and Fishery Management." *North American Journal of Fisheries Management* 13:367–75.

Hardin, G. 1968. The tragedy of the commons. Science, 162:1243-48.

Hildén, M. 1992. "Boundary Conditions for the Sustainable Use of Major Fish Stocks in the Baltic Sea." Paper presented at the Second Meeting of the International Society for Ecological Economics, Stockholm.

Holling, C. S. 1986. "Resilience of Ecosystems; Local Surprise and Global Change." In W. C. Clark and R. E. Munn, eds., *Sustainable Development of the Biosphere.* Cambridge: Cambridge University Press. 292–317.

Löfgren, O. 1977. *Maritime Hunters in Industrial Society.* Liber Läromedel Lund. In Swedish, English summary.

McCay, B. M., and J. M. Acheson, eds. 1987. *The Questions of the Commons: The Culture and Ecology of Communal Resources.* Tucson: The University of Arizona Press.

Ostrom. E. 1990. *Governing the Commons: The Evolution of Institutions of Collective Action.* Cambridge: Cambridge University Press.

Perrings, C. A., and others. Forthcoming. *Biodiversity Conservation.* Dordrecht: Kluwer Academic Publishers.

Rosén, M. 1987. *Hasslöborna. En livsform i förändring. Etnologiska sällskapet i Lund.* Växjö: RMR Förlag. In Swedish, English summary.

Ruddle, K. 1989. "Solving the Common-Property Dilemma: Village Fisheries Rights in Japanese Coastal Waters." In F. Berkes, ed., 1989, *Common Property Resources: Ecology and Community-Based Sustainable Development.* London: Belhaven Press.

Schultze, E.-D., and Mooney, H. A. 1993. *Biodiversity and Ecosystem Function.* Berlin: Springer Verlag. 497–510.

Scotte, L. 1981. "Slutfiskat. En undersökning av yrkesfiskets villkor i Västernorrlands län." Akademilitteratur, Stockholm. In Swedish, English summary.

Smetacek, C. 1984. "The Supply of Food to the Benthos." In M. J. R. Fasham, ed., *Flows of Energy and Materials in Marine Ecosystems*. New York: Plenum Press. 517–48.

Zijlstra, J. J. 1988. "Fish Migrations Between Coastal and Offshore Areas." In B.-O. Jansson, ed., *Coastal-Offshore Ecosystem Interactions*. Lecture Notes on Coastal and Estuarine Studies (22). Berlin: Springer Verlag. Berlin. 257–72.

Figure 12–1: Coastal Fishing Areas in Sweden

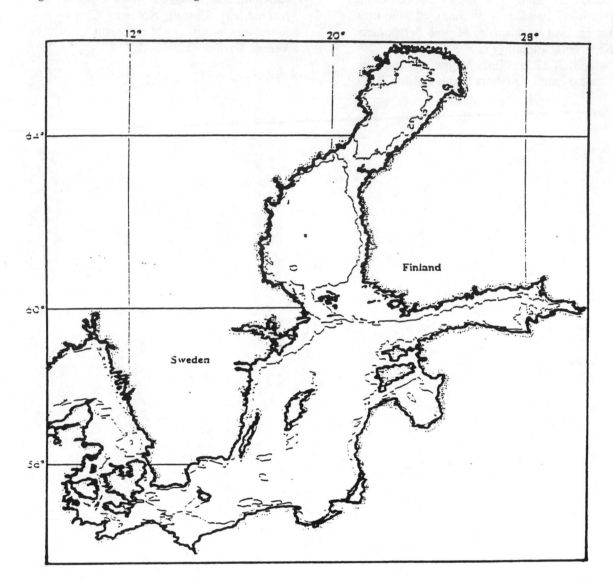

Figure 12–2: Major Factors Influencing the Development in Fisheries in Sweden

VIEW OF NATURE

"FREEDOM OF THE SEAS"	FISH A LIMITED RESOURCE	FISH AS A PART OF AN ECOSYSTEM
unlimited resources	but the ecosystem a black box	the life-support functions of ecosystems

MANAGEMENT OBJECTIVES IN FISHERIES

EXTRACTION maximize catches	INCOME standard of living as equal groups in society	CONSERVATION overfishing environmental degradation

STRUCTURAL TRENDS IN FISHERIES

INDUSTRIALIZATION agriculture and fisheries follows the industrial sector	CENTRALIZATION national fisheries administration	INTERNATIONALIZATION fish part of a trade package international cooperation

early industrialization   post industrial society

Figure 12–3: Fish Species, Gear Used, and Annual Harvesting Periods on Hasslö Island

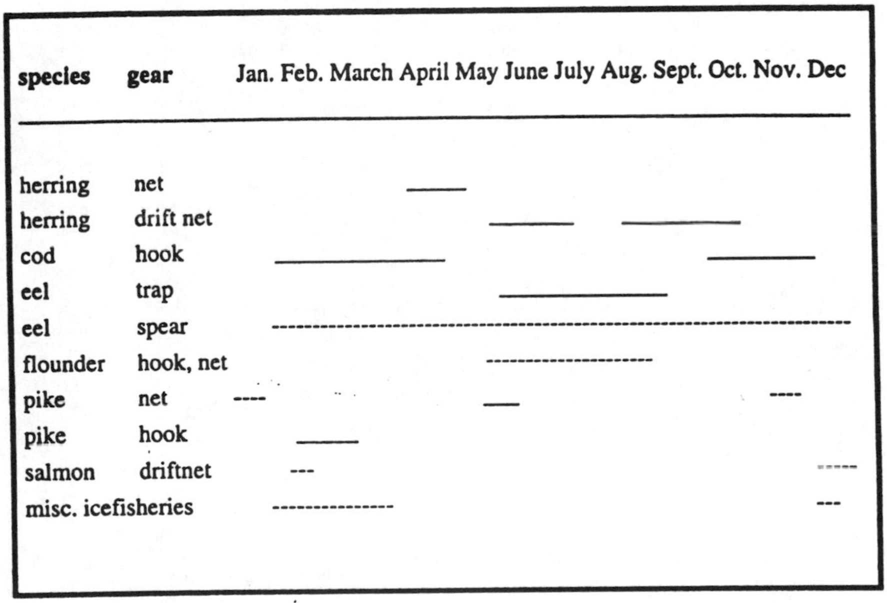

species	gear	Jan. Feb. March April May June July Aug. Sept. Oct. Nov. Dec
herring	net	
herring	drift net	
cod	hook	
eel	trap	
eel	spear	
flounder	hook, net	
pike	net	
pike	hook	
salmon	driftnet	
misc. icefisheries		

13

Parametric Management of Fisheries: An Ecosystem–Social Approach

James A. Wilson and Lloyd M. Dickie

Abstract

The immediate causes of over fishing are usually ascribed to the harvesting of too many fish to allow adequate spawning, recruitment, and sustainability. We argue that the actions that lead to overfishing are most probably to be found in the broader parametric effects of fishing on the whole biotic and environmental system. Fishing activity leads to a degradation of the biotic or physical environment of desirable species, upsetting their feeding patterns and disrupting normal life cycle sequences. These reduced opportunities for growth, reproduction, and survival alter the capacity of the whole system to maintain the organization of energy flows, on which the fishery depends.

The authors would like to thank Drs. S. R. Kerr, Robert Steneck, and James Leiby, and Edward Ames and Stephanie Watson for their valuable comments during the writing of this chapter. The Sea Grant Program of the Universities of Maine and New Hampshire, the U.S. Man and the Biosphere Program, and the Beijer Institute of the Swedish Academy of Sciences contributed valuable resources that made this work possible.

153

The fundamental cause of overfishing, however, lies in social institutions that either cannot conceive the complex biological interactions, or have insufficient authority to control the inputs. From a management perspective, this changed view of the overfishing problem suggests: (a) a shift to rules designed to address the parametric effects of fishing, rather than the species-specific effort controls of traditional management, and (b) creation of a multilevel governance system (of basic federalist structure) in order to match the scales and minimize the potentially large transaction costs of systemwide governance. Additionally, the difficult problem posed by uncertainty—our limited ability to tie particular restrictions to particular outcomes—means that hierarchical governance processes are needed to develop the basic requirements of credibility, incentive alignment, and individual assurances.

✧

Introduction

The term "parametric" refers to the constants in fisheries models. These constants, or parameters (habitat, genetic structure, life processes, patterns, and so on) characterize the system. That is, they describe the overall conditions under which the species dynamics operate, as well as the details of the system's internal organization. Parameters are distinguished from the dynamic variables, such as rates of change in numbers of fish, that act over relatively short time periods. In current fisheries management, the variables are regarded as needs that are to be explicitly measured and controlled for sustainability. In this chapter, we argue that management or protection of the parameters of real fisheries systems is the primary key to sustainable fisheries.

In the current approach to fisheries management, the rate of fishing mortality on a specific stock, relative to its rates of reproduction and growth, is held to be the chief cause of changes in population size. This theory predicts that when fishing removes too many fish before they have had a chance to produce eggs, the adaptive, density dependent mechanisms that can compensate for moderate rates of fishing, are no longer capable of restoring the productivity on which sustained catches depend. It follows that man-

agement must address the problem by reducing fishing mortality, to permit the stocks to rebuild. The almost complete emphasis on the mortality effects of fishing also leads current management to address the fishing problem at a single scale—a very large scale, corresponding with the range of the stock.

In contrast, parametric management draws attention to a different and more comprehensive explanation for the declines. Specifically, it implies that the failures in recruitment of fish stocks are not simply the result of changed variables controlling production of individual stocks. It argues that fishing activity has led to a degradation of parts of the biotic or physical environment of desirable species, reducing opportunities for growth, reproduction, and survival. Changes of this sort alter the capacity of the whole system to maintain the partitioning of the energy flows on which the fishery has depended, and lead to a situation in which a reduction in fishing mortality cannot guarantee the recovery of a particular fishery.

Parametric management also argues that the scales at which we address management problems need to be altered. Some rules still need to affect all parts of the fisheries system. Others must target smaller-scale events and processes. Rather than a sole emphasis on the thousands of square miles of the stock range, very local phenomena also may need to be considered. Even local factors, such as those that affect the integrity of local spawning grounds, are the concern of parametric fisheries management.

In drawing attention to multiple scales of concern, parametric management has very important implications for the kinds of tools (or rules) used. In particular, it emphasizes the importance of the scale at which we organize our fisheries management institutions. The need to address biological phenomena at many different scales, not just the large scale, implies a need to develop management institutions scaled appropriately to similarly scaled biological phenomena they are designed to address (Wilson, and others 1994).

The idea of parametric management also raises questions about the appropriate scientific agenda for fisheries research and information. A newly conceived scope for the factors of change has implications for both the time scale and the intensity of acquiring knowledge. Traditional knowledge gained by generations of fishers addresses many of the biotic and abiotic factors of concern to parametric management. It helps to set the framework of a fishery system, within which testable scientific hypotheses can be drawn. The challenge posed by parametric management is to find practical means to wed these two sources of understanding into a system of governance that meets the needs of the fishing communities, while simultaneously protecting the health of the fisheries. In this chapter, we examine several aspects of a parametric approach to management:

- A review of biological evidence, showing that the abundance of species varies in relation to parametric constraints, so that individual species are not independently controllable entities

- An inquiry about the kinds of rules that would be appropriate to the parametric approach to fishery system control

- An examination of the kinds of social organization that would be appropriate for efficient management, using the parametric approach

Evidence for Ecosystem Controls on Fish Production

The mortality effects of fishing effort have been cast traditionally as the principal source of overfishing. In contrast, the parametric view argues that the sources of overfishing are to be found in the broader effects of fishing on the system, such as affects on habitat, spawning behavior, de facto refugia, and so on. For example, in the Gulf of Maine, fishers estimate they are now able to fish perhaps 50 percent more territory than ten years ago. Their ability to find and fish local concentrations has been so improved by new navigation, sonar, and roller gear, that areas that were once refuges for the young or for the old spawning fish are so no longer.

Oral histories now being gathered in Maine point to the progressive extinction of inshore and nearshore spawning grounds, beginning as early as the 1920s. These effects are unrecognizable in the conventional mortality rate calculations. Yet, their accumulated effects on the productivity of the entire fishery can be substantial. The same effects are evident in Canada, where the advent of ice-capable draggers and newly mobile long-liners now brings disturbances to areas and to seasons that were previously exempt from fishing. These changes in the qualitative capabilities of fishing technology adversely affect the resilience of populations; "different" elements of the populations are removed, the safety of multiple spawning areas is eroded, and the habitat is made less favorable.

In addition to the expected changes in abundance, fishers have seen unanticipated changes at both large and small scales. They have noticed that young commercial fish are scarce and that the pockets of large, old spawners have disappeared. Although the efficiency of their gear has improved, they have seen changes in local and seasonal patterns of distribution that have increased the difficulty of catching fish. These changes have not been confined to the commercial stocks. Nonfished species have commonly increased their abundance and distribution to fill areas once occupied by desirable species. The abundance of dogfish and skates on Georges Bank is only one example of changes in the species composition of stocks that have been seen worldwide, wherever there are intense fisheries. In the Great Lakes, after the salmon, lake trout, and whitefish had been virtually eliminated, massive quantities of small fish appeared. In the mid-1970s, off Peru, the anchovies were replaced by sardines, and, in the North Sea, a generation of European fishers experienced abrupt and unexpected collapses of traditional pelagic and demersal stocks and increases of "industrial" fish. To understand these changes brought about by fishing, the parametric view seems a necessary, not an arbitrary, choice.

Science does not have any uniquely objective methodology for composing new models of fishery systems. Just the same as all of our understanding, it depends on analogy and metaphor to frame appropriate models (Rosen 1991). This is why inclusion of fishers' knowledge can be critical to developing relevant images. The special strength of science rests in its ability to study the larger consequences of experience of the many interrelated local changes that are identified. In this area, science has made significant progress along two lines that contribute to a parametric perspective. One has been to study large-scale factors, such as climatic parameters, that help explain dramatic changes in a species, or class of species, within the system. The other has been to define the ecosystem of the fishery in a manner that clarifies the evidence of stability in overall biomass, or output, indicative of parametric balancing of its organization. In a balanced system, changes in the structure, or the organization of one part, are certain to have effects on others. In recent years, science has seen increasing evidence that, in such systems, apparently small causes may lead to large effects. We need to take account of both of these lines of study.

Effects of Large-Scale Environmental Parameters

The search for explanatory environmental parameters includes the extensive changes in climate in the North Atlantic that have been common knowledge for over a century. It has been reflected in both the distribution and spawning success of the stocks of cod, herring, seals, and other species that were the mainstays of the fisheries. Mann and Drinkwater (1994) showed that, for recent years, changes in environment are associated with trends in fish catches along the Labrador and Newfoundland coasts. Their interpretations are supported by the widespread coincidence of similar trends in landings for many different species in widely separated geographic localities. We cannot avoid the conclusion that environmental parameters with a climatic scope may have been very important in the developing crises.

However, some of the fishery changes began before the environment changed, and, in some cases, similar past changes in environment have had lesser effects on catches. Large area correlations obscure important variations within and between stock units, so that Mann and Drinkwater (1994) warn that factors apparently related to heavy fishing also must be involved in the recent trends. Similar conclusions of a joint responsibility between environmental parameters and fishing variables were made for the collapse of the Peruvian anchovetta fishery, once the largest in the world (Dickie and Valdivia 1981), and in other smaller fisheries worldwide (Iles 1973). Effects of the environment amplify the fishing-related demographic alterations of populations.

The mortality effects of fishing had been measured by the early 1970s. Garrod (1973) showed that fishing on the Arcto-Norwegian cod already was sufficient to remove more biomass than could be resupplied by the observed density-dependent responses of production by the fish. Using similar methods, Hutchings and Myers (1994) have calculated that fishing has been more important than environment in the collapse of the northern cod fishery, that the fishery would have collapsed soon even without environmental change. Similar calculations explained the collapse of the California sardine fishery (Iles 1973), as well as the collapses of the Norwegian and North Sea Down's herring stocks (Cushing 1973). The fact that rates of fishing are now higher than they were in the early 1970s can only underline the necessity for consideration of the environmental and organizational parameters of fisheries systems jointly with the dynamic variables customarily used as management guides in the models.

Overall Ecosystem Responses

The value of overall ecosystem models in fisheries was first demonstrated for the Great Lakes of North America. Regier (1973) showed that, as the rate of fishing increased, large and valuable species that dominated in the 1850s, by 1950 had been replaced by an abundance of small "trash" fish. The especially notable observation was that, despite increased fishing, the total landings of fish had changed little. The change was in the quality of the species taken. Sutcliffe, Drinkwater, and Muir (1977) found a similar phenomenon for Georges Bank.

These observations were based on commercial statistics and, so, did not reflect the whole fish community. However, they directed attention to the suggestion of Sheldon, Prakash, and Sutcliffe (1977), that the body size composition of the total biomass of aquatic ecosystems might be stable, even if single species abundances were not. Accordingly, Pope and Knights (1982), using research vessel data that reflected the whole fish community, showed that, in the North Sea, comparable areas with different fishing intensities had very different proportions of large and small fish but similar overall biomasses. Murawski and Idoine (1989), using groundfish surveys of the Northeast Coastal Shelf from

Cape Hatteras to Georges Bank, showed that over a twenty-five-year period up to 1987, there were large changes in abundance of species and a variable fishing rate, but a stable density by body size of the whole fish community. Duplisea and Kerr (forthcoming), using research data for the Scotian Shelf, showed the same phenomenon over a period of twenty-two years, up to 1991. Wherever the data exist, they show that, as fishing intensity has increased, individual species have varied in abundance, but biological density and production of the total fish community have remained constant.

Following the lead of Sheldon, Prakash, and Sutcliffe, Boudreau, and Dickie (1992) compiled data on the biological particle-size spectrum from plankton to fish for seven different ecosystems, including three major fisheries systems: Georges Bank, the North Sea, and the Scotian Shelf. The level of production of the systems was related to the level of initial nutrient input, but the resulting biomass was distributed among body sizes of organisms, including fishes, in the same way in all ecosystems. That is, ecosystem production is under the overall parametric constraint of nutrient supply, with the many different species acting together as a stable producing system. From the point of view of parametric management, the important conclusion is that if one part of the system is reduced, the other parts capitalize on the opportunities opened up to them.

Ecosystem Organization

Fishing on one species affects the whole biotic environment, not just the species of interest. Evidently, there are compensatory changes among the remaining species and size elements that act to stabilize the total energy flows through ecosystems. Within this broadly stable system, therefore, there are organizational factors that make the elements interact as a whole, but equally there are connections that, if upset, may lead to unpredictable changes within the biological hierarchies.

Some of the implications of the details of biological system organization have become appreciated through specialized scientific models, such as the complex community organization models of cod, herring, capelin, and seals. All four interacting species are commercially

desirable and heavily fished. The models predict that fishing will create unexpected changes in species balance, a conclusion borne out by experience of the corresponding real systems in both Norway and Newfoundland.

These results are in keeping with the experience of the multispecies fisheries of the Great Lakes, Georges Bank, and Scotian Shelf. In all these instances, the species structure is highly variable and apparently sensitive to small changes in the initial conditions. If alteration in one species element of the system goes beyond a certain point, there is no guarantee that an original balance can be restored simply by reducing the level of fishing effort. In the Great Lakes, for example, the lake trout seems to defy persistent efforts to re-establish it, but the introduced species of salmon from the West Coast have become highly successful predators on small fish. Management of one part is critically dependent on management of the others (Hennemuth 1979; Wilson, and others 1991).

As we learn more in detail about the life histories of the organisms in relation to their environment, we appreciate better some of the instinctive apprehension of fishers at the alterations in the biological and physical environments they know by experience. We need to incorporate their more comprehensive and more detailed knowledge in management. A particular example is afforded in the effects of the massive migrations of fish within the continental shelves. These migrations are poorly known and rarely considered in management rules, yet they dwarf the migrations of salmon in highly regulated Pacific Ocean rivers. In British Columbia, runs may total seventy thousand to eighty thousand tons of fish per year. But, in the Gulf of St. Lawrence, annual migrations of mackerel alone vary between 100 thousand and four million tons. In addition, there are annual migrations of 500 thousand tons of herring and cod. These massive migrations are characteristic of almost all major oceanographic current systems. Adult fish move from feeding grounds to up-stream spawning areas, where the newly hatched young are able to feed on locally high biological productivity, before being carried back to the areas where the adults live.

Fishers' livelihoods have depended on knowing these patterns in great detail, including the precise times and locations of runs. Thus, they understood a relation between the offshore and inshore fisheries in many areas before it was established scientifically. They have also recognized the importance of certain details, such as the fact that the older, larger spawners migrate farther and at different times than smaller spawners. This knowledge led fishers to become alarmed when certain runs of fish disappeared with heavy fishing, years before mortality measurements showed the effects, and before scientific studies established the importance of such special stock elements to year-class success (Lambert 1990). They also recognize the potential impact of fishing activity on the behavior of fish in their spawning concentrations, and the vulnerability of the migrating fish at particular times and places along their path. Unless the special features of these population behaviors are understood and maintained by management, changes in them may render irrelevant the efforts to improve yields through control of mortality rates.

Implications for the Rules of Management

This chapter is not the place to examine detailed phenomena of system behavior or organization. It is necessary, however, to draw attention to the fact that, as fisheries science has come closer to an appreciation of ecosystem characteristics known to fishermen, there has emerged a growing consensus that intense fisheries cannot be managed on the generalities of single-species stock dynamics alone. To be fully responsible, management institutions have to develop a means of identifying the relevant parametric features in system organization, additional to controls on mortality. The needs for special protection at other scales require attention to new ways of utilizing fishery information or new methods of measuring effects within the whole system.

Even to be aware of the existence of some local factors requires improved input and evaluation from experienced individuals. However, no one can ever know the significance of all local features to fishery survival, and although each environment has special features, and each ecosystem faces unique disturbances, the sciences of ecology, economics, and sociology are rich with knowledge that helps establish whether

historical and local observations can explain the results of interaction. That is, in concert with the different sources of knowledge about fisheries, we are increasingly able to determine the consequences of neglecting certain classes of details in management. Our problem may then be primarily one of adaptation (Holling and others 1978), in which we work to find the organizational rules that bring the diverse sources of information and policy formation together with the means of implementation and evaluation.

There are a number of obvious examples of what is required of parametric management on the largest scale. A perception of almost everyone touched by the current fisheries crises is that the general level of fishing is too high. Detailed responses to the heavy fishing vary among areas, but the trend of the last twenty-five years is now very clear. Remarkably, however, it is only in the face of the recent catastrophic adjustments within the biological system that we have been able to reach consensus on the problem. It can now be seen that at a minimum, reductions in the overall intensity of fishing need to be coupled with attention to details of the methods and timing of the fishing. The need to find the means of bringing about appropriate reductions, before blanket closures are forced upon all fisheries, is paramount.

The changes in ecosystem organization attending fishing call, however, for a more comprehensive look at the effectiveness of management institutions and the rules by which they must work. In general, parametric change implies a need to shift the focus of management to both broader and finer scales of detail than are considered in the overall control of fishing mortality. The details that need to be taken into account will vary from place to place and from one biological and one human community to another. The main problem is to find methods of reaching a working consensus based on the most comprehensive judgment.

Social/Organizational Implications for Fisheries Management

The social rules that fall out of that judgment, and the social organization necessary to implement such rules, depend critically on our sense of the biological bases of overfishing. If these depart greatly from traditional explanations, as the parametric view argues, the foundations of much of social, especially economic, policy regarding fisheries and the organization of fisheries management are in need of revision. Social institutions need to be adapted to their environment; or, perhaps more accurately, we need to adapt our social institutions to our perception of the environment in which they are embedded. As our perception of that environment changes, so, too, does our sense of the appropriate institutions for management.

The causes of overfishing are social in origin. From the economists' perspective, they are generally to be found in the absence of a property right or other institution that might otherwise provide exclusive control over the productive capability of the resource and, as a consequence, an incentive to conserve. In the absence of exclusive control, one person's actions (harvesting) have detrimental impacts on others who respond in a similar manner (more harvesting and so on, with escalating positive feedback). Economists label these unwilling (nonmarket) exchanges, "externalities." The generally accepted solution to externalities is to create institutions that provide exclusive control over the sources of long-run sustainability.

In traditional single-species approaches to fisheries management, the problems of long-run sustainability are well-addressed by institutions that restrain total catch of the species. For this reason, the broad preference for individual transferable quotas (ITQs) that has emerged among managers and economists is mainly attributable to the idea that ITQs meet the requirements for well-designed institutions: that is, ITQs provide the basis for control over catch of the species and, at the same time, generate individual incentives that are consistent with the social object of long-run sustainability (Anderson 1992; Copes 1986). If, however, the mechanism leading to overfishing is to be found in the effects of fishing on the basic biological and environmental parameters of the fishery or ecosystem, it is very unlikely that institutions such as ITQs will lead to long-run sustainability. ITQs simply address the wrong externalities.

The parametric hypothesis regarding the effects of fishing identifies numerous nonspecies specific externalities occurring at various spatial and temporal scales. In other words, the problems of degradation of habitat, disruption of basic life cycle processes, removal of essential "patches," and so on, that occur at lower levels in the system hierarchy are all associated with discrete acts at particular times and places, and all have a cumulative impact on system structure. Changed ecosystem organization, which is manifest in the species composition problems that beset so many heavily fished systems, then tends to reinforce the lower-level effects upon which it is based. An institution that is able to exercise effective control over these numerous externalities at the various scales at which they occur is, by necessity, going to be very different from an ITQ designed to address a single externality at a single scale.

The Scale Problem in Management

The parametric explanation of overfishing exposes three problems that shape an approach to defining an appropriate management institution: the multiple scales at which the causative factors of overfishing arise, the nonspecies specific nature of those factors, and the resulting uncertainty of outcomes (the complexity of the system precludes the ability to unambiguously manipulate outcomes).

Together, the three problems suggest why it is difficult to encompass the relevant externalities with the kinds of institutions we have been using, that is, a government agency acting as much as possible as a sole owner, often in conjunction with quasi-property rights, such as limited entry or ITQs.

In the last two decades, social scientists have made important progress on the problem of institutional design. (See, for example, V. Ostrom and E. Ostrom 1977; E. Ostrom 1977, 1992; Williamson 1985; Eggertsson 1990). In the context of parametric overfishing, the basic requirements that new institutions must meet are:

- The ability to fully encompass the causes of overfishing (the externalities) within their control: that is, the restraining rules of the new institutions have to be applied to all behavior relevant to overfishing. In terms of the parametric view, institutions must be able to develop rules that (a) control total effort at a level that is consistent with total system productivity, (b) apply to and involve all users in the governance process, (c) control a potentially large number of interacting phenomena (both biological and human) at a variety of spatial and temporal scales, and (d) avoid creating a situation in which control at one scale leads to undesirable results at another scale or another site at the same scale. Where the causes of overfishing lie outside the institution's control, it will fail.

- The ability to credibly tie the application of rules to an intended outcome. Even if there is uncertainty about cause and effect, there has be a sense among users that the rule is a reasonable step to take. Furthermore, participants must be convinced that restraint on their part will likely lead to the intended individual or collective result. In a complex, unpredictable environment such as fisheries, if it appears that the intended result is not forthcoming, users have to know that a reasonable process of revision and new rule development will or can take place (Pinkerton 1989; E. Ostrom 1992). In the face of uncertainty, institutions must be able to go through a continuous learning process at a variety of scales, complete with active feedback about failure or success. In a sense, institutions are faced with the need to follow a learning process very similar to the scientific process. To the extent that credibility and an ongoing learning process cannot be established, administrative and enforcement costs can be expected to rise, or the success of the institution to decline.

- The ability to align private and social incentives: that is, the ability to develop rules that are simultaneously seen to be in the long-run best interests of society and the individual participants (E. Ostrom 1977; V. Ostrom and E.Ostrom 1977). In the face of the uncertainty arising from the complexity of fisheries systems, either the rules themselves, or the process of arriving at and changing them, must generate an atmosphere of belief that, on net, they are worthwhile. To the extent that individual interests cannot be harmonized with social interests, enforcement costs will rise.

- The ability to provide individuals with reasonable assurance that others will follow the rules (or face effective sanctions). In a para-

metric approach, this means the ability to go through a process of rule development and negotiation that leads to reduced uncertainty about the intent of other participants with regard to compliance (E. Ostrom 1992). Again, to the extent these assurances about rule compliance cannot be generated, the effectiveness of the institution declines or its enforcement costs rise.

- The ability to carry out efficiently the transactions required of management. Extensive transactions will be associated with maintaining exclusive control (measurement, monitoring, exclusion) and developing credible rules and maintaining harmonious incentives and assurances (especially when there is uncertainty about cause and effect and ambiguity in any result). More than any other criterion, the ability to minimize the costs of these transactions will determine efficient, workable institutional structure (Williamson 1985). To the extent that transactions cannot be conducted effectively, all the other functions of the institution can be expected to suffer.

It is unlikely that any institution can perfectly meet these criteria, but it is also the case that there can be better and worse institutional solutions. A sole owner corporation, a government agency acting as a sole owner, a decentralized property rights system, or a (community) governance approach, or some mix of all these might be created to manage a parametric fishery. However, the success or failure of these alternatives will depend greatly on how well their particular strengths and weaknesses as institutions match the circumstances of the fishery. Design of the most appropriate institution or mix of institutions depends heavily on the particulars of the problem.

Given the parametric explanation of overfishing, our current institutional approaches do not appear well adapted to either the scales or activities relevant to the overfishing problem. For example, property rights embedded in the resource, as in a species-specific ITQ or limited entry license, do not confer complete or meaningful control over those factors that determine the long-run sustainability of the resource to which the right is attached. Consequently, a property right holder is not in a position to influence the factors that contribute to the asset value of the right. As a result, the outcome of rational economic behavior may be no different from that found under open access. The property right becomes nothing more than privileged access, with no corresponding capability or incentive to deliver conservation. Even well-intentioned individuals who believe that such schemes lead to conservation, sooner or later have to come to grips with the fact that multiple factors external to the control explicit in the ITQ are the likely sources of sustainability.

The alternative of full property rights encompassing the entire system, accorded to a government agency or a private corporation, leads to a somewhat similar lack of control and inappropriate incentives. In this instance, the problem arises not because of the inadequacy of the property right, but because of the transactional impairments a single entity encounters in dealing with the complexity of the system. The biological and corresponding human details, occasioned by the uncertainty, multiple scales, and nonspecies specific nature of the problem, lead to either an overwhelming information problem, if the entity remains centralized, or the typical severe problems of inharmonious and conflicting incentives (what economists call "problems of agency") if the entity adopts a decentralized organizational structure (Williamson 1985).

Towards a Solution— A Hierarchical Approach

Without going into a long assessment of possible alternatives, let us suggest that the problems posed by parametric control of fisheries are very similar to those faced in the everyday governance of human activity. There, a great many human interactions have to be managed, at widely differing spatial and temporal scales and with various levels of certainty with regard to cause and effect. Outcomes from public policies are never unambiguous; we have to devise rules that people feel will reasonably address the various problems at their appropriate scales, and we have to do all this through a process that people find reasonable and that assures participants there is a reasonably uniform, fair, and equitable application of laws as well. What might otherwise be a monstrous transactions problem that would lead to inefficiencies and strong tendencies towards corruption, is resolved by erecting federalist-type hierarchies, in which responsibility for rulemaking and enforcement is assigned to the lowest possible unit in the hierarchy, and beggar-thy-neighbor activity is constrained by a set of rules governing interactions among the various units in the hierarchy (V. Ostrom 1971, 1991).

The circumstances of parametric management call for a similar approach in fisheries. In particular, the fishery's complexity and its derivative, uncertainty, put a premium on the solution of the very human problems of generating credibility, developing assurances, and aligning incentives, all within the context of minimizing potentially high transaction costs. A governance process that involves users (all stakeholders) from the bottom up seems most likely to efficiently address these problems (Pinkerton 1989, 1994; E.Ostrom 1992; McCay 1994).

Briefly outlined, we would suggest a federalist organization at three or more levels, starting with fairly local governance units, going through sub-regional, and finally regional units. (For example, in terms of the current U.S. system, this implies at least two governance layers below the current regional council.) The responsibilities accorded each level should correspond with the human and biological externalities that occur at that same or approximate scale. Similarly, the boundaries that define different units at each scale need to be defined in terms of the boundaries of the externalities at that scale. Each unit should be representative and nonspecies specific and, in keeping with federalist principles, independent. Between units at each level and between levels, there is a need for rules to prevent one unit from bringing harm to another or to prevent the equivalent of open-access myopia. Figure 13–1 illustrates parallel ecological and institutional hierarchies.

To briefly illustrate this hierarchical structure, consider the kinds of rules that might be required with parametric management:

Rules to Sustain the Fishery

- Higher-level system rules: Rules to restrain the total fishing effort on all species together, so that the effective mortality will be at or below the total biomass recovery rate. This may include rules to help control species balance.

- Species-specific rules related to life cycle and behavior: This includes minimum age of capture, no capture during spawning or along certain migration routes, and so forth.

- Lower-level environmental rules: closed areas, refugia, gear types, and restrictions (when, where, and how).

Rules Regarding Human Activity

- Human interaction rules: gear and territorial conflicts, and so forth, at all levels.

- Governance rules: enforcement, assignment of responsibilities to various governance levels, the process of development of new or changed rules, voting, representation, rights transfers, and so forth, at all levels.

At a local level, to take an example, rules restricting fishing in particular habitats (permanently or as temporary closures) may be required for the purposes of protecting spawning grounds, nurseries, or whatever. Under most conceivable circumstances, it is not likely that clear, unambiguous evidence will connect such actions with a particular outcome in the fishery. Rather, the intent and effect of such rules would be to create a generally more hospitable environment for the fishery as a whole. Because any restrictions of this sort encroach upon the present profitability of fishing, the development of credibility, assurances, and incentive alignment becomes very dependent on the process by which the rules are developed.

Because a local or community-level governance process brings to the table the varied interests and knowledge of users and creates an arena where assessments of individual intentions can be made, it is much more likely to address the human side of the problem than a centralized institutional arrangement. And to the extent that that can be done, the likelihood that the choice and design of rules will conform with what are thought to lead to the best collective outcomes is increased. Put differently, users who are knowledgeable about local circumstances (both biological and human) are not likely to agree to rules they feel are pointless with regard to results, that they feel will be wantonly disregarded by others,

or that contain incentives that pit the individual against the collective well-being.

At what might be called sub-regional levels (one above the local), rules of two sorts can be expected to develop. First, there are the rules governing externalities relevant to biological phenomena occurring at the sub-regional level. For example, for a particular species, it may be desirable to have a single minimum size of capture, or there may be habitat problems at the sub-regional scale that need to be addressed. Here again, the process can be expected to follow much the same pattern as at the local level, but most probably with representatives of local areas rather than direct involvement of all users. A second and very important kind of rule required at the sub-regional level concerns the prevention of beggar-thy-neighbor behavior between units at the local level. For example, fish that grow in local nursery areas may leave those areas before they are catchable adults; as a result, local fishermen may have little incentive to protect such areas. Consequently, general rules regarding the local treatment of region-wide externalities are also required.

Parallel kinds of rules would be required at the full regional level. But, at this level, a unique rule requirement might arise if, in fact, it was felt necessary to restrain total biomass removals or to constrain total effort consistent with biomass recovery rates. In this instance, a market in, for example, tradable generalized inputs, might well complement the governance structures required for the other kinds of externalities. However, because other rules at other scales, such as refugia, gear design, and so on, have clear economic impacts and consequent limits on the total amount of effort in the fishery, it is not clear that total effort controls would be necessary.

In general, it should be clear how a federalist approach can adapt to the various scales at which the fishery problem occurs. Less obvious is an equally important aspect of the governance process, the continuity or repetitiveness of the process itself. This is especially important in the uncertain environment of fisheries for two reasons: to suppress or minimize individual strategies that defect from the common interest (that is, individual gain at the expense of conservation), and to encourage learning about the environment.

In both these cases, feedback about the experience of individuals is essential. For example, one would expect as a normal course of events that some actors in this environment would attempt to avoid the effect of restraints that impinged on their immediate well-being. This might occur during the process of rule making or afterwards. It might be the result of deliberately cynical behavior or, perhaps more likely, a wishful belief that restraints are unnecessary. Whatever the source of the belief, if incorrect, there must be ways for the institution to flush it out, or reinforce it if correct. For this to occur, however, there must continuing and repeated decisions that allow individuals to recognize the patterns of behavior of one another. Then, defection can be sanctioned. Decentralized governance processes strongly increase the likelihood of this outcome because of the direct and continuous feedback they provide.

Similarly, with regard to institutional learning, over the long haul, the great danger to the governance process (or any other institution) comes from an inability to demonstrate or actually create a situation in which the restrictions on individual actions produce the desired results. This is why, for example, we would expect ITQs to fail as a credible institution, if and when it became apparent that the sources of sustainability lie outside the species-specific factors governed by the ITQ.[1] In the case of parametric management, this is a potentially large problem, especially because our state of knowledge of ocean ecosystems is fairly rudimentary and under any circumstance, as we have mentioned several times above, the complexity of these systems will always make it difficult to unambiguously connect cause and effect. We can expect and must anticipate mistakes. Consequently, the long-term legitimacy of the process will depend to a great extent upon a continuing process of learning with regard to the marine environment (Holling and others 1978). In this instance, also, decentralized governance structures provide the kind of direct and continuous feedback that is likely to generate the information necessary to make institutional learning workable.[2]

Conclusions

The immediate causes of overfishing are usually ascribed to the harvesting of too many fish to allow adequate spawning, recruitment, and sustainability. We argue that the actions that lead to overfishing are most probably to be found in the broader parametric effects of fishing on the whole biotic and environmental system. However, the fundamental cause of overfishing lies in social incentives that either cannot conceive the complex biological interactions, or have insufficient authority to control the inputs.

From a management perspective, this changed view of the overfishing problem suggests that a shift be made to rules designed to address the parametric effects of fishing, rather than the species-specific effort controls of traditional management; and that, because of the non-species-specific characteristic and various scales at which these rules must operate, a multi-level governance system (a basic federalist structure) be created in order to minimize the potentially large transaction cost problem. Additionally, the difficult problem posed by uncertainty—our limited ability to tie particular restrictions to particular outcomes—means that hierarchical governance processes are needed to develop the basic requirements of credibility, incentive alignment, and assurance.

Bibliography

Anderson, L. G. 1992. "ITQ Study Group Report: Volumes 2–5." NOAA ContractNo. 40AANF101849.

Boudreau, P. R., and L. M. Dickie. 1992. "Biomass Spectra of Aquatic Ecosystems in Relation to Fisheries Yield." *Can. J. Fish. Aquat. Sci.* 49: 1528–38.

---

1. The monopoly or cartel-like benefits that accrue to ITQ holders in this circumstance might, however, provide sufficient incentive for collective enforcement.

2. Fishers carry a great deal of knowledge about this environment, but as they would all readily admit, it is knowledge that could be greatly supplemented, refined, and even overturned by good scientific work. Deliberate steps taken to incorporate a scientific component within the governance structure would undoubtedly enhance the usefulness of fishers' knowledge and the feedback necessary for management success.

Copes, P. 1986. "A Critical Review of the Individual Quota as a Device in Fisheries Management." *Land Economics* 62(3):278–91.

Cushing, D. H. 1973. "Dependence of Recruitment on Parent Stock." *J. Fish. Res. Bd. Canada* 30:1965–76.

Dickie, L. M., and J. E. Valdivia G. 1981. "Investigacion Cooperativa de la Anchoveta y su Ecosistema (ICANE) between Peru and Canada. A Summary Report." *Boletin Instituto del mar del Peru* Vol. Extraordinario: XIII–XXIII.

Duplisea, D. E., and S. R. Kerr. Forthcoming. "Application of a Theoretical Biomass Size Spectrum Model to Demersal Fish Data from the Scotian Shelf." *J. Theor. Biol.*

Eggertsson, T. 1990. *Economic Behavior and Institutions.* Cambridge, United Kingdom: Cambridge University Press.

Garrod, D. J. 1973. "The Variation of Replacement and Survival in Some FishStocks." In B. B. Parrish, ed., *Fish Stocks and Recruitment.* ICES. Rapp. et Proc. Verb. 164. pp. 43–56.

Hennemuth, R. C. 1979. "Man as a Predator." In G. P. Patil and M. L. Rosenzweig, eds., *Contemporary Qualitative Ecology and Related Econometrics.* Fairland, Maryland: International Cooperative Publishing House.

Holling, C. S., and others, eds. 1978. *Adaptive Environmental Assessment and Management. 3rd International Series on Applied Systems Analysis.* New York: J. Wiley & Sons.

Hutchings, J. A., and R. A. Myers. 1994. "What Can Be Learned from the Collapse of a Natural Resource? Atlantic Cod, Gadus Morhua, of Newfoundland and Labrador." *Can. J. Fish. Aquat. Sci.* 51: 2126–46.

Iles, T. D. 1973. "The Interaction of Environment and Parent Stock Size in Determining Recruitment of the Pacific Sardine as Revealed by the Analysis of Density-Dependent O-Group Growth." In B. B. Parrish, ed., *Fish Stocks and Recruitment.* ICES. Rapp. et Proc. Verb. 164, pp. 228–40.

Lambert, T. C. 1990. "The Effect of Population Structure on Recruitment in Herring." *J. Cons. int. Explor. Mer.* 47:249–55.

Mann, K. H., and K. F. Drinkwater. 1994. "Environmental Influences on Fish and Shellfish Production in the Northwest Atlantic." *Environ. Rev.* 2:16–32.

McCay, B. J. 1994. "A Framework for Fisheries Management." Paper presented at the Coastal Communities Network Provincial Conference, Shaping the Future Fishery, Dartmouth, Nova Scotia, Canada, March 10–12.

Murawski, S. A., and J. S. Idoine. 1989. "Multi-Species Composition: A Conservative Property of Exploited Fishery Systems?" Northwest Atlantic Fisheries Organization, SCR Doc. 89/76.

Ostrom, E. 1977. "Collective Action and the Tragedy of the Commons." In G. Hardin and J. Baden, eds., *Managing the Commons.* San Francisco, California: W. H. Freeman.

———. 1992. *Crafting Institutions for Self-Governing Irrigation Systems.* San Francisco, California: ICS Press.

Ostrom, V. 1971. *The Political Theory of a Compound Republic.* Lincoln: University of Nebraska Press.

———. 1991. *The Meaning of American Federalism: Constituting a Self-Governing Society.* San Francisco, California: ICS Press.

Ostrom, V. and E. Ostrom. 1977. "A Theory for Institutional Analysis for Common Pool Problems." In G. Hardin and J. Baden. eds., *Managing the Commons.* San Francisco, California: W. H. Freeman.

Pinkerton, E. 1989. *Cooperative Management of Local Fisheries.* Vancouver: University of British Columbia Press.

———. 1994. "Local Fisheries Co-Management—A Review of International Experiences and Their Implications for Salmon Management in British Columbia." *Can. J. Fish. Aquat. Sci.* 51(10):2363–78.

Pope, J. G., and B. J. Knights. 1982. "Comparisons of Length Distributions of Combined Catches of all Demersal Fishes in Surveys in the North Sea and at Faroe Bank." In M. C. Mercer, ed., *Multispecies Approaches to Fisheries Management Advice.* Can. Spec. Publ. Fish. Aquat. Sci. 59, pp. 116–18.

Regier, H. A. 1973. "Sequence of Exploitation of Stocks in Multispecies Fisheries in the Laurentian Great Lakes." *J. Fish. Res. Bd. Canada* 30:1992–99.

Rosen, Robert. 1991. *Life Itself.* New York: Columbia University Press.

Sheldon, R. W., A. Prakash, and W. H. Sutcliffe, Jr. 1977. "The Size Distribution of Particles in the Ocean." *Limnol. Oceanogr.* 17:327–40.

Sutcliffe, W. H. Jr., K. Drinkwater and B. S. Muir. 1977. "Correlations of Fish Catch and Environmental Factors in the Gulf of Maine." *J. Fish. Res. Bd. Canada* 34:19–30.

Williamson, O. E. 1985. *The Economic Institutions of Capitalism.* New York: The Free Press.

Wilson, J. A, J. French, P. Kleban, S. R. McKay, and R. Townsend. 1991. "Chaotic Dynamics in a Multiple Species Fishery: A Model of Community Predation." *Ecological Modeling* 58:303–22.

———, J. M. Acheson, Mark Metcalfe, and Peter Kleban. 1994. "Chaos, Complexity and Community Management of Fisheries." *Marine Policy* 18:291–305.

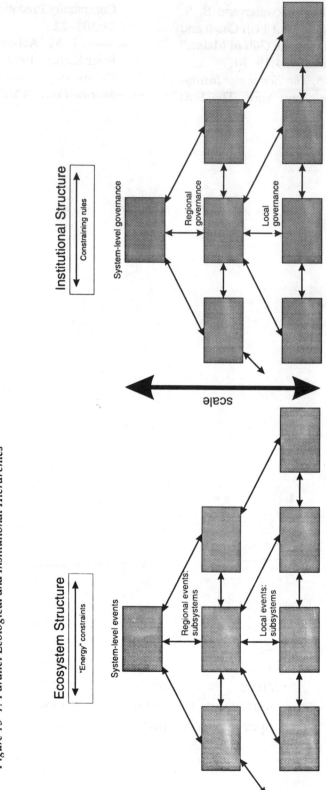

Figure 13–1: Parallel Ecological and Institutional Hierarchies

14

Environmental and Socioeconomic Linkages of Deforestation and Forest Land Use Change in the Nepal Himalaya

Ajay S. Pradhan and Peter J. Parks

Abstract

Nepal's rural farming communities depend on forests for products such as fuelwood and fodder. These communities have often been blamed for deforestation and its environmental consequences (for example, forest fragmentatation and degradation, accelerated soil erosion). Until recent years, the government's forest policy has been to change the forest property regime and protect forests as a state-owned resource. This effort to exclude local communities from using and protecting forests distorted land use incentives, and prompted individuals and communities to view state-owned forests as open-access resources.

Although the subsistence activities of farming communities are probably responsible to some extent for deforestation, the root cause has been the failure of government's policy regarding forest property regime and lack of effective decentralization in forest management. Policy initiatives taken by the government in recent years include handing back some of the state-owned forests to local communities for community management. This represents movement in the right direction, but the government must (a) show adequate willingness to transfer property and use rights to local communities and (b) recognize the capacity of local communities for self-governance in managing their resources.

✧

Introduction

More than half of Nepal's population lives in ecologically fragile watersheds of hills and mountains with marginal agricultural lands. Increases in population have resulted in large-scale forest degradation and in widespread use of marginal and highly erodible lands for cultivation and livestock grazing. Crop production depends on livestock systems sustained by fodder from the forests. Forests are also the prime source of household energy (fuelwood) and timber supplies.

As the forests have declined, the consumption of biomass and nutrients has exceeded the additions to stocks, causing agriculture to stagnate and making present practice of land use unsustainable and environmentally destructive. The total forest area is estimated to have declined from 6.4 million hectares in 1964 to 5.5 million hectare in 1985. It is estimated that about 0.2 million hectares of the *terai* and Siwaliks forests were cleared through planned settlement and illegal felling from the 1950s to 1985. Out of 5.5 million hectares of forest land, only 0.81 million hectares have over 70 percent crown cover. About 25 percent of the forest land is degraded, and has less than 40 percent crown cover. The loss and degradation of forests is one of Nepal's most serious resource management problems, and influences the environmental conditions in many other sectors of economy.

Forests are an integral part of rural society and the subsistence economy, providing fire-

wood, which is the main source of energy for cooking and heating, grass and leaves for animal fodder, and timber for building materials (Mahat 1987). Nepal's subsistence agricultural system is invariably based on the combined use of land, animal, and forest resources. There is a close-knit interrelationship between crop production, livestock, and forest resources in traditional subsistence agricultural systems in the mountains and hills of Nepal. From 1 to 2.8 hectares of forest are required to support one hectare of arable land (Wyatt-Smith 1982, Mahat and others 1987a, Ives and Messerli 1989).

Fuelwood is Nepal's major energy source, meeting 90 percent of all energy needs. Leaves from trees, understory plants, and grasses are major sources of fodder. In fact, the forest is most heavily used to provide fodder for livestock. The need for animal feed from the forest is three times as great as the need for fuelwood (Wyatt-Smith 1982). The collection of fuelwood and fodder, the grazing of animals, and the conversion of forests to agricultural land have all contributed to a greater or lesser extent to deforestation, forest degradation, and land use change in Nepal, particularly in the middle hills region.

Deforestation has had far-reaching consequences. Scarcity drives up the price of fuelwood that is sold in urban areas; livestock suffer from an inadequate and nutrient-poor food supply; erosion contributes to declining soil productivity; streams and rivers fill with silt and sediment, reducing their hydroelectric potential and their use for drinking water; landslides carry away entire villages; and floods wipe out crops and damage property not only in the flood plains of Nepal but also of India and Bangladesh. This situation points a bleak picture of the country's future.

Many observers think that Nepal is on the brink of a crisis that may cause irreversible damage to the fragile mountain ecosystem. However, not all agree with this prevailing view. This conventional view is now being questioned by an increasing number of scholars. The scrutiny of the conventional view has identified uncertainties and weak causal and consequential linkages of deforestation and land use change.

This chapter characterizes socioeconomic factors of land use change from forest land to agricultural land, and critically analyzes the conventional hypothesis that (a) the constraints to resource development and economic needs of the local people and mountain subsistence farmers have caused extensive deforestation and a rapid change in land use from forestry to agriculture, and (b) this land use change has consequently given rise to environmental problems, such as soil erosion and land degradation. The chapter examines public policies and institutional mechanisms that have been created to govern natural resources under different property regimes, including common-pool resources. These mechanisms have created or influenced the linkages between natural resource exploitation, particularly forest resource exploitation, and environmental problems, with land use change as an interface.

Land Use and Management in Nepal

The most complete study of land use and land resource base was undertaken by the Land Resources Mapping Project in the early 1980s (LRMP 1986). Land use in Nepal can be categorized into six different types: cultivated lands, noncultivated inclusions, grasslands, forested lands, shrublands and degraded forests, and other lands (LRMP 1986).

Table 14–1 presents the LRMP estimates for the major land use categories for the five physiographic zones. Forest land constitutes 37 percent of the total land area of the country, whereas cultivated land constitutes 21 percent. Grassland and shrubland constitute 7 and 5 percent, respectively. Noncultivated inclusions, which are small pockets of land close to cultivated lands and which may contain barren areas, trees, shrubs, or grass, constitute 7 percent. Almost all of the lands shown in the table as forest, shrub, or grasslands are under the control of the government (Gilmour and Fisher 1991).

Forest lands are those with at least 10 percent crown cover, and may include small pockets of plantation and burned areas. "Other lands" include rocky areas, water bodies, or settlements, and constitute 18 percent. This would place forests as the biggest land-using sector, although a quarter of the nation's forests are degraded to varying degrees, with less than 40 percent crown cover (MPFSP 1988). Much of the forest is poorly stocked, and potential productivity is severely impaired (Gilmour and Fisher 1991).

Recent Land-Use Change

A number of studies are available that show that Nepal's forest area is declining and some of the forest lands are probably being converted to agricultural lands (for example, LRMP 1986, WECS 1983). Table 14–2 shows the changes in the area of forested lands and shrublands (forest area) in two physiographic zones. The figures for the mountain areas were excluded by LRMP, since WECS had concluded that the area of forests in the mountain zones had not changed significantly during the study period. It was, however, noted that overcutting for fuelwood and fodder had resulted in the degradation of accessible forests in the mountain zones.

The land use changes between 1979 and 1986 were also estimated by the MPFSP (1988) by taking into account the opening of *terai* and Siwalik forests to settlements, forest cutting to meet wood demands, and the development of plantations during the period (Table 14–3). A total of 103,968 hectares of forests in the Siwalik and *terai* were cleared under government settlement programs from the 1950s to 1985. About 22,700 hectares of these were cleared from 1978-79 to 1984-85. It was also assumed that equal area of forest was lost due to illegal settlements during this period. MPFSP (1988) found that during the seven-year period between 1978-79 and 1985-86, the forest area slightly increased in high Himalaya and high mountain zones, but decreased slightly in middle mountains and Siwalik, and significantly in the *terai*. Not all of the deforested lands were converted to agriculture; some remained as degraded forests and grasslands. Forest area (including natural forests, degraded forests, shrublands, and new plantations) declined by only 84,900 hectares, or 1.3 percent, in 1979–86. As an annual rate, this is only 0.2 percent, half of the 1964–79 period.

The main causes of forest degradation were attributed to overcutting of trees for fuelwood and lopping of trees for fodder. Another cause of forest degradation was said to be illicit felling of trees in the *terai* for commercial timber for illegal export across the border to India. It was also reported that more than a quarter of the forests are degraded, with less than 40 percent crown cover. Between 1964-65 and 1978-79, and again between 1978-79 and 1985-96, the forest area decreased, particularly in the Siwalik hills and the *terai*.

During approximately the same period, the area of agricultural lands increased significantly (Table 14–4). Between 1965 and 1985 the estimated area under cultivation increased by 31 percent and the annually cropped area by 100 percent. The cropping intensity had risen from 108 percent in 1965 to 166 percent by 1985; however, at the same time, the yield remained stagnant or even declined (Hrabovszky and Miyan 1987). Although the time-series data on land use change in general and increasing deforestation and expansion of agricultural land in particular are not yet strong, available data suggest a positive linkage between deforestation and agricultural expansion.

Forestry-Agriculture Linkages

Nepal is facing two fundamental land-resource issues: (a) the final limit of land suitable for cultivation is rapidly being approached; and (b) the speed at which suitable land can be brought into cultivation, or at which its intensity of use can be increased, is constrained by available technology.

Nepal still has about 730,000 hectares, in addition to the 2.41 million hectares presently under cultivation, that could be converted to arable land (Ives and Messerli 1989). All this land is currently under forest cover and nearly all is in the *terai*. Demand for forest products such as fuelwood will probably prevent all of this land from being converted. Moreover, removal of forest reduces nutrient supply to farm lands and animals due to the shortage of fodder, and forest litter for the supply of organic matter to the arable lands. Taking these considerations into account and allowing for the increased area of settlements and roads, Hrabovsky and Miyan (1987) estimate that only about 160,000 hectares could be added to total cultivated land; this amount is seven percent of the presently cultivated area. The limited potential to increase the cultivated area clearly points to land use intensification as the main means for raising agricultural output.

The traditional method for maintaining the fertility of the land is running into resource constraints, not only because of the declining forest/cultivated land ratio, but also because the supply of farmyard manure is rather inelastic. There are opportunities to increase the share of manure which is available for cropland (for example, through zero grazing and stall-feeding systems); however, there is a consensus that Nepal should avoid increasing the number of animals because fodder is already scarce and increased grazing will further damage forests and grasslands. Thus the ultimate resource for increasing production is technological change, through low-cost, appropriate technology, and improved and expanded irrigation.

When land resources are constrained and technological change does not provide enough relief from the pressure of population on food resources, most societies adapt the pattern of distribution of the limited resources, or they establish rules about sharing labor and thus the total product of society. Nepal shows some of these signs, but also a growing landlessness among the agricultural population. Given the limits on all the above means of adaptation, when possible, the reaction of the farming population to a declining per capita land base is to migrate from hills to the plains, both in the form of rural-to-rural and rural-to-urban migration.

Indigenous Forest and Farm Management

Deforestation is often claimed to result from mismanagement of the environment by local users (Griffin and others 1988). Villagers are almost never thought of as having the ability to recognize the problems, let alone do something about them. Identifying and resolving land use problems is seen to be the sole prerogative of outside interventionists (for example, government, foreign experts). Efforts to halt and reverse the loss of forest cover in the hills are not a lost cause; the farmers themselves have already realized the nature of the problem and are doing something about it (Gilmour 1988).

Contrary to the claims by many professionals, there are documented as well as anecdotal examples that show that local subsistence farmers are aware of the problem of declining forest resources and productivity, and are willing to respond to the problem by way of indigenous forest and farm management practices. Many examples of indigenous forms of forest management have been cited by Arnold and Campbell (1985) and Molnar (1981).

These examples vary considerably, but generally involve locally devised and operated rule-ordered institutional mechanisms to ensure protection of the forest in conjunction with controlled access for harvesting and collecting forest products. Protection is frequently accompanied by paying a forest watcher (guard) in either cash or in kind (generally grain), with the payment coming from the families that form the use group (Gilmour and others 1989).

Historical and contemporary evidence indicates that subsistence farmers in the villages of Nepal are very aware about the linkages of forestry and agricultural systems, and have responded to the resource depletion problems from community and household levels. At the community level, they have engaged in collective management of common-pool resources, most significantly forest resources. Gilmour and Fisher (1991) report that there are many places in the hills of Nepal where local people have—without outside guidance—made arrangements to protect and regulate access to forest resources for which there is no single owner.

Those who blame the subsistence farmers for over-using forest resources may confuse common-pool forest resources and with open access forest resources. The open access situation actually developed as a result of the failure of state property rights enforcement by the government due to the lack of capital and human resources. Although the villagers may have overused the open-access forests, the origin of the problem lies in the government policy of not seeking people's participation until recently. Successful indigenous and common-pool forest resource management systems have been identified in many villages of Nepal (for example, Campbell 1978; Campbell and others 1987; Fisher 1989; Gilmour and Fisher 1991; Messerschmidt 1986, 1987; Molnar 1981). Local systems of management are increasingly acknowledged as central to the conservation and sustained utilization of Nepal's upland natural resources (Exo 1990).

The *Shinga naua* system is a classic example of a successful common forest management system practiced by the local Sherpa community in the Solukhumbu region of Nepal. The *Shinga naua* were locally appointed officials with responsibility for allocating forest resources and enforcing compliance to locally crafted rules. Later this indigenous system was replaced by the government apparatus, which led to a conversion of property rights regime of forests from a common-pool resource to open access resource. This example offers a very good case in which a successful common-pool resource management regime was replaced by a system that ignored the local people's need.

Subsistence farmers have also taken private initiative at the household level by planting trees on their private farm lands to tackle the problem of forest resource depletion. A study of tree cover and density on the private farmlands in rural village offers an appropriate insight into the perception of subsistence farmers about the importance of forests and trees in a rural agricultural system. While national studies on this topic do not yet exist, studies carried out to estimate the change of tree density on private farmlands in the hill villages in central Nepal can be considered to represent the situation in the hill areas of Nepal. Gilmour and Fisher (1991) and Gilmour and Nurse (1991) provide examples that indicate subsistence farmers have employed indigenous management practices to integrate forestry and farming.

Forest Management and Policy Initiatives

Recent History of Forest Management

The Nepal government has recognized severe inadequacies and impracticabilities of the centralized, command-and-control bureaucratic model of forest management. Since 1988, it has ostensibly sought to decentralize the policy process and to provide for greater community participation in forestry policy (IUCN 1991). Community forestry, which is a form of common-pool resource management, was practiced in the hills of Nepal before the nationalization of forests in 1957 (Bonita and Kanel 1988) through the enactment by the government of the Private Forests Nationalization Act. The Act was passed ostensibly to protect, manage, and conserve the forests of the country, but it ignored the traditional communal practices and rules that regulated forest use (Basnet 1992). Because of the Act's adverse effect on forest resources, and consequently on the environment, it was realized that without the cooperation of local communities, Nepal's forests cannot be conserved and developed (Bonita and Kanel 1988).

As recognized by MPFSP (1988), forest management in Nepal can be said to have gone through three phases during the last fifty years. The first phase can be characterized as management by local people of forests near their villages to meet household needs for fuelwood, fodder, and other timber and nontimber forest products. The forests were communally managed and people could generally obtain enough forest products for their needs. This was what can be called common property resource management.

The second phase was characterized by a reduction of the forest area, and degradation of the remaining stands. Initially, the decline was slow, but it rapidly accelerated. In 1957, forests were nationalized in Nepal. The preamble of the enabling act states that forests are an important part of the national wealth and that it is necessary to nationalize them in order to protect, manage, and utilize them so that they may not be depleted. While the objective of the act was noble, in many instances its effects were opposite to what was intended.

The act allowed private ownership of up to 1.25 hectares of forests in the hills or 3.5 hectares in the *terai*. To prevent their private forests from being nationalized, people who owned forests converted their forests to farmlands. Moreover, the remaining forests virtually became nobody's property, since the government had no resource to protect them effectively, let alone manage them. With the increase in population and demand for forest products, the forests, particularly those in the hills, were put under heavy pressure. In the *terai*, the situation was no better. With the eradication of malaria, people from the hills migrated to the plains and converted large tracts of forests into settlements and farms.

The National Forestry Plan of 1976 marks the beginning of the third phase. It recognized the critical forestry situation and laid down as objectives for forest management the restoration of the balance of nature, economic mobilization, practice of scientific management, development of technology, and promotion of public cooperation. The initiation of community forestry practices also characterizes the third phase. This

system was started in a village in Sindhu Palchok, a district to the southeast of the Kathmandu District. A forest committee comprised mostly of local people makes decisions about the use and management of forests. This system is proving to be an effective rural institution, and has encouraged greater self-reliance.

Decentralization Program

Given the enormous diversity in geography, resource endowment, and socioeconomic characteristics in Nepal, central government is poorly placed to identify local needs or implement natural resource management programs in the rural areas. The Decentralization Act of 1982 was enacted for the implementation of decentralization programs to deal with this shortcoming. This program provided a broad basis for community forestry projects, among other planning and management activities at the local level. However, a study completed for the World Bank in 1989 by Environmental Resources Limited (ERL) indicates that the results for forestry have been disappointing (ERL 1989). The main mechanisms provided by the decentralized program were designed to to encourage local participation in natural resource management.

Forest Management By User Communities

In the forestry sector, the user groups are the foundation of the community forestry program. The user groups manage the common-pool forest resources for the common benefit of the user community. The forests that are managed by the user groups can either be community forests or state-owned forests that have been handed over to the local community. Such user groups are legally assigned use and access rights over the forests.

Under this mechanism, direct beneficiaries of a certain forest are identified and organized into user groups. Each group elects a user committee that writes a management plan and rules for the management and protection of a portion of national forest or for afforestation of badly degraded national forest. Upon approval of the management plan by the district forest officer and the chairman of the village development committee, which is the politically elected local government body, the legal tenure of the forest is given to the user group in the custody of the village development committee. The regulation gives the village development committee all rights to forest resources.

Overall achievements in establishing groups as a result of these provisions are not well documented. Details about the successes or failures of user group establishment are sketchy. Lack of local people's participation and support is a major barrier to the success. Although the user groups elect user committees that are supposed to develop management plans and rules, in practice, the plans and rules are often written by the district forest office staff. Therefore, the objective of enabling user groups is to guarantee their long-term involvement, but this objective remains unfulfilled.

Since 1979, some 28,000 hectares of plantation forests and 35,000 hectares of protected forests have come under the management of formal user groups. However, this only represents one percent of the forests. Nevertheless, about one-third of the country's forests is actively managed by indigenous, informal user groups that are largely not recognized or ignored by the government.

The Decentralization Act and the Community Forestry regulations allow for the establishment of user groups. The concept of user groups for forest management combines the basic concept of community forestry with that of the Decentralization Act, and has been based around the village development and user committees. Most formal user groups have been set up under projects with a community forestry program. User groups have been established by various forestry-related development projects as well as by the government's Department of Forests.

The Community Forestry Program is intended to set up two nurseries and at least one forestry committee in each village. The aim of the Community Forestry Development Program is to improve management practices with the intention of halting all deterioration of forest stocks, which are being depleted at two percent per annum (ERL 1989). Since the introduction of the Community Forestry Program in 1979, user groups have been established to carry out plantation forestry to plant 63,000 hectares of forest by 1988. This is equivalent to one percent of Nepal's forests.

Locally self-organized indigenous groups have existed in many areas of the country, and they provide important lessons for establishing self-sustaining user groups. There are a large number of indigenous self-governing user groups that are managing community forests, with little or no assistance from anyone outside the community. There is no reliable estimate of the number of indigenous user groups, but a number of surveys show that the existence of community-protected forests is common and growing.

Thirty-three percent of forests are under the management of informal user groups (Dani and Campbell 1986), and 22 to 50 percent of villages have such user groups (Campbell and others 1987). Fisher and others (1989) suggest that management activities may be cyclical, appearing and disappearing in relation to scarcity, suggesting that the objective of local group activities is to achieve local balance in demand and supply of forest products rather than conservation.

There are several advantages of having user groups in the management of forest resources. As they write their own plans and rules, define their duties and privileges regarding forest protection and use, there is a strong sense of stewardship and a long-term interest in sustainable management based on local knowledge of demand and supply of forest products. They can ensure the participation of all direct users, including women and poorer households, in protecting and benefitting from the management of local resources. Their activities have to be endorsed by the village development committees, therefore making them accountable to the most local unit of political representation. They are expected to mobilize their own resources for management activities.

The success of user groups depends on a number of factors, such as good motivation, assurance of rights, and effective resource mobilization. In order to establish user groups widely, it is important to know what motivates a community to form a group to manage its resources and how this can be facilitated. User groups must be given assurance of rights over the use of forest resources.

Instituting Forest User Groups

Several provisions are available under community forestry programs for establishing and supporting user groups through legal and financial means. The legal provisions give the village development committees the right to form user groups and committees, and also empower them to formulate working plans and utilize forestry revenues for forestry activities. The specific provisions include assignment of property rights, establishment of user committees, and development of management plans and rules.

The framework recognizes that where people do not have recognized rights and therefore a guarantee of benefits, they will make little effort to manage the forests. The user group is therefore given the property and user rights over some state-owned forests under the supervision of the village development committee. The group has a responsibility to protect the forest from unscrupulous use by enforcing rules that are designed by its committee. The committee designs a management plan that contains detailed rules, which is implemented by the group for the effective management of resources and for equitable distribution of products.

The plan demarcates and describes the state of the resource, and identifies the beneficiaries. The plan also serves as a contract between the district forest officer, the village development committee, and the user group. The plan provides mutual assurance that no one in the group can consume more than others. In the case of disputes, the district forest officer arbitrates and helps achieve equity. The district forest officer is actually accountable to the government. If the village development committee, which is the local government, judges that the user committee is failing in its duties, then the user committee can be dissolved. The village development committee, therefore, has an important role in the establishment and operation of user groups.

In practice, the provision of this framework mechanism has not proven to be a sufficient incentive for communities to establish user groups without external support. Such support is often provided by development projects having a community forestry program component. Potential members of the user groups are identified by field-level staff of the district forest office in collaboration with the village development committee.

Gilmour (1987) has found that as long as ample forest resources are available, there was practically no interest in protecting or managing the forests. However, communities showed emerging interest in the management and protection activities as forest resources began to be depleted. As the shortage of forest products became more acute and it took much longer for the people to get to the nearest forest than before, they became aware of the situation, showed genuine interest in management activities, required little or no convincing through extension work, and welcomed outside assistance.

Motivation for establishing a forest user group emerged for two reasons. First, degradation and depletion of forests and their resources have prompted people to get organized to tackle the problem collectively. Second, the long-established management system to protect religious forests has always required group cooperation. The first is most important and has happened where rotational or seasonal harvesting breaks down because of population pressure, or because people have other sources of income and are no longer interested in managing forest resources. As the resources are depleted, people become aware of the need for action.

The conditions that can be expected to act as an incentive or motivation exist in many areas, but there is no evidence of user groups approaching the line agencies for assistance in starting work. In some cases, user committees had been established without the knowledge of the users or even those whose name had been put on the committees (ERL 1989). In these cases, plantation and protection were carried out by government employees without any involvement of the villagers. This suggests that "user groups" were established only to meet project targets. This is an example of the typical target mentality of the government bureaucracy.

In order to help establish user groups, the line agencies provide cash and noncash, credits or grants to groups. Noncash assistance can include land, seedlings, saplings, nursery materials, and watchman services, among other things. The line agencies provide technical expertise for preparing and implementing forest management plans. As local villagers lack technical knowledge and expertise, this is an important form of assistance.

Obstacles to Forming User Groups

Several problems that may be encountered in successful establishment and operation of user groups can be identified. These are chief among them: conflicting political interests within the user community; overemphasis on formal decisionmaking; lack of mechanisms to encourage involvement of women and minorities, especially the so-called "low-caste" people; lack of effective participation of users in designing plans and rules; lack of motivation among government field agents; lack of extension work; and lack of support to informal and indigenous user groups.

Often the interests of the elected representatives do not really represent the interests of the villagers. Usually, only those people can get elected to public office who have social and economic influence due to caste, religion, and landholding factors. Hobley and others (1988) suggest that women and minority groups are not well represented on indigenous committees either, which tend to be dominated by "higher-caste" men.

Dani and Campbell (1986) suggest that although user group committees are supposed to make decisions regarding forest use, often the decisions are made by staff of district forest officer's office. This may create situations where decisions may not be acceptable to many user group members. In this respect, indigenous groups seem to be better organized, as all of their decisions are made by informal committee that meets on an ad hoc basis as the need arises. Decisions may take longer to reach but are likely to reflect a consensus.

Lack of consensus is a problem. For instance, where community grazing land has been converted to community forestry without broad consensus, grazing restrictions are often not respected. Where rules are based on consensus and well understood by everyone, they are seldom broken; where there is fear that they may be broken, a forest watcher is appointed and paid by the group. The management plans drawn up by indigenous groups are simple and often effective because they are based on consensus and group understanding. In a Community Forestry Development Project study, Shrestha and others (1986) suggest that the management plan must be simplified so as to be comprehensible for the users. Support of local political leaders is crucial for the success of user groups.

If legal property rights are in question, conflicts may arise. Specifically, the conflicts arise when several groups lay conflicting claims on forest resources. Conflicts arise also because the control of resources offers political and economic power. Campbell and others (1987) suggest that some villagers use several forests for different products, while other prices of forests are used by several village development committees. This suggests that it would be far more desirable for the groups to hold the property rights to the resources. ERL (1989) reports that where the existence of indigenous user groups has not been recognized, any effort to replace them with formal user groups cannot gain local support. Besides, such an initiative tends to stifle indigenous efforts to organize informal groups.

Conclusions and Policy Implications

Conclusion

Subsistence activities of rural farming communities may have been responsible for deforestation in Nepal, but their behavior has been driven by misguided incentive structures and policy initiatives. Study of historical and contemporary government initiatives and policies has influenced the behavior of farmers. Historically, the government has engaged in surplus extraction and rent-seeking by increasing the tax revenue base in the agriculture sector by allowing and encouraging—and in some cases, even by granting—incentives to people to convert forest lands into agricultural lands.

Such incentives often included granting of lands as personal reward. In addition, recent policy initiatives in Nepal designed to reduce forest cutting have had the reverse effect. For example, the enactment in 1957 of the Private Forests Nationalization Act prompted the alarmed villagers to convert their forests to farmlands because the nationalization reduced security of tenure and usufruct, and the villagers who converted their forests into farmlands could still claim those lands as private (see, for example, Bajracharya 1983; Mahat and others 1987b). Moreover, in the absence of effective enforcement of the newly nationalized state property regime, coupled with the villagers' perception that their forest lands had been expropriated by the government, the forest became—for all practical purposes—an open access resource which villagers felt free to squander.

The nationalization policy, in effect, prompted destruction of traditional conservation systems in the villages. This policy began a legacy of distrust and suspicion that defined relations between hill farmers and their government (Metz 1989; FAO/World Bank 1979). The nationalization policy was a top-down approach; the government took control of all the forests and promoted a hierarchical system. Local people's participation was not sought, there was no incentive for local community development, the revenue collected from the forests was not utilized for local development, and it was costly for the government to maintain an efficient infrastructure (NAFP 1976). Moreover, the real target of the nationalization policy—the landlords who owned vast tracts of forest lands—converted the forests to farmlands as much and as quickly as they could to keep their lands from being nationalized.

The foregoing conclusion does not mean that subsistence farmers are not responsible at all for deforestation in Nepal; it only means they are not the only ones to blame. Among the most important causes of deforestation and forest land use change into agricultural land is the deliberate action of the government to increase tax revenue by expanding agriculture into forests, and misguided government policies that ignore or discourage the participation of local people in the management of forests.

Policy Implications

Property Rights and Self-Governance

After the nationalization of forests in 1957 and until the late 1970s the government expected that placing the forests under the control of the Forest Department would ensure proper management and protection. The effort to ensure conservation of Nepal's forests through command and control by the national government has been largely unsuccessful. Therefore, local people's participation and self-governance is essential if conservation and management of forests are to be effective and successful. Priority should be given to the local community and their indigenous knowledge, views, skills, and methods of resource utilization (Mishra and Sherpa 1987). Local people often have detailed knowledge about their resources, which is invaluable for the planning and management of local natural resources.

Therefore, the legacy of distrust and suspicion between local people and the government must be broken down by designing policy that encourages self-governance. Rather than viewing the subsistence farmers as ignorantly destroying their environment, policymakers should view them as people with sufficient understanding about their environment, about the environmental and socioeconomic consequences of deforestation and forest land use change. Villagers know what needs to be done; they simply lack means to do it (Ives and others 1987). Social and physical problems of the Himalaya cannot be alleviated without utilizing the knowledge, experience, and cooperation of hill farmers. Despite the reorientation in national policy which seeks to elevate the role of local people in managing crucial resources, significant expansion of local initiatives has yet to occur. Until local people are empowered to reclaim and renew the dwindling resource base on which they depend, their already marginal existence will continue to worsen. The legal and organizational basis for local control of resources must be strengthened, and barriers must be removed.

More recently the policy has shifted course, and the current approach is to devolve control of forests back to local people. For the most part, this has been conceived of in terms of setting up new local organizations to manage forests (Gilmour and Fisher 1991). Devolving control of forests back to local people means shifting the forests from the management by the government and placing them under the management of the local people themselves who use the forests and forest products. However, the process of devolution should be accompanied by incentives to local people.

The most important incentive is the recognition of people's rights to use forest resources. Once such rights are assured, the local people will form formal and informal institutional structures necessary for the proper management and protection of forest and forest resources. Formation of user groups, user group committees, and appointment of forest watchmen are some of the components of such institutional structure. Others are development and imposition of formal or informal rules and regulations. Therefore, in order to place forests under the effective management of the forest users themselves, their use rights must be defined and appropriately recognized.

Integration of Forestry and Agricultural Planning

Over 90 percent of Nepal's people are engaged in subsistence farming, which is critically dependent on the forestry system. In other words, Nepal has a mixed farming system. Forestry and agriculture are both major land-using sectors of the country's economy. Therefore, the planning for one sector must be invariably linked with the other sector. For example, land use facilities must be planned and implemented in such a way as to take into account the strong interrelationship that exists between these two sectors.

Limits on extensive land use in the agriculture sector have been reached, or even exceeded, in many parts of Nepal. In the meantime, the pressure of a growing population on the land continues to rise. Since agriculture cannot be expanded, the only solution to an increasing demand for food is intensified agricultural land use. This will curtail the pressure to clear forest for agriculture.

Intensification must, however, be carried out with proper regard for ecological concerns. Intensification must be achieved not only in agriculture, but also in the other two major land-using sectors: grazing lands and forests. Land must be allocated to uses which are not degrading and which represent the best and most productive use of that land. Within each of the main categories, there must be a drive to use the most productive and least degradation-prone lands most intensively, so as to reduce the pressure on marginal lands, which then can be put to appropriate nondegrading uses.

Bibliography

Arnold, J. E. M., and J. G. Campbell. 1985. "Collective Management of Hill Forests in Nepal: The Community Forestry Development Project." Paper presented at the Common Property Resources Management conference, April 21–27, Annapolis, Maryland.

Bajracharya, D. 1983. "Deforestation in the Food/Fuel Context: Historical and Political Perspective from Nepal." *Mountain Research and Development*, 3(3):227–240.

Basnet, K. 1992. "Conservation Practices in Nepal: Past and Present." *Ambio*, 21(6):390–393.

Bonita, M., and K. Kanel. 1988. "Some Views of the Master Plan for Forestry Sector Project on Community Forestry." *Banko Janakari* 1(4):76–88.

Campbell, J. G. 1978. "Community Involvement in Conservation: Social and Organizational Aspects of the Proposed Resource Conservation and Utilization Project in Nepal." Report to U.S. Agency for International Development, Kathmandu.

Campbell, J. G., R. J. Shrestha, and F. Euphrat. 1987. "Socioeconomic Factors in Traditional Forest Use and Management: Preliminary Results from a Study of Community Forest Management in Nepal." *Banko Jankari* 1(4):45–54.

Dani, A. A., and J. G. Campbell. 1986. *Sustaining Upland Resources: People's Participation in Watershed Management.* ICIMOD Occasional Paper No. 3. International Center for Integrated Mountain Development, Kathmandu.

ERL. 1989. "Natural Resource Management for Sustainable Development: A Study of Feasible Policies, Infrastructures and Investment Activities in Nepal with Special Emphasis on the Hills." A Study for the World Bank. London: Environmental Resources Limited.

Exo, S. 1990. Local Resource Management in Nepal: Limitations and Prospects. *Mountain Research and Development* 10(1):16–22.

FAO/World Bank. 1979. *Report of the Nepal Community Forestry Project Preparatory Mission.* FAO/World Bank Report No. 16/79 NEP. Washington, D.C.: The World Bank.

Fisher, R. J. 1989. "Indigenous Systems of Common Property Forest Management in Nepal." Working Paper No. 18. Environment and Policy Institute, East-West Center, Honolulu, Hawaii.

Gilmour, D. A. 1988. "Not Seeing the Trees for the Forest: A Reappraisal of the Deforestation Crisis in Two Hill Districts of Nepal." *Mountain Research and Development* 8(4):343–350.

Gilmour, D. A., and R. J. Fisher. 1991. *Villages, Forests and Forestry: The Philosophy, Process and Practice of Community Forestry in Nepal.* Kathmandu: Sahayogi Press.

Gilmour, D. A., and M. Nurse. 1991. "Farmer Initiatives in Increasing Tree Cover in Central Nepal." In *Workshop on Socioeconomic Aspects of Tree Growing by Farmers*. Anand, Gujarat, India: Institute of Rural Management.

Gilmour, D. A., G. C. King, and M. Hobley. 1989. "Management of Forests for Local Use in the Hills of Nepal—Changing Forest Management Paradigms." *Journal of World Forest Resource Management* 4:93–110.

Griffin, D. M., K. R. Shepherd, and T. B. S. Mahat. 1988. "Human Impact on Some Forests of the Middle Hills of Nepal, Part 5. Comparisons, Concepts, and Some Policy Implications." *Mountain Research and Development* 8(1):43–52.

Hobley, M., D. A. Gilmour and G.C. King. 1988. Management of Forests for Local Use in Nepal. 3: Participatory Forest Management: Who Benefits? Nepal-Australia Forestry Project, Kathmandu.

Hrabovszky, J. P., and K. Miyan. 1987. "Population Growth and Land Use in Nepal." *Mountain Research and Development* 7(3): 264–270.

IUCN. 1991. "Environmental Review of Existing Legislation, Administrative Procedures and Institutional Arrangements Relating to Land Use and Resource Development." Draft Report. Nepal National Conservation Strategy Implementation Project, National Planning Commission and IUCN-The World Conservation Union, Kathmandu.

Ives, J. D., and B. Messerli. 1989. *The Himalayan Dilemma: Reconciling Development and Conservation*. London: Routledge.

Ives, J. D., B. Messerli, and M. Thomson. 1987. "Research Strategy for the Himalayan Region: Conference Conclusions and Overview." *Mountain Research and Development* 7(3):332–344.

LRMP. 1986. Land Utilization Report. Land Resources Mapping Project, His Majesty's Government of Nepal, Kathmandu. Appendices.

Mahat, T. B. S. 1987. *Forestry-Farming Linkages in the Mountains*. ICIMOD Occasional Paper No. 7. International Center for Integrated Mountain Development, Kathmandu.

Mahat, T. B. S., D. M. Griffin, and K. R. Shepherd. 1987a. "Human Impact on Some For-ests of the Middle Hills of Nepal. 3: Forests in the Subsistence Economy of Sindhu Palchok and Kabhre Palanchok." *Mountain Research and Development* 7(1)53–70.

_____. 1987b. "Human Impact on Some Forests of the Middle Hills of Nepal. 4: a Detailed Study in South East Sindhu Palchok and North East Kabhre Palanchok." *Mountain Research and Development* 7(2):111–134.

Messerschmidt, D. A. 1986. "People and Resources in Nepal: Customary Resource Management Systems of the Upper Kali Gandaki." In *Proceedings of International Conference on Common Property Resource Management*. Washington, D.C.: National Academy Press, pp. 455–480.

_____. 1987. "Conservation and Society in Nepal: Traditional Forest Management and Innovative Development." In P. D. Little and M. M. Horowitz, eds., *Lands at Risk in the Third World: Local Level Perspectives*. Boulder, Colorado: Westview, pp. 373–397.

Metz, J. J. 1989. "Himalayan Political Economy: More Myths in the Closet?" *Mountain Research and Development* 9(2):175–186.

Mishra, H. R, and M. N. Sherpa. 1987. "Nature Conservation and Human Needs: Conflicts and Coexistence: Nepal's Experiment with the Annapurna Conservation Area Project." Fourth World Wilderness Congress, September 11–18, Denver, Colorado.

Molnar, A. 1981. "The Dynamics of Traditional Systems of Forest Management: Implications for the Community Forestry Development and Training Project." Report to the World Bank, Washington, D.C.

MPFSP, 1988. "Master Plan for the Forestry Sector Nepal." Main report in *Master Plan for the Forestry Sector Project*. Kathmandu: Ministry of Forests and Soil Conservation.

NAFP. 1976. "Nepal's National Forestry Plan." Technical Note 1/82. Kathmandu: Nepal-Australia Forestry Project.

Shrestha, B. K., P. B. S. Pradhan, R. Shrestha, and M. B. Dahal. 1986. "Integrating the Forestry Sector Within the District Development Plan Under the Decentralization Policy. HMG/UNDP/FAO Community Forestry Development Project." Kathmandu: Ministry of Forests and Soil Conservation.

WECS. 1986. "Land Use in Nepal: A Summary of the Land Resources Mapping Project

Results." Report No. 4/1/310386/1/1, Seq. No. 225. Kathmandu: Water and Energy Commission Secretariat, Ministry of Water Resources, His Majesty's Government of Nepal.

Wyatt-Smith, J. 1982. *The Agricultural System in the Hills of Nepal: the Ratio of Agricultural to Forestland and the Problem of Animal Fodder*. APROSC Occasional Paper 1. Kathmandu: Agricultural Projects Services Center.

Table 14–1: Land use in Nepal, 1985–86 ('000 hectares)

Physiographic Zone	Cultivated Lands	NCIs	Grass Lands	Forested Lands	Shrub Lands	Other Lands	Total
High Himalaya	8	1	885	155	67	2234	3350
High Mountain	244	148	508	1639	176	245	2960
Mid-Mountain	1223	667	278	1811	404	59	4442
Siwaliks	269	59	16	1438	29	75	1886
Terai	1308	123	58	475	30	116	2110
TOTAL	3052	998	1745	5518	706	2729	14748
Percent	21	7	12	37	5	18	100

Source: LRMP (1986) and MPFSP (1988)

Table 14–2: Changes in Forest Area (Forested Lands and Shrublands) ('000 Hectares)

Physiographic Zones	Forest Area 1964–65	Forest Area 1978–79	Difference	% Change 1964–79	% Change Annual
Siwaliks	1739	1476	-263	-15.1	-1.1
Terai	784	593	-191	-24.4	-1.8
Nepal	6689	6307	-382	-5.7	-0.4

Source: LRMP (1986) and WECS (1983).

Table 14–3: Changes in Area of Natural and Enriched Forests, 1978-79 to 1985-86 ('000 Hectares)

Physiographic Zone	Forest Area 1978–79	Forest Area 1985–86	Difference	% Change 1979–86	% Change Annual
High Himalaya	154	155	+1	0.6	0.0
High Mountain	1628	1634	+6	0.4	0.0
Middle Mountain	1791	1781	-10	-0.6	0.0
Siwalik	1445	1434	-11	-0.8	-0.1
Terai	587	445	-142	-24.1	-3.9
Nepal	5605	5449	-156	-2.8	-0.4

Source: MPFSP (1988)

Table 14–4: Increase in Area under Cultivation in Nepal Between 1965-66 and 1985-86 ('000 Hectares)

Year	Cultivated Land	Cropped Area	Cropping Intensity
1965–66	1,840	1,995	108
1970–71	2,030	2,231	110
1975–76	2,161	2,410	112
1980–81	2,272	2,459	108
1985–86	2,410	4,002	166

Source: Hrabovszky and Miyan (1987)

Poverty and Population

15

Environmental Crisis
and Unsustainability in Himalayas:
Lessons from the Degradation Process

Narpat S. Jodha

Abstract

As revealed by the persistent negative trends in the health and productivity of natural resources bases, the current pattern of resources use in the Himalayas is not sustainable. An understanding of the emerging unsustainability processes suggests that replacement of traditional conservation-oriented resources management systems by more extractive systems is responsible for the current situation. This change, interpreted as a part of the dynamics of nature and society interactions, helps in identification of objective circumstances and driving forces that induced or forced the communities to treat natural resources differently under the traditional and the present-day contexts.

Social Policy and Resettlement Division, Environment Department, the World Bank, Washington, D.C.

Because the reestablishment of traditional circumstances (manifested, for example, by semiclosed, subsistence-oriented communities with total dependence of sustenance on local resources), is not possible, this chapter suggests an approach to explore their present-day functional substitutes to help conservation and sustainable use of resources. In concrete terms, the issues addressed include how to alter resources users' and decisionmakers' perceptions and diagnoses of stakes in natural resources; how to ensure users' understanding of and sensitivity toward natural resources; and how to facilitate local control of community resources. All of these were key elements of traditional systems. This formulation is applicable to the situations beyond the Himalayan context.

Introduction:
Previewing the Argument

The Policy Context

A major challenge faced by the national and international development agencies is rapid resources degradation and declining resources productivity, particularly in the ecological fragile resources zones, such as the Himalayas. Equally important problems are the limited effects of remedial measures on the process of decline and accentuation of resources degradation as a side effect of development and welfare interventions. Even the remedial measures incorporating rationale of traditional resources management systems (with high-sustainability potential under low-demand pressure on resources), failed to stick because of the changed demographic, institutional, and technological contexts.

This chapter attempts to explore the approaches that can be taken to identify present-day functional substitutes of the objective circumstances that induced or forced traditional communities to evolve and adopt measures conducive to sustainability of natural resources. For this, the Himalayan case is used here as an illustration, focusing on unsustainability of the current patterns of natural resources use in the Hindu Kush-Himalayan (HK-H) region, the factors contributing to this process, and possible

approaches to arrest and reverse the current process of resources degradation. In a wider context, the Himalayan case reflects the changing dynamics of nature and society interactions, or the patterns of ecosystem and social system linkages that, in turn, are manifested through changing resources usage practices and the factors dictating them. An understanding of these dynamic processes is a first step toward evolving strategies for sustainable natural resources management.

As a part of such effort, even a quick look at the traditional resources use patterns and practices in the Himalayas reveals several usable lessons for reconciling resources conservation concerns and extraction needs in the present-day context. However, potentially usable rationales of traditional or indigenous resource management practices are not completely context free (Redford 1990) and hence easily transferable. Equally important are the objective circumstances and driving forces that induce or dictate the use of particular measures and practices for resources management. This suggests the need for exploring the present- day functional substitutes of the driving forces and incentive structures that characterized the traditional systems and facilitated balancing of resources conservation concerns and society's production needs.

The Dynamic Context
of Nature-Society Interaction

For operational purposes, the whole dynamics of change or nature and society interactions can be seen as a two-way adaptation process. The latter implies adapting human needs and resources use practices to satisfy them to the features of natural resources bases and adapting or amending the latter to suit the former (Gadgil and Berkes 1991). In a given socioecological context, the nature and composition of adaptation measures, for example, those directed to rationing and diversifying needs, or those focused on manipulating and extracting resources to meet unrestrained demands, represent a society's responses to the objective circumstances created by specific features of natural resources on the one hand and the socioeconomic driving forces on the other.

Factors such as resources users' and decisionmakers' direct and total, or crucial, dependence on local resources, or their control of local resources, their close proximity and intimate functional knowledge of the resources, and so forth (as found in isolated or semiclosed indigenous and traditional communities, such as those in remote mountain areas) tend to make natural resources management systems largely ecology-driven (Berkes 1989; Ellen 1981; Jochim 1981). An absence of these features, as in the case of open and externally linked areas, generates resources use systems that more often are insensitive to the limitation of resources, are highly extractive, and are potentially unsustainable in their orientation as well as application. Dictated by a variety of internal and external driving forces, the extra active orientation of resources usage systems disrupts the ecosystem and social system linkages, which are not only functionally crucial for co-evolution of the two-way adaptation mechanisms, but also are helpful in balancing the resources conservation and production needs of a community.

Restoration of the aforementioned features (crucial dependence on local resources, close physical proximity, functional knowledge of the resources, and so on) that characterized traditional, semiclosed, isolated, small communities and facilitated evolution of effective ecosystem and social system links and sustainable management of natural resources, seems almost impossible in today's world with complex socioeconomic realities. The latter creates a variety of intersystem linkages, hierarchies, and interdependencies. These changes, in turn, create and widen the distance between resources, as well as resources users, and the decisionmaking about resources, between users of resources and final users of resources products, between creators of resources knowledge (research and development, for example) and users of knowledge, and between natural processes and social processes influencing the same resources base. Finally, they dilute or erode the local communities' concerns and abilities for sustainable resources use.

Closer examination of the traditional and present-day resources use systems and their underlying factors can help in identifying some present-day functional equivalents or substitutes for the aforementioned features (close proximity, direct total dependence, and so forth), on which a strategy for sustainable resources use can be built. The above formulation is illustrated by a situation observed in the selected areas of the HK-H region. This chapter presents a synthesis of the studies of microlevel situations, rather than a descriptive and statistical account of the variables in different administrative units covered by the studies. The essence of the argument presented in this chapter can apply to other ecosystems, where resources use patterns are conditioned by relative isolation or closed nature of a system, where users have close proximity to and knowledge of resources bases, and have direct dependence on, as well as local control over, the local resources.

To reiterate, this chapter focuses on the foregoing circumstances (or their present-day functional substitutes) because the frequently advocated incorporation of the rationale of traditional resources use practices in present-day resources management systems is difficult unless the objective circumstances or driving forces conducive to such change are created. In this sense, the argument of this chapter may represent a small step toward the understanding of processes and approaches required for operational use of rich and progressively enlarging inventories of traditional knowledge for environmentally and socially sustainable patterns of natural resources use.

The Empirical Base of the Reasoning

The Geographical Context

The formulation of the issues and approaches presented by this chapter are based on the field level understanding received through studies, including action research on farming systems and resources use practices and attempted replication of successful mountain development experiences, in the selected areas of four countries, as a part of the work program of ICIMOD during 1988-93 (Jodha, Banskota, and Partap 1992; Jodha and Shrestha 1994). The areas studied included West Sichuan and Tibet in China, Himachal Pradesh and the hill areas of Uttar Pradesh states in India, the middle mountains of Nepal, and the North West Frontier province of Pakistan.

Resource Focus

The primary focus of the work at ICIMOD was on mountain and hill agriculture, covering all land-based activities, such as cropping, horticulture, animal husbandry, and forestry and their support systems. However, because of the interrelationship of mountain resources conditions represented by inaccessibility, fragility, marginality, and diversity, and their effects on mountain agriculture, the work encompassed the broader microlevel and macrolevel issues of natural resources management and changes therein. Accordingly, it focused on the totality of resources, including land (soil), vegetation, and water and other related aspects, such as mountain slopes and biodiversity, human adaptation experiences reflected through traditional practices, and mountain development interventions that accelerated indiscriminate usage intensification of fragile and diverse mountain resources.

Dominant Scenarios in HK-H: Emerging Indicators of Unsustainability

Early in the process of the fieldwork and knowledge reviews on mountain agriculture, some persistent negative trends characterizing most of the areas became evident. These verifiable or measurable negative changes, with varying degrees of visibility, which are described as indicators of unsustainability (Jodha 1990), relate to the resources base (for example, decline of topsoil and waterflows or reduced extent of agro- biodiversity), resource productivity (persistent decline in crop and animal yields, as well as in production of biomass), and resource management options and production practices (disappearance and infeasibility of various forms of diversification, facilitating resource regeneration, and disappearance of institutional arrangements to enforce resources conservation measures).

Although some negative changes, such as declines in yields, changes in the composition of vegetation in the forest, and so forth, are clearly visible, others are concealed by human responses to negative changes (for example, substitution of shallow-rooted crops for deep-rooted crops because of topsoil erosion, or increased dependence on chemical fertilizers following the reduced regeneration of organic matter as a result of declines in farming-forestry-livestock linkages). Furthermore, some of these changes are visible at macrolevels, whereas others are visible at microlevels.

Finally, by nature, some indicators of unsustainability represent a process of negative change, and others are negative consequences of the process. For instance, decline of diversification and resources regenerative practices following the promotion of new technology-based monocropping are "process types" of indicators. The decline in productivity following these changes is a "consequence type" of indicator. Table 15–1 summarizes the findings and observations relating to the above aspects reported by more than 45 studies conducted in different contexts by different researchers and agencies in different countries of Hindu Kush-Himalayan region over last two decades or so (Jodha and Shrestha 1994). ICIMOD's focus was on understanding the factors and processes contributing to unsustainability indicators in order to identify measures to reverse these trends. The key message of different studies (Shrestha 1992; Singh 1992; Dev 1992; Bajracharya 1992; Yanhua 1992; Shutain and Chunru 1989; Ruizhen and Yuan 1992; Hussain and Erenstein 1992) that are relevant to the theme of this chapter was the emergence of imbalance between ecological context and social and economic forces affecting use of mountain resources.

These persistent negative changes are indicators of unsustainability because they represent a situation where the production or resources use systems have failed to satisfy the conditions associated with sustainability, namely enhancing the performance (output, services, or range and quality of options) without depleting the resources base (Jodha 1995a).

In the final analysis, unsustainability is manifested by the ultimate consequences of the above trends, in terms of interrelated social and environmental effects with serious long-term negative implications. They are reflected through decisions and actions of the communities faced with unsustainability prospects, such as acceptance of inferior production and consumption options, an intense degree of "desperation" in resources use and production practices leading to over-extraction of the resources base, acceptance of external dependency (charity, subsidy, and so forth) as a normal basis of survival, and loss of resilience or capacity, in terms of culturally determined collective sharing and caring mechanisms through group action, to deal with emergencies.

The consequences are reflected also through the worsening conditions of natural resources and production processes using these resources, such as loss of "systematic integrity," implying disappearance, or weakening, of resources regenerative, resources protective practices and measures, and intrasystemic and intersystemic linkages; ever-increasing biochemical and economic subsidization of the production processes to maintain the same or lower levels of performance; marginalization, decline, and disappearance of a production system or its component due to loss of its identity and efficacy in the changed context; and loss of recoupment capacities of the resource base. Jodha (1995a; 1995b) provides practical life situation examples of the change.

Viewed in the context of the thematic framework of nature and society interactions, the aforementioned negative changes reflect a complex of disruptions. Where social systems tend to behave independent of the imperatives of ecosystems, the two-way adaptation process is converted to a one-way adjustment where resources manipulation and extraction are stretched to meet increasing human demands rather than adjusting the latter to resources situation. This has led to a break down of resources regenerative, diversified production systems, indiscriminate resources use intensification (often maintained through a high level of chemical, biophysical, and economic subsidization), and depletion of environmental resources. The following section comments on the factors and processes contributing to this change.

Environmental Degradation and Unsustainability Processes

The factors and processes contributing to unsustainability indicators involve: (a) the specific features of mountain areas, which can be called "mountain specificities" (that is, an incredibly high degree of features such as fragility, inaccessibility, marginality, diversity, and so forth that separate mountains from other ecosystems); (b) the imperatives of mountain specificities, or rather the objective circumstances created by them; and (c) the human response to the

above circumstances as reflected through resources use and management practices representing, in different contexts, both the elements supporting as well as disrupting the two-way adaptation processes (Jodha, Banskota, and Partap 1992). These aspects are summarized in Table 15–2.

Based on the synthesis of descriptive or quantitative accounts of different mountain areas reported in more than 50 studies, the details in Table 15–2 describe the situation in relatively broad terms. The concrete practices incorporating the rationale conveyed by the general features of the situations involved in Table 15–2 are too numerous and too varied to be meaningfully accommodated by this chapter Even a quick glance at traditional farming systems in mountain areas will furnish a range of examples on the aspects highlighted by Table 15–2 (Pant 1935; Price 1981; Guillet 1983; Bjonnes 1983; Hewitt 1988; Brush 1988; Whiteman 1988; Sanwal 1989; Carson 1992; Yanhua 1992; Jodha, Banskota, and Partap 1992; Jodha and Partap 1993; Jodha and Shrestha 1994).

However, the extent of the extent of traditional practices declines as one moves from relatively remote to more accessible villages, where improved accessibility and linkage with the outside world have influenced the traditional systems. The consequences of these changes were visible, and in most cases people realized and conveyed them as part of their concerns and vision of the future of their children (Jodha 1995b).

Traditional Patterns of Nature and Society Interactions

Traditional Systems

Based on the understanding provided by different accounts of situations in mountain areas, we can recapitulate the dynamics of ecosystems and social systems linkages and address issues such as what governs these linkages, how they operated in the traditional context, and how they are disrupted in the present-day context. The involved issues are summarized in Table 15–3. Although the context is mountain areas, the formulation and analysis presented may have general applicability to traditional or indigenous communities with semiclosed situations.

Accordingly, the information in Table 15–3 indicates (a) the nature-dominated key objective circumstances under which small and relatively isolated communities lived and managed their natural resources (that is, most of the communities in remote areas prior to their integration with the mainstream though improved accessibility); (b) key driving forces and factors that shaped the societal responses to the said objective circumstances; (c) broad social responses in terms of concerns and adaptation strategies; (d) technological and institutional mechanisms evolved and adopted for implementing the said strategies; and (e) consequences of (b) to (d) in terms of evolution of nature and society interactions and sustainability of resources use.

The above features of traditional systems are contrasted with the changes following the physical, administrative, and market integration of hitherto semiclosed and isolated systems or areas with the mainstream situation, which despite several gains has adversely affected the traditional resources management system (Banskota 1989; Collier 1990; Jodha 1995a).

Table 15–3 is self-explanatory. However, its key highlights can be briefly summarized. The biophysical environment of communities characterized by high degree of inaccessibility imposed a certain degree of isolation and semi-closeness for them. In the absence of effective outside linkages, their sustenance or welfare depended totally or crucially on local resources. This made them adapt their requirements or resources use systems to the limitations and potentialities of local resources rather than attempt to manipulate or overextract resources to satisfy uncontrolled human needs. They had a high stake in the health and productivity of local natural resources. Close proximity to natural resources, local control of the resources, and intimate functional knowledge about them, again largely because of the closed nature of the system, helped the communities to evolve folk technologies and institutional arrangements and enforce them without external interference for protection, regeneration, and regulated use of the resources.

In the process, the gradually evolved attitudes and norms of socioeconomic behavior, relative to biophysical resources of the community,

helped in linking social systems with ecological systems to ensure sustainable use of resources in a subsistence context (Guillet 1983; Hewitt 1988; Jochim 1981; Redford 1990).

The Changed Situation

With the changed circumstances, beginning with the increased integration of these areas and communities with mainstream areas, the ecology-driven social responses and resources management systems faced a rapid decline. Although the integration of isolated and indigenous areas may be justified on several grounds, the process of doing so, using the norms and procedures characterizing the mainstream, marginalized the areas and communities in question. As a result, although the biophysical context remained largely unchanged, the socioeconomic circumstances following integration changed rapidly (Bjonnes 1983; Ives and Messerli 1989; Jodha, Banskota, and Partap 1992; Gadgil and Guha 1992).

The local level ecosystem and social system linkages were disrupted because of an emergence of a complex of internal forces, chiefly population growth, and external forces. The pressure on resources encouraging their overextraction increased. The total dependence on local resources ceased to be a key driving force to sustain people's stake in resources stability. The positive effects of local autonomy or control over local resources, close proximity to resources, and functional knowledge of resources, which in the past helped in development of technologies and institutional responses, became marginalized. With the process of integration, the imposition from above, whether technologies or regulatory framework or resources planning decisions, became the rule.

In the changed circumstances, unlike in the past, local communities were left with neither sufficient lead time nor control over their resources and community affairs to amend or evolve their age-old coping strategies against change. Furthermore, they also did not have capacities or even incentives to resist internal and external forces released by their integration with stronger, external systems. Their knowledge system, social sanctions, and collective sharing system became less effective or less feasible, and in some cases less attractive, particularly to younger generations, in comparison with externally supported arrangements, at least in the short run. As a final consequence, the whole complex of driving forces—their type and nature—and patterns of responses to them changed (Jodha 1995b).

Unutilized Elements of Traditional Systems

Although Table 15–3 highlights the key features of resources management systems under two situations, it also indicates the possibilities for picking up relevant elements from traditional systems for integration into present-day resources management strategies to reverse the unsustainability prospects in mountain areas described earlier. A brief inventory of such elements has been presented elsewhere (Jodha 1990; Jodha, Banskota, and Partap 1992). The important elements include the combination of product and resources concerns in production systems; a high extent of diversification and flexibility, and a focus on local resource regeneration and recycling.

However, follow-up efforts to the above findings through policy advocacy and action research, including work done under the institutional strengthening project of ICIMOD, indicated that despite recognition and appreciation of the rationale of traditional practices, their incorporation and application for actual decisions and action could not take place. The primary reason for this gap was found to be linked to a lack of circumstances and incentives structures, conducive to their adoption at different levels, ranging from policymaking to community action. Hence, the key challenge is how to create such circumstances. This is elaborated on in the next section.

Exploring Usable Elements from Traditional Resources Use Systems

Through a synthesis of the factors indicated by Table 15–4, some key elements of circumstances and processes can be identified that generated community concerns, commitments, and incentives for protection and regulated use of natural resources; enhanced community capacities, both technical and institutional, to appropriately respond to circumstances by combining production and protection-centered measures; motivated and facilitated enforcement of measures that helped in adapting community

needs to resources, rather than manipulating and overextracting the latter to meet unrestrained demands.

Accordingly, three elements can be identified that individually or jointly contributed to the natural resources-friendly traditional management systems. They include (a) total dependence-driven stake in protection of natural resources; (b) close proximity and functional knowledge-driven approach to resource use; and (c) local (resources) control-determined sanctions and facilities governing the resources use. The following discussion elaborates on these elements, with a view to exploring some possibilities of reinstating the elements or identifying their present-day functional equivalents as parts of an incentive structure to facilitate sustainable resources use in mountain areas, in the changed context.

The key premise behind this exercise is that even when the isolation or semiclosed nature and physical proximity, as parts of the key objective circumstances characterizing the traditional communities, were the basis of the aforementioned elements (for example, stake and sensitivity toward natural resources), the latter's relevance and viability are not confined to small and isolated groups. By changing the forms of their manifestation and their operating mechanisms, these elements can be integrated into any resources management system and can prove effective in any context.

Dependence-Driven Community Stake in Resources Health

According to the information in Table 15–4, in the relatively less accessible mountain areas, exclusive or total dependence for sustenance on local resources was the key incentive behind communities' concern and follow-up actions leading to protection and regulated use of their natural resources. To reiterate, activities ranging from the combining of production and conservation measures to rationing and regulating of demand, including recycling and collective sharing, as well as adherence to social sanctions regulating resources use, can be linked to such uniqueness of the situation or the incentive system it created.

Reinstating such incentive or disincentive systems by creating exclusive dependence of survival on local resources is neither desirable nor feasible in the context of the changed situation of mountains. However, other approaches can be explored to strengthen the total or crucial dependence-driven stake of a community in its natural resources base. Two possibilities can be indicated: by changing the "product context" of dependence and by changing the "scale context" of dependence.

Product Context

Changing the product context of dependence involves substituting, at the local community level, the traditional security of sustenance with the security of ecological "niche," or comparative advantage (due to specific high-value options) that is potentially available to the community through physical and market integration of its area with the mainstream systems. There are cases of transformed areas in the HK-H region and other mountain regions where niche-based gains have worked as new incentives for protection and regulated use of overall natural resources bases by the communities (Jodha and Shrestha 1994).

For example, in areas such as Ningnan county in West Sichuan, China, where sericulture recently has become a lead activity with a high payoff and comparative advantage to the area, communities attempt to manage and protect hill slopes, shrubs, and waterflows on a priority basis because it helps in strengthening the sericulture activities. Other examples are in Himachal Pradesh in India, especially the apple zone, and the Ilam district of Nepal where multiple new activities are sustained through better management of natural resources in general. In areas where the mountain environment and landscape have become major tourist attractions, including the Alps and pockets of the Himalayas, the same logic of incentive through stake has helped in better management of natural resources by the communities. One can multiply such examples where a stake in the lead sector and lead activity, owing to biophysical and economic interlinkages, has induced and initiated a process of better management of overall resources by the communities. The exceptions to process include cases where niche is identified and harnessed, or extracted, without involving the local communities.

Scale Context

Changing the scale context of dependence implies that the phenomenon of local resources dependence, that is, a crucial if not a total dependence, as a source of stake becomes relevant and operational at a much higher or macrolevel, rather than at a small community level. In other words, in place of small isolated communities, the much wider social economic entities become the units in the context of which dependence-centered stakes are perceived and diagnosed and responded to.

For example, the sustenance of the hitherto isolated communities may not be completely ruined by the degradation of mountain resources. Because of external linkage, their degree of dependence on local resources is reduced today, but the bigger areas or ecologically integrated entities, sustained through biophysical and economic upland-lowland linkages, may have the problem owing to mismanagement of mountain resources by microentities. For example, in the changed context, the downstream areas, which also produce food surplus available to mountain areas and have a crucial dependence on the stable hydrology of mountain areas, may have a much stronger stake in the protection and regulated use of upland resources. The recurrent debates on "Himalayan waters"—blaming Nepalese farmers for Bangladesh floods—is one concrete manifestation of the issue. Any action conceived and implemented in such larger areas context will represent the perception and diagnosis of a stake at a higher scale.

It is not difficult to count many more examples of shifting product, or spatial context, and hence group context of dependence-driven stake in better natural resources management. But in both cases, because of enlarged size and increased diversity of user groups (stakeholders), dilution and diffusion of perception and diagnosis of stake to induce positive community responses poses a serious problem. In a diverse and widely spread group of resources users, perception of stake that is based on the understanding of association between cause (resource extraction) and consequence (resource degradation) cannot be uniform and strong enough to induce community responses for resources conservation (Rosser 1995).

In the case of small and isolated communities, their physical proximity and firsthand knowledge of the resources features shaped people's perception and diagnosis of stake. The present-day resources users normally do not have such facility.

Viewed in terms of the thematic framework of this chapter, the dilution and diffusion of perceptions of stake imply an absence of the circumstances facilitating co-evolution and smooth working of ecosystem and social system linkages. Although the ecological context remained relatively unchanged and spatially confined to specific areas, the social systems not only have expanded but have become more complex, owing to multiplicity of stake holders and external linkages, and have ceased to evolve by way of responding to feedback from below or to the ecological imperatives of the situation.

To explore the scope for altering the resources users' perceptions of stake in conservation of natural resources and to clarify the involved issues, it may be helpful to compare the present-day situation with the traditional situation. Two key differences are involved, relating to (a) an individual's time horizon, and (b) feedback mechanisms and sensitivities as they influence resources use practices.

Resource Users' Time Horizon

A community's perception of its stake in its natural resources base, as the biophysical foundation of the society, is determined largely by formers' concerns for long-term survival and welfare of community members. Although the community deals with the long-term concerns, most of its individual members may not do so, as long-term sustainability falls outside the realm of an individual's life cycle decisions, which are dictated by one's short planning horizon.

In this respect, the traditional peasant or pastoralist did not differ from present day resources users or even the serious scientists engaged in pursuit of sustainability-related issues. All individually have a short time horizon in the sense that their private, life cycle decisions and activities seldom go beyond the concerns for their grandchildren. Sustainability-related concerns are a mandate of the society as a collective entity. The latter collectively establishes social norms of behavior reflecting the community's long-term concerns, which in turn provide a framework for the conduct of individuals' short-term activities. Absence of such a framework and its enforcement, leads to the domination of short-sighted activities and to degradation of the production base of the society. This can explain the difference between traditional and present-day systems of natural resources use in the Himalayas.

Under traditional systems, the communities through trial and error over several generations evolved certain approaches to natural resources use and codified them into routine practices followed by the individual resources users, guided by their short-term considerations (Jodha 1995b; Davis 1993; Ostrom 1990; Guillet 1983). Examples may include cereal-legume mixed cropping sustaining soil fertility, farming and forestry linkages facilitating nutrient cycling directed to local resources regeneration and ecological balancing, and traditional forms of rural cooperation for collective sharing and product and resources recycling to help ration pressure on natural resources.

Routine adherence to these practices to fulfill short-term needs simultaneously satisfied the long-term conservation needs of resources, often without explicit and conscious concern for the latter on the part of individual resources users. Thus, the process aspect of sustainability got built into the folk agronomic practices, or resource use systems, and helped to ensure positive long-term effects of activities undertaken with short time horizons.

The present-day resources users unfortunately do not have or normally do not follow such norms of behavior involving usage of natural resources. Things have changed drastically in contrast to the traditional situation. In the present-day context, the local community has been replaced by the state, or its agencies, for designing and enforcing resources use norms to be followed by individuals or groups. The state is endowed with more resources, powers, and formal mechanisms to frame norms and enforce them.

However, despite all the resources and enhanced scientific, fiscal, and administrative capacities and means to understand the natural resources characteristics and approaches to manage them sustainably, the present-day decisionmakers have not been able to provide an effective and widely usable framework, where short-term activities of individuals could be focused to achieve both short- and long-term goals of the society. The elaborate exercises on perspective planning, proactive policies, and wide range and hierarchy of incentives, support systems, and even coercive measures created to guide or dictate the people to undertake activities that are compatible with the long-term social concerns do not seem to have succeeded. An important reason behind this, in fact, is that in the mountain areas and elsewhere, in practice, the governments provide contradictory messages to different resources users (Jodha, Banskota, and Partap 1992). For instance, one provision of state intervention promotes protection of natural vegetation, but another in the same area subsidizes land use intensification through annual cropping; one provision calls for integrated resource use, but another effectively divides the mandates, support, and authority sector-wise.

Devoid of a mountain perspective (Rhoades 1988; Banskota and Jodha 1992), the state policies and programs focus more on enhancing supplies to meet rising demands, due to population growth and market forces, rather than adapt demands to resources limitations. Consequently, they promote indiscriminate use intensification and overextraction of natural resources. Even the declared intentions of resources conservation neither involve local people's perspectives nor get codified in agricultural technologies or rural development projects, because of the latter's product-centered rather than resource-centered focus. Thus, in the changed context of mountain areas, both the individual resources users and the state, representing the people as a collective entity, as facilitators of resource harnessing, seem to operate with a short planning horizon. To redress the situation, especially in the mountain context, a beginning can be made by sensitizing the policymakers to the nature-determined objective circumstances of mountain areas and imparting mountain perspective to development intervention, and involving the local communities and elements of traditional knowledge systems while designing and implementing development intervention. This will be considered in later sections.

Proximity-Based Feedback Mechanisms and Sensitivity to Natural Resources

Under the traditional resource use systems, the people's adherence to long-term concerns, as codified into short-term activities, was further reinforced by their firsthand functional knowledge and understanding of the natural resources. This was facilitated by their close proximity to resources. Because of proximity-based instant feedback, they more easily could perceive the risks of resource mismanagement and degradation. Understanding of the real costs involved in the process further sharpened their perceptions of stake in resources management and acted as a part of the incentive-disincentive system guiding their decisions and actions.

In today's context, owing to a wider spread of resources users, their diversity, and the emergence of a multiplicity of intermediaries between resources users and resources planners and decisionmakers, all of the factors facilitating understanding of stakes and using it as basis for resources management in the past have become largely dysfunctional. It hardly needs elaboration that the wider and more diverse the group context is, the less is the direct visibility of association between cause and consequences of resources mismanagement. This is more the case because of the lack of effective feedback arrangements to replace the traditional proximity-based spontaneous visibility of effects of resource mismanagement. As elaborated in the next section, the possible solution to the above problems lies in (a) enhancing resource users' and decisionmakers' sensitivity and understanding of the natural resources base by using modern means of information collection, synthesis, and dissemination (Jodha, Banskota, and Partap 1992), despite their physical distance from resources; (b) association of local communities in decisions relating to their natural resources (Proffenberger 1995); and (c) reorientation of fiscal and resource and product costing norms, to reflect the real worth of environmental costs of resources use (McNeely 1988; Munasinghe 1993).

Physical Proximity and Functional Knowledge as Facilitators

As previously mentioned, under traditional systems, a community's stake in its natural resources was an important driving force behind conservation-oriented resources management. Equally important was the role of site and season specific functional knowledge of the resources. This, in turn, was gained through a close proximity and access to resources. Comment has been made above on the complementary role of physical proximity and functional knowledge in enhancing and sharpening people's perceptions of their stake in better management of natural resources. The following discussion elaborates on the proximity and knowledge of resources as driving forces, or rather facilitators, of traditional resources management systems.

Proximity, direct access, and functional knowledge of local resources facilitated the evolution of environment friendly resources usage systems, folk technologies, demand management measures, and the institutional arrangements to facilitate their adoption and enforcement. The balancing of extensive and intensive types of land uses, various forms of resources use diversification and flexibility, resource regenerating, recycling practices, methods of resource upgrading (such as terracing), seasonal periodic restrictions on product gathering, and so forth are some of the concrete examples where closer understanding of resources features and availability of longer lead times for informal experimentation helped the communities.

Absence of any gap between decisionmaking and actual use of resources, as well as between resources users, or producers, and product users, again facilitated by proximity and access, helped in flexible approaches to resources management to meet site and season specific differences and contingencies. This also helped in adjusting people's requirements, such as animal grazing intensity and collection of food, fuel, and fodder, to the specific situation of the resources base. This is illustrated by restrictions on collection of specific products during specific periods, or from specific areas, and grazing rotations enforced by local communities in some villages even today.

Unlike in the past, the present-day resources use situation is characterized by several factors:

(a) a wider spread of users of the resources products, owing to market integration, and an equally wide gap between producers (resources users) and products consumers (the final users, for example, of herbs, horticulture products, and hydropower from mountain areas); (b) disassociation between usership and ownership of resources, because of an increased number of absentee landlords in many areas; (c) disassociation of legal, fiscal, and administrative decisionmaking agencies from resource using agencies, such as farmers or the communities; and (d) distances and differences between technology developers and technology users.

The above circumstances restrict the scope for reinstating and strengthening the resources management practices that are closely tied to physical proximity, direct involvement, and accessibility to resources bases and their close firsthand knowledge. However, to take fuller advantage of the knowledge and understanding of resources bases for designing and implementing relevant usage and management systems, it is not necessary to re-create the traditional situation characterized by semiclosedness and physical proximity to resources.

One of the key contributions of physical proximity, direct involvement, and accessibility to resources bases has been in terms of generating sensitivity toward and understanding of resources bases, which in turn shaped people's responses leading to conservation-oriented resources use systems. In the present context, with better means of information acquisition, verification, and synthesis, as well as communication and dissemination, the above goals can also be achieved differently.

To benefit from the firsthand feel of the field situation and accumulated traditional knowledge about the resources and their usage systems, there are well-tested methods of involving local communities (for example, through RRA/PRA and others) in the process of collection, analysis, and utilization of information to create among diverse stake holders (policymakers to urban consumers) a sensitivity toward the natural resources.

The key constraint in this regard is that the aforementioned facilities and means have not been utilized for building sensitivity and understanding of the mountain resources to develop and adopt technological and institutional measures relevant to their conditions. The focus of policy and program interventions, whether agricultural research and development or integrated rural development, have lacked the mountain perspective, implying understanding and incorporation of imperatives of mountain specificities, such as incredibly high degrees of inaccessibility, fragility, diversity, marginality, and mountain niche, in the conception, design, and implementation of development and welfare activities in mountain areas (Jodha 1990). If these interventions and their dynamics are seen as a part of the broader social systems characterizing and influencing mountain areas, they once again reflect the rapidly vanishing links between social systems and ecosystems and their co-evolution in mountain areas.

A beginning towards filling this gap can be made by initiating a process directed toward the following (Jodha, Banskota, and Partap 1992): (a) sensitization and reorientation of the decisionmakers to create a policy environment sensitive to mountain conditions; (b) involvement of the local communities in decisionmaking and actions relating to local resources, to ensure relevance of interventions to the field situations; (c) recognition and utilization of traditional knowledge systems by the formal research and development agencies engaged in development of technologies for these areas; (d) reorient the whole process of project planning, designing, and implementation by making it a bottom-up approach involving local communities and user groups.

Community Control and Resources Use Rationing

Regulation of resource use, rationing of pressure on resources, mobilization of community, and focused group action, which helped in sustainable use of natural resources in mountain areas in the past, were greatly facilitated by full control by communities of local resources. This was a positive consequence of isolation and semicloseness of communities, which prevented impositions from outside. As shown in Table 15–4, this sort of autonomy available to communities was conducive to evolution of both institutional and technological measures suited to local resources and survival needs. The close proximity and knowledge of local resources complemented the process.

With the integration of mountain areas with the mainstream, the state authority, executed through different agencies, was extended to hitherto semiclosed areas. In the name of development, welfare, social and political integration, and even national security in many cases, the state usurped the resources and mandates that historically belonged to the people. With this process, both formal and informal control by communities over local resources weakened or disappeared. The same thing happened to the resources management arrangements supported by the community autonomy and social sanctions.

In such a situation, restoring of traditional autonomy and control over resources enjoyed by isolated communities does not look possible. Its revival may seriously conflict with the ruling culture and approach of the modern state that is oriented toward greater centralization. Even the genuine efforts by some states toward decentralization and participatory development may not go so far as providing the traditional type of autonomy to village communities and, thereby, disempower themselves or their bureaucracy. However, despite the above constraints, some form of diluted autonomy and functional control of local resources by local communities within the framework of overall legal control of the state is possible. Such possibilities are further strengthened by some emerging trends. First, it is increasingly realized that management and protection of local level resources through state agencies, such as forest departments, is progressively becoming more difficult and costly. On the other hand, involvement of local communities in the local resources management has improved the situation in many areas (World Bank 1995). Second, the awareness and mobilization of local communities for their rights and resources, enhanced through nongovernmental organizations (NGOs), are emerging features of communities even in less accessible areas. Successful negotiations of forest user groups and community irrigation groups, which are helped by NGOs, to acquire control of resources in countries like Nepal, India, and Pakistan is one case in point (Ostrom 1990; Husain 1992; Proffenberger 1995).

However, without belittling the potential of the above possibilities that favor community control of local resources, it may be noted that the envisaged transformation may not be an easy and straightforward task. There may be many hurdles in the process. In addition to their quantitative increases, the qualitative changes in mountain populations (Sharma and Banskota 1992), reflected through rapid erosion of community cohesion, weakening of the culture conducive to group action and collective sharing, rapid growth of individualistic tendencies, and economic differentiation of communities, may obstruct the effective use of restored community authority over local resources for regulating resources use.

The internal weaknesses of the present-day village communities, constraining the community initiatives for resources use regulation, may be complemented by external forces generated by market and political economies and manifested through a range of fiscal and pricing arrangements. An overextraction of mountain resources driven by the above forces may continue despite regulatory powers of the community. This calls for a gradual process of change, focused on the following steps: (a) making constant efforts for greater involvement of communities and user groups supported by NGOs for planning and implementation of resources management initiatives, use of resources regenerative technologies, and regulation of resources use (Daly and Cobb 1989; Cernea 1991); (b) taking examples from successful cases of participatory, decentralized resources management projects and focusing on their replication and mainstreaming (World Bank 1995); (c) helping build capacities and incentives for local communities to adapt to changed circumstances and reviving traditional practices for resources management in the changed contexts (Jodha, Banskota, and Partap 1992); (d) introducing different norms for products and resources pricing, reflecting their true worth or environmental cost by building on the conceptual leads provided by recent thinking in this area (Munasinghe 1993; Dasgupta and Mäler 1994; McNeely 1988); and (e) introducing biophysical measures of compensation for resources extraction, such as planting the same type of tree when one is cut for the timber market (Jodha and Shrestha 1994)

The suggestions for creating present-day functional equivalents of traditional circumstances presented in this chapter are indicative of the new possibilities. However, their design and implementation presumes fulfillment of several preconditions, including commitment of the decisionmakers and site specific preparations.

Conclusions and Policy Implications

Summing Up

Using the Himalayan case as an illustration, this chapter has tried to show that indifference or insensitivity of policymakers toward the imperatives of specific features of natural resources is the primary reason for overextraction and degradation of resources. The traditional communities under low pressure of demand managed the resources more sustainably. The rationale of traditional management systems is relevant in the present context as well. But, despite its relevance and frequent advocacy, the present-day resources management systems or development strategies in general have not been able to incorporate the elements of traditional systems. This is partly due to a lack of fuller recognition and internalization of traditional knowledge systems by policymakers and planners.

The main constraint to adoption of traditional elements, however, is the absence of objective circumstances conducive to their application. The traditional circumstances represented by relative isolation and closedness of systems, as well as subsistence orientation of production, are neither desirable nor feasible in the present-day context. Similarly, close physical proximity and total local control over local resources, as factors shaping resources management in the past, cannot be reinstated today.

Hence, one has to look for functional substitutes for the traditional circumstances that generated people's concerns and stakes in natural resources and responses thereto. This chapter has tried to indicate some of them. Accordingly, for the first element of traditional systems, namely dependence-driven stake in natural resources, it is suggested that the source of dependence be shifted from security of sustenance to security of niche. It also is suggested that the scale context of stake be changed from small, microlevel entities to macrolevel units. However, both the suggested changes imply a multiplicity and diversity of stakeholders, which lead to dilution and diffusion of perception and diagnosis of stakes. To counter this problem, approaches have been suggested that generate sensitivity and feedback mechanism to help conservation-oriented responses of diverse user groups of natural resources and their products.

As functional substitutes for the second element of traditional systems, namely, physical proximity-based understanding and responses to ecological circumstances, reorientation is suggested of policy environment and program activities, which depend on closer and better understanding and sensitivity to natural resources and involve local communities in resource management decisions and actions. Finally, in place of the third element of traditional systems, namely total community autonomy, approaches have been discussed to enhance community control over local resources that can facilitate resources use regulation and participatory development.

Any progress in the above mentioned directions would mean a step toward rehabilitation of ecosystem and social system linkages, which is a key to sustainable resources management. However, the involved process of changes is faced with serious constraints. In the preceding sections, including Table 15–4, some of the key constraints and possible measures to handle them have been indicated. The suggestions made in this chapter are indicative of new possibilities of natural resources management in the changed context. However, their design and implementation presumes fulfillment of several preconditions, including commitment of policymakers and site specific preparations. They are recapitulated in terms of focused policy issues in the following section.

Policy Implications

The natural resources degradation in regions such as the Himalayas is the product of a mismatch between the features of a resources base and attributes of its usage systems. This fact seems to be ignored by development policies and programs, as well as the people using the resources, because of their overemphasis on production growth rather than the resources base that ensures production flows. Hence, there is a need for a strong resources focus of development interventions.

To reverse the unsustainability trends indicated by resources degradation, the product-centered interventions need to be balanced with the resource-centered measures. In this regard, the formal policies and programs can greatly benefit from the recognition and use of rationale or knowledge systems underlying the traditional resources management systems that ensured sustainability of resources and production under low- demand pressure in the past. By implication, this means better recognition, documentation, and use of traditional knowledge systems by development interventions.

Because the traditional measures were not context free, their application in the current situation is seriously constrained by the changed demographic, institutional, economic, and technological circumstances. The objective circumstances (isolation, physical proximity, local resource control, and so forth) characterizing traditional management systems, created for the people of strong dependence-driven stake in the natural resources, ensured close understanding of the resources base and instant feedback on consequences of its mismanagement, and facilitated resources use and regulation through community sanctions. Reinstating the traditional circumstances shaping people's approach to resources use is not feasible in the present context. Hence, a major challenge for policy and operational work is to identify functional substitutes for the traditional circumstances conducive to sustainable resources management.

A useful approach to identify functional equivalents of the traditional circumstances is to focus on the functions they performed, rather than their forms, which are difficult to reinstate. Thus, the relative isolation or semiclosed nature of traditional communities helped generate (sustenance based) dependence-driven stake in resources. The changed product, or service, context and scale context of dependence can help generate new forms of users' dependence on resources and stakes therein, and facilitate sustainable management of resources in the changed circumstances. Similarly, sensitivity and understanding of resources that facilitate resource friendly usage systems can be promoted without re-creating the semiclosed systems. Similarly, enhanced local participation and planning from below can ensure sustainable resources management without traditional types of local autonomy. However, much more thinking has to be invested to multiply functional substitutes of traditional arrangements.

The key constraints to the above possibilities may be the existing perspectives and orientations of policymakers and development planners. They may not be very innovative and supportive of the new ideas that are based on learning from the traditional resources management systems. This calls for changing the overall perspectives on development goals and development processes.

The situation can be helped by designing and using the learning processes, whereby through concrete examples, such as a few field projects, the message and process of change can be demonstrated.

Bibliography

Bajracharya, B. B. 1992. *A Review of Literature Focused on Indicators of Unsustainability of Mountain Agriculture in Nepal.* A report for ICIMOD. Kathmandu, Nepal: ICIMOD

Banskota, M. 1989. *Hill Agriculture and the Wider Market Economy: Transformation Processes and Experience of the Bagmati Zone in Nepal.* ICIMOD Occasional Paper No. 10. Kathmandu, Nepal: ICIMOD.

Banskota, M., and N. S. Jodha. 1992. "Mountain Agricultural Development Strategies: Comparative Perspectives From the Countries of the Hindu Kush-Himalayan Region." In N. S. Jodha, M. Banskota, and T. Partap, eds., *Sustainable Mountain Agriculture.* New Delhi, India: Oxford and IBH Publishing Co., Pvt. Ltd.

Berkes, F., ed. 1989. *Common Property Resources: Ecology and Community-Based Sustainable Development.* London: Belhaven Press.

Bjonnes, I. M. 1983. "External Economic Dependency and Changing Human Adjustment to Marginal Environments in High Himalaya, Nepal." *Mountain Research and Development* 3(3).

Brush, S. B. 1988. "Traditional Agricultural Strategies in Hill Lands of Tropical America." In N. J. R. Allen, G. W. Knapp, and C. Stadel, eds., *Human Impacts on Mountains.* New Jersey: Rowman and Littlefield.

Carson, B. 1992. *The Land, the Farmer, and the Future: A Soil Fertility Management Strategy for Nepal.* ICIMOD Occasional Paper No. 21. Kathmandu, Nepal: ICIMOD.

Cernea, M. M., ed. 1991. *Putting People First: Sociological Variables in Rural Development.* New York-London: Oxford University Press.

Collier, G. A. 1990. *Seeking Food and Seeking Money: Changing Relations in Highland Mexico Community.* United Nations Research Institute for Social Development (UNRISD) Discussion Paper 11. Geneva: UNRISD.

Daly, H. E. and J. B. Cobb, Jr. 1989. *For the Common Good: Redirecting the Economy Towards Community, the Environment and Sustainable Future.* London: Merlin Press.

Dasgupta, P., and Karl-Göran Mäler. 1994. *Poverty, Institutions and the Environmental Resource Base.* World Bank Environment Paper No. 9. Washington, D.C.

Davis, S. H. 1993. *Indigenous Views of Land and the Environment.* World Bank Discussion Paper No. 188. Washington, D.C.

Dev, S. M. 1992. *A Review of Literature Focused on Indicators of Unsustainability of Mountain Agriculture in Indian Himalayan.* ICIMOD Commissioned Report. Kathmandu, Nepal: ICIMOD.

Ellen, R. 1981. *Environment, Subsistence and System: The Ecology of Small Scale Social Formations.* Cambridge: Cambridge University Press.

Gadgil, M., and F. Berkes. 1991. "Traditional Resource Management Systems." *Resource Management and Optimization.* 18:127–41.

————, and R. Guha. 1992. *The Fissured Land: An Ecological History of India.* New Delhi: Oxford University Press.

Guillet, D. G. 1983. "Towards a Cultural Ecology of Mountains: The Central Andes and the Himalayas Compared." *Current Anthropology* 24:561–74.

Hewitt, K. 1988. "The Study of Mountain Lands and Peoples: A Critical Overview." In N. J. R. Allen, G. W. Knapp, and C. Stadel, eds. *Human Impacts on Mountains.* New Jersey: Rowman and Littlefield.

Hussain, S. S., and O. Erenstein. 1992. *Monitoring Sustainability Issues in Agricultural Development: A Case Study in Swat in North Pakistan.* PATA Working Paper No. 6. Saidu Sharif, NWFP, Pakistan: PATA Integrated Agricultural Development Project.

Husain, T. 1992. "The Aga Khan Rural Support Programme: An Approach to Village Management Systems in Northern Pakistan." In N. S. Jodha, M. Banskota, and T. Partap, eds. *Sustainable Mountain Agriculture.* New Delhi: Oxford and IBH Publishing Co., Pvt. Ltd.

Ives, J. D., and B. Messerli. 1989. *The Himalayan Dilemma: Reconciling Development and Conservation.* London: Routledge.

Jochim, M. A. 1981. *Strategies for Survival: Cultural Behavior in an Ecological Context.* New York: Academic Press.

Jodha, N. S. 1990. "Mountain Agriculture: The Search for Sustainability." *Journal of Farming Systems Research Extension* 1(1):55–75.

———. 1995a. *Sustainable Development in Fragile Environments.* Ahmedabad, India: Center for Environment Education. Forthcoming.

———. 1995b. *Transition to Sustainability in the Next Century: Hopes and Dismays in Mountain Regions.* 2050 Project. World Resource Institute, Washington, D.C.

———, M. Banskota, and T. Partap, eds. 1992. *Sustainable Mountain Agriculture.* Vol. 1, *Perspectives and Issues*; Vol. 2, *Farmers' Strategies and Innovative Approaches.* New Delhi, India: Oxford and IBH Publishing Co. Pvt. Ltd.

———, and T. Partap. 1993. "Folk Agronomy in the Himalayas: Implications for Agricultural Research and Extension." In *Rural People's Knowledge, Agricultural Research and Extension Practice.* IIED Research Series, Vol. 1, No. 3. London: International Institute for Environment and Development.

———, and S. Shrestha. 1994. "Sustainable and More Productive Mountain Agriculture: Problems and Prospects." In *Proceedings of the International Symposium on Mountain Environment and Development.* Kathmandu, Nepal: ICIMOD.

McNeely, J. A. 1988. *Economics and Biological Diversity: Developing and Using Economic Incentives to Conserve Biological Resources.* Gland, Switzerland: IUCN.

Munasinghe, M. 1993. *Environmental Economics and Sustainable Development.* World Bank Environment Paper No. 3. Washington, D.C.

Ostrom, E. 1990. *Governing the Commons: The Evolution of Institutions for Collective Action.* Cambridge: Cambridge University Press.

Pant, S. D. 1935. *The Social Economy of Himalayas: Based on a Survey in the Kumaon Himalayas.* London: George Allen and Unwin.

Price, L. W. 1981. *Mountain and Man: A Study of Process and Environment.* Berkeley: University of California.

Proffenberger, M., Betsy McGean, A. Khare, and others. 1995. *Village Voices, Forest Choices: Pioneering India's Forest Management into the 21st Century.* New Delhi, India: Oxford University Press. In press.

Redford, K. H. 1990. "The Ecologically Noble Savage." *Orion* Summer:25–9.

Rhoades, R. E. 1988. "Thinking Like a Mountain." *ILEIA News Letter* 4(1).

Rosser, J. B., Jr. 1995. "Systemic Crises in Hierarchical Ecological Economics." *Land Economics* 71(2).

Ruizhen, Y., and W. Yuan. 1992. *Poverty and Development: A Study of China's Poor Areas.* Beijing, China: New World Press.

Sanwal, M. 1989. "What We Know About Mountain Development: Common Property, Investment Priorities, and Institutional Arrangements." *Mountain Research and Development* 9(1).

Sharma, P., and M. Banskota. 1992. "Population Dynamics and Sustainable Agricultural Development in Mountain Areas." In N. S. Jodha, M. Banskota, and T. Partap, eds. *Sustainable Mountain Agriculture.* New Delhi, India: Oxford and IBH Publishing Co., Pvt. Ltd.

Shrestha, S. 1992. *Mountain Agriculture: Indicators of Unsustainability and Options for Reversal.* MFS Discussion Paper No. 32. Kathmandu, Nepal: ICIMOD.

Shutain, G., and H. Chunru. 1989. *Problems of the Environment in Chinese Agriculture and a Strategy for Ecological Development (an Overview).* Beijing, China: Ministry of Agriculture and Beijing Agricultural University.

Singh, V. 1992. "Dynamics of Unsustainability of Mountain Agriculture." Unpublished report on U.P. hill areas, India. Kathmandu, Nepal: ICIMOD.

Whiteman, P. T. S. 1988. "Mountain Agronomy in Ethiopia, Nepal, and Pakistan." In N. J. R. Allan, G. W. Knapp, and C. Stadel, eds., *Human Impacts on Mountains*. New Jersey: Rowman and Littlefield.

World Bank. 1995. *World Bank Participation Source Book*. Environment Department. Washington, D.C.: World Bank.

Yanhua, L. 1992. *Dynamics of Highland Agriculture*. (A Study in Tibet, China), ICIMOD Occasional Paper No. 22. Kathmandu, Nepal: ICIMOD.

Table 15–1: Negative Changes as Indicators of Emerging Unsustainability in Hindu Kush–Himalaya Region

Visibility of change	Changes related to [a]		
	Resource base	*Production flows*	*Resource use management practices/options*
Directly visible changes	Increased landslides and other forms of land degradation; abandoned terraces; per capita reduced availability and fragmentation of land; changed botanical composition of forest/ pasture. Reduced water flows for irrigation, domestic uses, and grinding mills.	Prolonged negative trend in yields of crop, livestock, etc.; increased input need per unit of production; increased time and distance involved in food, fodder, fuel gathering; reduced capacity and period of grinding and saw mills operated on water flow; lower per capita availability of agricultural products.	Reduced extent of fallowing, crop rotation, intercropping, diversified resources management practices; extension of plough to submarginal lands; replacement of social sanctions for resource use by legal measures; unbalanced and high intensity of input use, subsidization.
Changes concealed by responses to changes	Substitution of cattle by sheep and goats; deep-rooted crops by shallow-rooted ones; shift to nonlocal inputs. Substitution of water flow by fossil fuel for grinding mills; manure by chemical fertilizers.	Increased seasonal migration; introduction of externally supported public distribution systems (food, inputs); intensive cash cropping on limited areas.	Shifts in cropping pattern and composition of livestock; reduced diversity, increased specialization in mono-cropping; promotion of policies and programs with successful record outside, without evaluation.
Development initiatives, etc., processes with potentially negative consequences[b]	New systems without linkages to other diversified activities and regenerative processes; generating excessive dependence on outside resource (fertilizer and pesticide-based technologies, subsidies), ignoring traditional adaptation experiences (new irrigation structure); programs focused mainly on resource extraction.	Agricultural measures directed to short-term quick results; primarily production (as against resource)-centered approaches to development; service-centered activities (e.g., tourism) with negative side effects.	Indifference of program and policies to mountain specificities; focus on short term gains; high centralization; excessive, crucial dependence on external advice, ignoring traditional wisdom; generating permanent dependence on subsidies.

a. Most of the changes are interrelated and could fit into more than one block.

b. Changes under this category differ from those under the first two categories, in the sense that they are yet to take place, and their potential emergence could be understood by examining the involved resources use practices in relation to specific mountain characteristics. Thus, they represent the "process" dimension, rather than consequence dimension of unsustainability.

Source: Table is adapted from Jodha (1990) and Jodha and Shrestha (1994). It is based on data or descriptions by more than 45 studies from Nepal (18), China (15), India (7), Pakistan (3), Bhutan, Bangladesh, and Myanmar (1 each), as synthesized by Jodha and Shrestha (1994).

Table 15–2: Mountain Resource Characteristics, Their Imperatives, Objective Circumstances, and Driving Forces behind Human Response

Resource features and objective circumstances	Imperatives and driving forces	Responses, resource use practices
Inaccessibility (caused by physical, terrain factors) imposing high degree of isolation, poor mobility, and limited external linkages, semi-closeness.	Survival strategies with direct and total dependence on local resources and high stake in their protection, regulated use, and regeneration; local control of local resources, culture of self-management, evolution of systems from below based on closer proximity and knowledge of resource base.	Ecology-driven resource management, using conservation and protection technologies, and institutional arrangements, evolved with closer feel of the resources and enforced through local autonomy and control of local resources; rationing of demand pressure on resources, and restricting extraction levels in keeping with subsistence needs.
Fragility (caused by biophysical, topographic, adaphic characteristics) making resources highly vulnerable to irreversible degradation with small disturbance, restricting usage options, intensity levels.	High risk of rapid resource depletion owing to usage intensification inducing measures to balance extraction and conservation of production base, narrow range of production options (only land extensive users).	Technologies and usage practices combining intensive and extensive uses of natural resources, provision of institutional arrangements (e.g., common property resources) against overextraction of fragile and marginal resources, spatially and temporarily differentiated resource use systems, rationing, knowledge, and capacity-based resource upgrading (e.g., by terracing, agro-forestry, etc.).
Diversity (created by huge variations in biophysical features and elevations at shorter distances) creating opportunities for diversified and interlinked production and consumption activities.	Local knowledge, skill, and capacity-based diversification of resource use as a key element of both survival strategies and approach to sustainable productivity and health of natural resource base.	Spatially and temporarily diversified and interlinked activities with varying levels of intensification; diversification of demands to match the diversity of products and supplies, especially in a semi-closed situation.
Niche (created by unique agro-climatic, biophysical situations), imparting comparative advantage to mountain areas in some activities and products (forests, horticulture, herbs, hydropower, etc.)	Potential for trade-based external linkages restricted by levels of knowledge, capacities to harness, etc.	A limited range of diversified activities directed to petty trading to supplement subsistence activities; local demand and extraction facilities and capacities as key factors governing the exploitation of niche situations.
Implication	Adherence to two-way adaptation process.	Ecology-driven systems of resource use conducive to sustainability (under low-pressure population and external demand).

Source: The table is based on synthesis of accounts of concrete situations described in over 50 studies about mountain areas (Jodha and Shrestha 1994).

Table 15–3: Factors and Processes Associated with the Nature-society Interactions under Traditional and Present-Day Systems of Resource Use in Mountain Areas

Situation under traditional systems	*Situation under the present-day systems*
A. Basic objective circumstances 1. Greater degree of inaccessibility, isolation, and semi-closeness of systems; poor mobility and external linkages, etc. creating total and exclusive dependence on local resource base and high concern for its health and sustainable use.	1. Greater physical, administrative, and market integration of traditionally isolated areas and communities with the dominant, mainstream systems, reducing critical dependence of farmers on local resources and hence the degree of their stake in the conservation of the local resources.
B. Key driving forces/factors generated by (A) 1. Social survival and welfare strategies totally focused on local, diverse, fragile resources. 2. High collective stake in protection and regeneration of local natural resources. 3. Functional knowledge and closer understanding of limitations and potential of resources due to closer proximity and access to resources, little gap between resource user and resource itself. 4. Autonomy, local control over local resources (owing to absence of external impositions).	1. External linkages-based diversification of sources of sustenance, welfare, and development, reducing the extent of critical stake in local resource maintenance. 2. Role of functional resource knowledge marginalized because of imposition of generalized approaches from above for local resource management; wider gap between resource users and decisionmakers. 3. Erosion of local resource control, autonomy following the extension of mainstream, legal, administrative, and fiscal arrangements to formerly isolated areas.
C. Social responses (concerns and adaptations) dictated or facilitated by B 1. Adoption and enforcement of production and extraction systems adapted to natural resource features through diversified usage, controlled usage intensity, regenerating, upgrading, and developing the resources, depending on capacities and needs. 2. Controlling or rationing the demand pressure on resources through social and institutional sanctions, collective sharing, recycling, outmigration ,etc.	1. Greater role of demand-driven measures leading to resource use intensification, over-exploitation with greater extractive capacities and technologies. 2. Increased role of (unregulated) external demands, which are insensitive to local resource limitation. 3. Resource upgrading measures more generalized and less location specific.
D. Mechanisms and means to execute social responses 1. Collectively evolved site- and season-specific norms of resource use facilitated by direct access and proximity to resources and little gap between decision makers and resource users. 2. Site, season, product, and resource component-specific folk technologies evolved over the generations, facilitated by functional knowledge and close proximity to resource base. 3. Formal and informal institutional arrangements guiding broad approach to resource management, access, and usage regulation, facilitated by group action or community participation, and autonomy and local control over local resources.	1. Largely externally evolved generalized rules guiding resource use, framed by legal and technical experts with little concern for local resource users' perspectives and limited knowledge of site specific situations. 2. High science-based modern research and development as a source of technologies, ignoring rationale of traditional practices; ignoring local resource perspectives. 3. Institutional interventions evolved, designed in incomparable situations and extended to these areas as a part of agricultural, rural development.

| E. Consequences
Ecology-driven natural resource management systems:
1. Evolved by the communities having high stake in sustainability of the resource base.
2. Facilitated by functional knowledge of resources, close proximity to resources, and community control over the local resources. | Resource usage system driven by uncontrolled pressure of demand:
1. Developed by experts without local participation;
2. Enforced (rather nonenforced) by formal state machinery. |

Source: Table based on synthesis of inferences from different studies; in particular, Brush 1988, Banskota 1989, Rieger 1981, Jochim 1981, Myers 1986, Price 1981, Jodha 1990, Rhoades 1988, Jodha and Shrestha 1994, and Whiteman 1984, Carson 1992, Yanhua 1992, Gadgil and Guha 1992, Guillet 1983, Ives and Messerli 1989. For more details, see Jodha 1990; Jodha and Shrestha 1994.

Table 15–4: Possibilities of Reorienting Current Resource Usage Systems in Mountain Areas by Incorporating Elements from Traditional Systems

Circumstances, driving forces, and response mechanisms characterizing traditional resource use systems	*Elements of traditional systems with scope for revival, reorientation, and substitution in the present-day context*	*Constraints to measures under "Elements" column and possible responses*
Total dependence-driven community stake in natural resource base: 1. Key factor: almost total and exclusive dependence on local resources for survival (in a semi-closed, isolated subsistence-oriented context), inducing protection, regeneration, and sustainable use of resources; the process was complemented by close proximity and functional knowledge of the resources that sharpened the community's perception and diagnosis of resource situation. 2. Infeasibility (and undesirability) of no. 1 in the changed context of reduced isolation and access to external sources, etc.	**Rediscovered areas of total and crucial dependence as sources of community stakes in natural resources:** 1. Change of product and service context of stake, i.e., substituting (traditional) sustenance security by security of "niche" (high-payoff products and services with comparative advantage to the local communities), and use them as lead sector influencing overall natural resource management (e.g., horticulture or tourism-led initiatives in mountains). 2. Change of spatial and socio-economic context of dependence as a source of stake, i.e., instead of an isolated community's sustenance (now met partly by external links), the crucial environmental products and services for larger entities (e.g., hydrological stability and productivity of total agro-ecological zone affected by resource mismanage-ment in small units (see text for illustrations).	**Constraints:** 1. Wider spread and diversity of resource users and other stakeholders *diffusing and diluting the perception and diagnosis of stakes*, reducing role of stake as incentives for resources management. 2. Lack of substitute arrangements comparable to traditional provisions such as (a) norms of routine resource use practices reconciling individuals' short planning horizon and the community's long time horizon; and (b) advantage of close proximity, first-hand knowledge of resource base. **Possible Responses:** 1. Reduce gap between resources as well as resource users and the resource planners, policymakers, development agencies, etc., by sensitizing the latter to mountain conditions. 2. Develop feedback mechanisms by involving local communities in resource-related decisions and actions. 3. Plan resource development and use with mountain perspective based on no. 1 and no. 2.

Close proximity, direct access to resources and their functional knowledge:	**Functional substitutes for close proximity and first-hand knowledge of resource base:**	**Constraints:**
1. Generated understanding and sensitivity to resource situation and its variability; helped in developing relevant folk technologies; encouraged institutional arrangements for resource use regulation (intensity, diversification, common property regimes, etc.); reduced gap between resource user and decisionmaker, producer, and produce consumer, and helped in regulating pressure on resources. 2. After integration with the mainstream (external systems), leading to distance between the resource and resource planners; multiplicity and diversity of resource users and pluralization of perception of stakes and marginalization of traditional knowledge systems, and physical proximity, dependent approaches are not feasible.	1. Focus on sensitivity (in place of proximity) to resource situation, as the latter contributed to evolution of resource management measures mainly by generating sensitivity toward the resources; reorient and sensitize policymakers and development agencies (even market forces) to make them understand imperatives of mountain resources and act accordingly. 2. Evolve feedback mechanisms (about resource situation) by involving local communities as a substitute for instant feedback provided by physical proximity; 3. Fill in knowledge gaps by collection, synthesis, and application of resource-related information on using facilities offered by information technologies and communications.	1. The culture of development interventions that emphasizes the extension, and imposition of measures developed for other areas; ignoring local resource base and its imperatives, local knowledge systems, and people's perspectives. 2. Missing mountain perspective of mountain development approaches. **Possible Responses**—Possible approach starts with reorientation of overall strategy of development interventions and resource management. Specific steps may include: 1. Sensitization and reorientation of relevant decisionmaking agencies about resource characteristics and their diversities. 2. Involvement of local communities in design, planning, and implementation of interventions involving resource management, i.e., bottom-up approach. 3. Recognition and use of traditional knowledge systems, and reorientation of research and development systems focusing on on-farm research, farmer participation, and bottom-up farming system research to help integration of knowledge generating processes rather than knowledge only.

Autonomy and community command over local resources:	Restoring community management of local resources:	Constraints:
1. A product of isolation or semi-closedness of areas and communities that facilitated effective community ownership of resources; helped in designing and enforcing resource use regulations; reduced gaps between decisionmakers and resource users; encouraged community participation and group actions; and helped in resource use rationing, collective sharing, resource recycling, and protection against pressure of (possible) external demand. 2. The local community control over resources and capacity to design and enforce usage regulation have vanished or weakened with the integration of isolated areas with the mainstream. Revival of the system conflicts with "centralization" and top-down approaches of the mainstream decisionmakers, governed more by the interests and perspectives of the mainstream.	1. Build on the emerging trends toward decentralization, community-based development, participatory and bottom-up approaches to development. Experiences of user group and NGO initiatives, etc., can help provide functional substitute arrangements for traditional community control of resources. 2. Take leads from successful experiences, community forestry, community irrigation systems, and other grassroots-level participatory initiatives, facilitate their replication and mainstreaming.	1. Loss of traditional collective sharing systems and culture of group action, emergence of social and economic differentiation and individualistic tendencies. 2. The states, agreeing to decentralization, community participation, etc., may not imply local control of resources: states' tendency to use community as a convenient agent (rather than an autonomous body) with little powers and capacities for rationing of demand on local resources or for pricing of products. 3. Market pressure (distant demand) may prove more powerful than community initiatives in adapting demand to resources features rather than the other way around. **Possible Responses:** 1. Exploration and use of constant possibilities to manage above constraints through (a) greater autonomy to communities and user groups, and (b) association of local communities with resource-related decisions. 2. Initiatives on product and resource pricing reflecting their true worth and sharing gains with local communities; introduction of biophysical measures for compensation for natural resource extraction.

Source: Author.